FRANKIE BOYLE

WORK! CONSUME! DIE!

★★★★★

HarperCollins*Publishers*

HarperCollins*Publishers*
77–85 Fulham Palace Road,
Hammersmith, London W6 8JB

www.harpercollins.co.uk

First published by HarperCollins*Publishers* 2011

1 3 5 7 9 10 8 6 4 2

© Frankie Boyle 2011

Illustrations by Nick Morley

Frankie Boyle asserts the moral right to
be identified as the author of this work

The novel element of this book (identified by the Nexus Typewriter font) is a work of fiction.
The fictional names and characters are the work of the author's imagination, as are the
incidents portrayed in it. Any resemblance to actual persons, living or dead, events or
localities is entirely coincidental.

The remaining chapters (identified by the New Century Schoolbook font)
contain previously published material.

p. iii John Dos Passos, *Manhattan Transfer* © the estate of John Dos Passos; p. 14 Slavoj Žižek,
Violence (Profile Books, 2009); p. 76 Hakim Bey, *Immediatism*, reproduced by kind permission
of Autonomedia; p. 76 R. D. Laing, *The Politics of Experience* © R. D. Laing, 1967. Reproduced
by permission of Penguin Books Ltd; p. 94 Bret Easton Ellis, *The Informers* © Bret Easton
Ellis, 1994; p. 122 Raj Patel, *The Value of Nothing*, published by Portobello Books © Raj Patel,
2009; p. 148 David Icke, *Children of the Matrix*, reproduced by kind permission of David Icke
books; pp. 161–162 Obituary of Jeff Conaway by Ronald Bergan, 30 May 2011 © Guardian
News & Media Ltd 2011; p. 168 C. P. Snow, reproduced by kind permission of Curtis Brown
Group Ltd; p. 182 Thomas Geoghegan, *The Law in Shambles*, reproduced by kind permission
of Prickly Paradigm Press; p. 190 and p. 302 Terence McKenna, reproduced by kind
permission of the estate of Terence McKenna; p. 228 Robert Anton Wilson, permission granted
by Writers House LLC as Agent for the Estate of Robert Anton Wilson; p. 252 Noam Chomsky,
What We Say Goes © 2007 by Aviva Chomsky and David Barsamian. Reprinted by
arrangement with Henry Holt & Co; p. 270 David Madsen, *Memoirs of a Gnostic Dwarf*,
reproduced by courtesy of Dedalus Ltd © 1995.

A catalogue record of this book is
available from the British Library

ISBN 978-0-00-742678-2 (hardback)
ISBN 978-0-00-742680-5 (trade paperback)

Printed and bound in Great Britain by Clays Ltd, St Ives plc

MIX
Paper from
responsible sources
FSC
www.fsc.org
FSC C007454

FSC™ is a non-profit international organisation established to promote
the responsible management of the world's forests. Products carrying the
FSC label are independently certified to assure consumers that they come
from forests that are managed to meet the social, economic and
ecological needs of present and future generations,
and other controlled sources.

Find out more about HarperCollins and the environment at
www.harpercollins.co.uk/green

His stomach turns a somersault with the drop of the elevator. He steps out into the crowded marble hall. For a moment not knowing which way to go, he stands back against the wall with his hands in his pockets, watching people elbow their way through the perpetually revolving doors; softcheeked girls chewing gum, hatchetfaced girls with bangs, creamfaced boys his own age, young toughs with their hats on one side, sweatyfaced messengers, crisscross glances, sauntering hips, red jowls masticating cigars, sallow concave faces, fat bodies of young men and women, paunched bodies of elderly men, all elbowing, shoving, shuffling, fed in two endless tapes through the revolving doors out into Broadway, in off Broadway. Jimmy fed in a tape in and out the revolving doors, noon and night and morning, the revolving doors grinding out his years like sausage meat. All of a sudden his muscles stiffen. Uncle Jeff and his office can go plumb to hell. The words are so loud inside him he glances to one side and the other to see if anyone heard him say them.
They can all go plumb to hell.

John Dos Passos, *Manhattan Transfer*

If rape, poison, dagger and arson
Have not as yet adorned with their pleasing artistry
the banal canvas of our piteous destinies
It is, alas, because our soul lacks boldness

Baudelaire

Introduction

I sincerely hope you will be disappointed by this book. To disappoint, anger and dismay has always been my ideal. Of course I've made the book a fairly commercial collection of light-hearted topical comments. This is so I can dismay you further by pocketing a huge advance and spending the rest of my life surfing, reading crime thrillers and fucking.

If I had it my way this book would be an impeccably researched novel about the friendship between Tom, a young white boy, and Jefferson, an old black gardener, set in turn-of-the-century Mississippi. It would possess an air of complete authenticity. The old gardener would have an encyclopaedic knowledge of herbs and their uses, but he would be an illiterate and solitary curmudgeon. He would heal the boy's broken arm with a poultice and later save his little brother from dying of a fever. Young Tom would convince Mr Bridges, his schoolmaster, of the gardener's gifts and together the three of them would start to write a herbal encyclopaedia. The three protagonists would come from very different worlds, so there would be a lot of conflict but also a lot of wry humour and wisdom.

After the first 50 pages the reader would wonder what kind of follow-up this was to the jokey autobiography of a panel-show contestant. After 100 pages they would be completely drawn into the world of Tom, Jefferson and Mr Bridges. After

150 pages they would be nervously wondering whether Tom's stepmother could really have been so spiteful as to burn the manuscript.

For the final 50 pages I would have a description of Old Jefferson surprising Tom in a hay barn and the two of them having brutal, unprotected consensual sex. As he fucked the boy, he would scream about how he didn't give a shit about plants. Perhaps in modern words, because he was a time traveller or something. His cock would grow to a fantastical size within the boy, and glow and hum like a lightsaber. The boy's arsehole would start to talk. 'I clench and unclench just like a vagina' it would note cheerfully in poor French.

Perspective would shift jarringly to a microscopic civilisation that lived in the hay under Tom's face. They would be a poetic, romantic people for whom time moved incalculably slowly. Tom's face would have hung in their sky like the sun for millennia before Old Man Jefferson started fucking him. Its gradual change to a rictus of pain would excite and disturb the minds of their greatest philosophers. Eventually, the glowing tip of a huge black cock emerging from his mouth would cause the whole society to commit mass suicide.

Ideally, the title of the book would be an endless binary number and it would scream when you opened it and then a brawny fist would shoot out from between the pages and rip the nose right off your face. As you fell to the ground squealing, the hand would hail a cab that would run over your head. A passer-by would film your death on a mobile, making it an internet phenomenon. Huge crowds of Japanese teens would gather at stadium events to masturbate each other as they watched it on overhead screens. This footage of your nonchalant and motiveless murder by a book would attract a billion YouTube hits and not a single sympathetic comment. In a million years a super-advanced civilisation of androids would misinterpret the film and you would become a figure in their culture analogous to a paedophile Guy Fawkes.

Through advanced scientific methods they would re-create your consciousness and you would re-live your whole life over and over again, but with all the enjoyable stuff taken out. On the day of your 18th birthday someone would hit you so hard on the back of the head with a polo mallet that your eyes would pop out. Crawling from your burning house you would have your arse clawed out by a mountain lion and when you reached the hospital you would be diagnosed with AIDS of the leg and cancer of your empty eye sockets. Through a synaptic quirk you would have one image frozen in your mind so it was as if you were looking at it constantly – your long-dead Chinese stepfather's dead arsehole. The only way to treat your eyes would involve, every night just before bed, playing the screams from a horror movie loudly to encourage a wolverine to fuck the sockets. Somehow its stinking cock would numb the holes even as its scrabbling feet shredded your face and scalp. You would continue to re-live this life in ever-increasing detail long after the universe had ended, praying for death to a God who was already dead himself.

★

I got into comedy because I loved watching comedy as a child. I later discovered that's a bit like loving burgers as a child and deciding to become a cow. I've never found anything in life particularly heart-warming or uplifting. Except the smiles of my children and even those are ruined by the knowledge that someday my children will die, their smiles having long gone as they struggled with the mental and social handicaps they developed from having a cunt like me for a dad. If you want to hear something uplifting go read something else. You are well catered for in our culture; there are hordes of halfwits who want to help you find an upside. One day both you and I will be hipbones and shinbones buried in a box being eaten by worms. You will find no solace here.

Just fuckin witcha! I've always had an instinct to laugh at everything, the good stuff, the horror, everything. With laughter comes perspective. You might be scared of the dark, you might be sitting alone in the woods in the dark but if you suddenly heard laughter ... no, wait a minute. Some people don't hold with the old 'gallows humour', it's not civilised, there's some stuff you shouldn't laugh about and so on. I think we're all in this trench together and everything is fair game. Do me a favour. Any time you have a problem with somebody having a laugh, have a think about where your grandparents went, look around and tell me what you think a gallows looks like.

'Slowed by the grass, the guys laugh as they spacewalk
on the suddenly deep carpet'

★★★★

I've been living at the top of a high-rise on the
outskirts of Glasgow. I can't say where exactly but
it's the tallest one in the city. The evening I moved
in I remember standing at the bottom just looking at
it, reaching up endlessly into the night. The partying
windows and the partied-out windows, a punch card for
the fifth dimension. One night me and my mate Paul Marsh
stop in the wee pub at the bottom of the flats. We're
supposed to be going round to our pal Murphy's to play
FIFA on the PlayStation and have a few joints, but the
Celtic game is coming on in the pub and it seems daft
to go play football. We phone Murphy to come meet us
and after the game we walk down to the high street,
Murphy's elongated frame casting a daddy-longlegs
shadow under the streetlamps. I get us all fish suppers
and, for a laugh, pickled eggs, 'cause we've not had
them in years and are genuinely fucking surprised they
still happen. We get the lift up to mine to have a few
beers and get MTV Base on.

Murphy is banging on about some show called *The Game*
and genuinely can't believe we haven't heard of it.
Cannot believe it. He's laughing and shaking his head
and chokes as he opens the wee bag with the pickled

eggs in. He's eating the third egg by the time the lift starts and then he realises. He looks up embarrassed with his face stuffed with eggs and says, 'Sorry guys, fuck, sorry.'

'It's OK,' I say, and fuck knows why but I tousle his hair, like he's a wee boy. 'I fucking hate eggs,' I say stupidly and we all laugh. We've had two joints outside the chippy and we're all stoned.

I'm staring at a football sticker someone's put on the intercom. It's Anthony Stokes, the Celtic player, with the bland smile of a waxwork. The smile that a millionaire in his early twenties conjures up for a contractually necessary photograph. Someone has scratched his eyes out with their thumb, really precisely, so with the perforated metal of the intercom underneath he seems to have the eyes of a robot beeman. As we go past the 14th floor the lift gives its usual shudder. Some really bad bastards on this floor.

I dig out some of those big plastic plates I have for when the kids come round, easier to clean. My flat looks like it's been furnished at a hoopla stall and I just think, fuck this, fuck playing it on the portable telly again, this is nuts. 'Wait till you see this, lads!' I yell, rising unsteadily and aiming at the far wall. I'm pressing at the wall and suddenly it flies open with a rattle, not the *Star Trek* whoosh I'd paid for.

Paul looks up from his chips and still has his hand in his mouth, like a baby. I'm standing with my arms wide and laughing. Behind me – the lights slowly rising – is a massive room going back an impossible distance in Victorian splendour.

It's an expedition down to the far wall where a huge plasma sits, still paused on a grimly realistic cup game I was playing as Celtic. Slowed by the grass, the guys laugh as they spacewalk on the suddenly deep carpet. The room is the whole floor down one side of the building and I've roughly modelled it on a stateroom on the *Titanic*. There are walnut panels, replica straight-backed chairs, an ottoman and three huge brass floor-to-ceiling portholes. Glasgow in the darkness is just lights.

I take them to the big oak table and there's the whole estate mapped out in a wax model. It's a proper belter too. All the local characters are there, wee white wax people, wee wax hardmen and wide-os, and wee wax shopkeepers (I just keep those ones in the shops, you never really see them anywhere). All the wee wax people are mostly in their houses because I haven't really fucked with it since last night. I notice that the wee Murphy, Marshy and me are all in my flat, right by the table.

All over the rest of the table are notes for the book, paragraphs in longhand on A4, scraps of paper, a stack of little notebooks for sitting in cafes.

'This the book?' says Paul, compartmentalising both the stateroom and voodoo neighbourhood with typical élan.

'Aye,' I laugh. 'That's "War" you're holding right there. I explain "war", man …'

It's like a wee neat pile of stress, those notebooks, so I just mumble, 'It's good for absolutely nothing,' but, like most references, this passes Marsh by. I take the notebook off him and put it back where it was.

'Some days I think it's brilliant, some days I think it's shite …' I offer over my shoulder while I'm plugging the controllers in.

'Like having a kid!' slurs Murphy, but he's got kids so we all groan at the harshness.

Murphy gets bored of the football. He can never get the shooting right, always just fucks it over the bar. He's sitting through in the lounge of the real flat watching MTV loudly, as Paul and I fight a gripping series of Old Firm encounters. I play as Celtic and the ref is even biased on the fucking PlayStation, Marshy getting away with several tackles Frank Miller's Batman would have been proud of.

I wake Murphy up when I'm going to bed and he phones a cab. As I'm saying goodnight to Paul, I notice the wee light flashing on my laptop. David Murphy doesn't even know any porn sites and has just pishedly typed the word 'groped' into Google.

I go into my room and start the big stretching session I always have before bed. No matter how long I do, my legs always ache when I get up. *Telegram from Mr Death! He's sorry he can't be with you right now! Telegram from Mr Death!*

★

I'm in the middle of a confused dream where I'm married to a Muslim woman who won't let me fuck her, when I hear the drill of the doorbell. I bang through to the living room and nearly fall over Paul, who for some reason is sleeping on the floor, right beside the couch. As I open the door, I look behind me and check we closed the wall, and when I look back I see two massive cops.

They're plainclothes, CID or what have you. The older one has those watery eyes some older Scottish guys have, like he's about to start greeting. In front of him is a man with a side-parting who looks like an enormous schoolboy.

'Mr Francis Boyle?' he asks, but it's not really a question. 'Alright if we come in?'

All the grass is through in the stateroom, I can see it in my mind's eye. It's on the big tarpaulin I put down so we wouldn't get burns on the carpet. 'Paul! We have visitors!' I shout, and he leaps up startled. Literally springs up like he's part of an ambush, then sits down suddenly on the couch, internalising a massive spasm of guilt.

The two cops are making a show of looking about, like explorers in a bad movie. I make them a cup of tea and we all sit down around the tiny kitchen table while Paul sits rigidly in the other room, too paranoid to leave. I expect some kind of introduction but there is none.

'This is a fairly unusual matter,' the younger one starts happily. 'I believe you know the TV presenter Dom Joly?'

I try to shrug but the mug I'm holding is too full, so it comes over like a twitch. 'Eh, not really. I met him a couple of times doing panel shows. We did a couple of panel shows together.'

'Panel shows,' agrees the older one mournfully, his eyes filling right up like tears are going to start rolling down his face.

'Mr Joly was the subject of a serious sexual assault over the weekend,' chirps the other guy. I don't really register what he says at first. I'm aware that I'm not really saying anything and I start to feel uneasy.

'Dom Joly?' I ask foolishly. They don't acknowledge this in any way, so I say, 'sexually assaulted?' and then there's a long pause.

'Dom Joly has been sexually assaulted,' the old policeman confirms sadly. 'Dom Joly from *Trigger Happy TV*.'

'God, I'm sorry to hear that,' I say, trying for a concerned look and tone. I actually feel nothing or – if possible – less than nothing. 'He's a big guy,' I add puzzledly.

'It's believed Mr Joly was drugged, although we are still looking for a physically powerful attacker,' side-parting confides excitedly.

'That's terrible.' I look blankly at the digestive beside my cup that it would now be inappropriate to dunk. 'Someone drugged his drink, or …'

'They somehow got the drug into food served in his dressing room,' he explains.

'A Chicken Kiev,' watery eyes announces.

I feel a rising, horrified excitement. The sort you feel when somebody dies. 'Am I a suspect?'

They both laugh.

'No, no, no, Mr Boyle.' They beam silently at me for a bit. 'You are on a list of, eh, celebrities we're contacting in case they may be in danger.'

'Danger? In danger of, eh …?'

'Of being sexually assaulted,' the old guy nods vigorously. 'Of being subjected to the same kind of sexual assault as Mr Joly … there have been other incidents like this involving other, eh, celebrities.'

'The suspicion is that this guy has been operating for several years, attacking people who have been famous but then slip below a certain level of public recognition,' his partner explains, inexplicably ending by smacking his fist into his open palm.

I hold my tea in both hands like I'm nursing a

Scotch. I try to think of a polite way of asking, then blurt out, 'Who? Who else has he raped?'

The old boy flips open a notebook. 'A lot of the presenters from *The 11 O'Clock Show*, Tony Slattery, Steve Punt, Sam Fox, Michael Greco, two … no, all three of the ladies from *Smack the Pony*, Frank Sidebottom, before he died. We can't really name people.'

'This has been going on for a while?'

'It seems to be getting more active. And he seems to be focusing his anger on comedy.'

'Everybody does,' I smile.

As I show them out, Paul gets up halfway as some sort of farewell and it ends up looking like a curtsy. They both shake my hand warmly and, as the younger cop heads out, the old guy grips me by the arm and forces some-thing into my hand. He fixes me with the liquid eyes of a dying spaniel and leaves without a word.

Half an hour later Paul and I are still smoking a joint on the couch, passing the picture back and forth. It's a dressing room. I reckon it's an ITV dressing room at LWT. In the foreground you can see part of a guy lying on the floor, his trousers off and a huge arse exposed. Is this Dom Joly? Is he fucking dead? Why would they take a photo while he was still unconscious? Did the rapist take it? On the wall is the real focus of the piece. Written in blood (presumably, we agree, Dom Joly's arseblood) is a slogan in block capitals.

'SHOWBUSINESS HAS NO BOTTOM.'

★ ★ ★ ★

Abu Ghraib was not simply a case of American arrogance towards a Third World people: in being submitted to humiliating tortures, the Iraqi prisoners were effectively *initiated into American culture*. They were given a taste of its obscene underside, which forms the necessary supplement to the public values of personal dignity, democracy and freedom. Bush was thus wrong: what we are getting when we see the photos of the humiliated Iraqi prisoners on our screens and front pages is precisely a direct insight into American values, into the very core of the obscene enjoyment that sustains the US way of life.

Slavoj Žižek, *Violence*

★ ★ ★ ★

01

It's interesting that war is the ultimate in reality television and yet the British public couldn't be less interested. Remember when they used to have to persuade the country to go to war? Fake up a dossier? Remember when they even used to announce a war? Now, it's just, 'Hey, we're bombing Libya!' Soon they won't even bother with that and we'll only find out who we're fighting when our friends send us a postcard saying that their hotel buffet just got destroyed by a pilotless attack drone, or when we accidentally read a tweet that Liam Fox has sent to Fearne Cotton.

Of course, war to us seems so brutal, so unnecessary. That's because we don't own shares in arms companies. Those guys live in palatial penthouses full of shrunken heads and wank to the news. Still, we are members of our society, so we are complicit in what it does.

Look at it this way. Personally, I think we should have much more open immigration arrangements, we should treat asylum seekers fairly, we shouldn't imprison them and we particularly shouldn't imprison their children. Perhaps I can hold that view because I live in a country that does the opposite. Because I have the security of knowing that it won't happen. It's the same with war. We might say, 'Not in my name', but it is in our name, and with our taxes.

We are told we fight consequence-free wars. Drone missions are 'targeted killings', of people who have never stood trial. 'Your judge is this flying bomb, your sentence is kaboom!' We drop bombs from miles up in the sky and say they are surgical strikes. Ignoring the fact that there is no way to safely drop high explosives into urban areas. That surgeons don't, for good reason, ever use explosives.

In the UK, as bailiffs cleared out protestors at the peace camp outside parliament, one was filmed stamping on a protestor. And with that one vicious act of violence, the area was officially no longer a peace camp and just another London park. The area is now going to be used as a holding pen for Boris Johnson's mistresses.

I never understood why men go to war. Then I thought, men have children. The average length of a war is four or five years, which is also the amount of time it takes for a child to stop being really fucking annoying. Men are saying to themselves, 'Do I want to be here, listening to this wee guy scream because I've cut his toast into triangles instead of squares? No, I'll go join the army. I'll send him a Christmas video message, when I'm beheaded on YouTube … screaming, 'How do you want my head cut off then? In triangles or in fucking squares?!'

Reading about Help for Heroes, I think it's sad that that's left to charity. Give it a couple of years and we'll be getting hassled in the high street to adopt a para for £5 a month. There was a story that a legless war hero couldn't get into a charity ball where he was guest of honour because it had no disabled access. Organisers apologised for the mix up, and invited him to have tea with the Queen – on a bouncy castle at the top of Blackpool Tower! How could we treat a man who lost so much for this country like that? Well, we sent him into an unnecessary war with inferior equipment and a breathtaking ignorance of historical precedent, so it was probably pretty easy.

★

I really don't understand the no-fly zone in Libya. How can we designate a no-fly zone and then whizz about it in our planes? It has all the logic of a parent in McDonald's telling their kids they're embarrassing them. Presumably the reason coalition forces have been blowing up tanks and buildings is because they're worried they might take to the skies like migrating geese. Instead of a no-fly zone, Cameron should just parachute in whoever was running Britain's transport network last winter. British Typhoons reduced some schools and hospitals to barely functioning messes. Not in Libya, over here – at a cost of £90 million each, they're bound to have.

William Hague said that Britain will stop bombing Libya when Gaddafi stops killing his own people. They've managed to turn a war into something akin to a loved-up couple not wanting to hang up the phone first.

'No, you stop shooting first …'

'No, you stop bombing first …'

'No, you stop shooting first … Hello? … Hello? … Are you still shooting …'

'Yeah …'

'Oh, you!! OK, let's both stop killing together … 3 … 2 … 1 …'

'Are you still bombing? …'

'Yeah.'

The debate is whether the war is legal. It has brought pain, misery and desperation to hundreds of thousands of people. Does that sound legal to you? To me it sounds like the dictionary definition of the legal profession. Tony Blair phoned Gaddafi twice to urge him to stand down. Apparently, the delusional lunatic rambled on for hours about not being a war criminal before Gaddafi managed to get a word in.

Hague confirmed that Britain is supplying the rebels with mobile phones. That's incredibly useful. It seems that they've been texting us saying, 'We're dying. Send guns please.' I hope we sent them iPhones. There's a wonderful app for finding your legs in a bomb crater.

People may be wondering where Britain is getting all these free mobile phones from that we are handing to the young radical Muslims in Libya. They're mainly confiscated from the young radical Muslims that we put in Belmarsh.

An American fighter plane crashed in a field near Benghazi. If you ask me, that was enforcing the no-fly zone a bit too strictly. What a laugh it would have been if it had landed on the house of Lockerbie bomber al-Megrahi. Not that he'd have been in; he spends most afternoons waterskiing.

The Scottish Parliament still argue they did stringent checks that al-Megrahi definitely had a note from his mum asking for him to be excused from prison. The claim is that it was the Scottish Parliament acting compassionately. Scottish and compassionate? Those words go together about as well as 'Premiership' and 'consensual'.

BP lobbied over the Libyan prisoner-transfer scheme. If you're one of those people who stick your finger in their ears and sing to themselves that Britain's foreign policy is nothing to do with oil, that must be quite difficult to explain. It seems like the two have nothing in common. It's like finding out that the manufacturers of Lynx shower gel had been demanding the release of Peter Sutcliffe.

The RAF pilots who flew on a rescue mission to Libya used maps printed straight from Google. Why bother? When I need a map of Libya I use a sheet of sand paper. Apparently, we have been dropping in troops as 'advisors'. It's all perfectly fine under international law so long as when they shoot someone they say, 'I advise you to die.'

The public doesn't seem to be behind the war in Libya. To engage them, maybe we should tally up the number of civilian casualties and use them as the numbers for the EuroMillions. You'll have Jenni Falconer in a morgue as Graham, the voice of the dead, reads the results. 6, 22, 11, 4, 9 and, because last night we hit a primary school, 40.

David Cameron said he undertook military action because it's 'not acceptable to have a situation where Colonel Gaddafi can be murdering his own people using planes and helicopter gunships'. It also invalidates the warranties the British arms manufacturers sold them with. Amusingly, David Cameron was roaming around the Middle East with arms dealers trying to flog weapons while calling for an end to violence. He's right. What these places need to solve their differences is more guns. The Tories see Gaddafi as a 'legitimate target' for them – after all he is elderly, Muslim and has children.

Gaddafi's also been accused of using human shields. He's going to have to do better than that. Our bombs will simply rip through them. He should have opted for steel or concrete. And they say he's a tactical genius! Yes, it's horrible that protestors are being fired on by jets, but what a way to go! Fighting a plane! It must be like unlocking a secret level of *Grand Theft Auto* coded by Raoul Moat.

Both sides have been accused of using rape as a weapon. The hardest part of using rape as a weapon is training the troops. The assault course is a very different thing at rape camp. You rarely see rape squads as part of military marches. You can hear David Dimbleby doing the voiceover at Trooping the Colour. 'Visiting from Scotland we have the 4th Rape Squad. They've been raping for their country since 1935. They're taking the salute from the Queen. Some of them have broken ranks, and are racing straight towards Her Majesty's box. And from here, I think I can see a flicker of a smile come across her face.'

NATO says Gaddafi's reign of terror is near an end – because we will soon have bombed everybody he's been trying to scare. It's an interesting policy. We just keep bombing everything around him, but not actually him. I presume if he gets captured they're going to execute him by knife thrower.

We were told that military action helped to prevent a bloodbath in Benghazi. Thankfully, with our help the bloodbath happened five miles outside Benghazi. Libyans are gathering around military instillations, not to act as human shields but in the knowledge that it's probably the last place that NATO bombs are going to land. Surprisingly, some people in Tripoli still support NATO. The undertakers. To most Scots, NATO's just a description of their feet after suffering a decade of Type 2 diabetes.

Is it wise to fill Libya with melting corpses while we look for Gaddafi? He's increasingly blending in. Gaddafi has a lot of money at his disposal – it can't have been cheap buying Michael Jackson's face after he died. He looks like the last surviving balloon from a children's party. If only he hadn't hoarded £60 billion abroad. He could have kept say £10 billion, and used the rest to create an unbreachable defence. Right now, a colossal golden robot bear could be lapping up the protestors like ants, its tortured attempts to sing 'Bear Necessities' in machine code sounding, to Libyans, like a series of garbled sex threats.

Our various wars are being fought purely to justify a £50 billion defence bill and maintain an army that is grossly oversized for the realistic needs of our country. Ours is the second largest military force in the EU. The last time Britain was successfully invaded was over a millennium ago in 1066.

And our military is used to attack not to defend. Some critics of this will say that Britain *has* been attacked, by terrorists. But we didn't need an army to prevent 7/7. We needed a bus conductor.

The bombs we're dropping cost more than the buildings we're dropping them on. In financial terms they're winning. First Sea Lord Admiral Sir Mark Stanhope says he's sure if we'd had enough money to send another warship we'd have finished this conflict. Yes, Sir Mark, and if we had enough money for jobs people could feed their kids. Who'd have thought that a navy as powerful as ours would struggle to win a war in a desert? So we sold Gaddafi weapons and now he has more than we do. How do we get out of this sticky situation? Surely we could launch a product-recall notice?

'An unfinished surface of the T-72 dashboard could cause a nasty cut. Please return, in person, to the nearest HM warship.'

Why should we believe the opinions of the First Sea Lord? I haven't trusted him since he told his daughter she couldn't marry a human and she ended up selling her voice for legs. Also, maybe saying we're running out of money to carry on isn't the best way of getting Gaddafi to surrender. Is this the Big Society? We all work for free to save lives while special funding is ring-fenced to kill people? We got stuck in Iraq for eight years, we've been stuck in Afghanistan for ten years and, for some reason, we set the timetable for a conflict in Libya at 90 days. You can't even get a sofa delivered in 90 days.

Gaddafi shut down all internet communications in the country. Which is a pity, as there are always thousands of people trying to get on Freecycle to pick up a coffin. Libya operated tight state control over the media, that's obvious. The rebels invited Britain to get involved in their war – they must have watched no television *at all*. Gaddafi banned the learning of the English language in Libyan schools, which is obviously why Libya did most of its diplomatic negotiations with the Scottish government. A succession of colourful noises was all the two parties needed to be understood.

Trumping even Libya, Tunisia had the harshest internet censorship outside of China. I wonder why so few of us knew that? The Tunisian revolution started when a street vendor set fire to himself. Ian Tomlinson's inquest ended and the British people were watching TV's *Most Shocking Talent Show Moments*, which was a revolution in a way, as you didn't get to vote on what won.

Tunisia's revolution inspired the uprisings across the Arab world, so maybe all the Arab refugees should go to Tunisia. Put all the exiled revolutionaries in one country and rename it 'Spirited Arabia'. It will have a lovely climate and be very close by plane, but the customer service will consist of someone shouting, 'Don't tell me what to do!' and shooting into the ceiling.

These Arab states have had to fight with their lives to install a hastily-decided-upon, cobbled-together, temporary government. We did it simply by not bothering to vote last year. The Arab League. It's not a patch on the Premiership. You just can't get the ball control with sandals.

It was reported that Leila Trabelsi, the wife of Tunisia's ousted ruler, left the country with 1.5 tonnes of gold, worth more than £35 million. The joke's on her, though, as she fled the country on easyJet. Her baggage allowance came to just over £40 million.

Israel killed a bunch of civilians in international waters for trying to bring aid to the Palestinians. According to the Israelis, their troops started shooting because people on the boats threw stones. That sounds proportionate. It's a bit like, well, someone throwing stones at you and you executing them in cold blood with a team of commandos. '20 soldiers airdropped onto the boat from a helicopter' – what surprised me is, if you type that into Google, you get a Charlie Sheen sex tape.

Israel still claims land rights based on the Bible. That's a bit like me pitching a tent beside your house and saying I want your garden because it belonged to King Arthur. I pity the Palestinians, who didn't do anything to deserve what happened to them. Israel should have been given some of Germany to start a country in. Anyway, I'd better leave it there. I get a lot of complaints when I write jokes about Israel, mainly from the Mossad agent who has to update my file.

There's a real sense of change taking place right across the Arab world as the old rulers are removed from power, making way for a whole new set of ruthless dictators. When will these corrupt rulers come to realise that guns cannot silence the people? Only reality television and talent shows can do that.

The people of Yemen have also overthrown their ruler, and now Syria is trying. The young lesbian from Syria who wrote an online blog was actually a 40-year-old fat American. As I discovered after arranging to meet her in a Travelodge car park. Despite common perceptions, lesbianism is actually becoming a more popular lifestyle choice for young women in Syria, now that all the men are dead.

What are all these Middle Eastern rulers going to do now they've been chucked out of a job? Become Northern Ireland peace envoys? Back home, people are asking why other Arab leaders haven't got involved; given that most Arab countries are currently being ruled by an 'out of office' email, that might be a bit of a problem. The leader of the UN wants the world to have one clear opinion. The world won't even buy the records of *The X Factor* winners they voted for – you expect consistency?

★

For all that I in my middle-class, lefty reality tunnel imagine that people aren't behind Britain's wars, I sometimes wonder if that's true. I look at the *Top Gear*-style news items about the rockets we use, the computer games where we symbolically join in, and I think maybe everybody is right fucking into this.

Britain sent over new Apache helicopters and Typhoons to Libya. Are we just parading what they could have bought had they not decided to make things awkward? Our Tomahawk missiles have a camera on the front, which provides great clip-show footage worth £250 a go to help pad out the defence budget. There's even talk of a couple of new ships if Channel 5's controversial *You've Been Maimed* gets the go-ahead. They use the latest sat-nav guidance system, replacing an earlier model where two mice sat in a transparent nosecone yanking at a joystick as they bickered over a tiny map.

Some of our troops are to be issued with special bomb-proof pants. Yes, I can think of nothing that will ease the pain and suffering of grief-stricken parents more after being informed of the death of their son than being handed his perfectly preserved cock and balls.

Meanwhile, US soldiers have started using a futuristic rifle that fires radio-controlled bullets that can travel round corners. Now, they'll be able to shoot British soldiers without even aiming at them. There are strict guidelines for their use and they'll only be sold to rogue Middle Eastern states if they're willing to pay more for them than their enemies.

The US army also wants all its troops to eventually carry military smart phones, with various battlefield apps. The apps will contain all sorts of useful military information, including phrasebooks. Though if you're out of signal, a bit of paper with 'You killed my wife, you western devil!' should cover most of the things you'll hear.

The US army are putting everything into this. They will have apps with training manuals, and the capability to order new equipment and downloadable maps of all the enemy's positions. British soldiers will be getting a text message saying 'Duck!' Some soldiers are killed when protecting their squad, and some soldiers are killed when patrolling the streets. Future soldiers will be killed by replying slowly to a text message asking if you'll definitely be home in time for Uncle Alan's retirement party.

It will take a few years before the technology is developed for every soldier to carry a military smart phone. By that time, they will probably be quite useful because we'll be placing phones in the hands of the first generation to have been raised by parents with mobiles. And if there's anything to inspire a lust to kill strangers, it's being given the object that prevented your mother from looking or communicating with you for the last 18 years.

I'm not sure why they say mobile phones are the weapons of the future? From where I'm standing, it looks like handing every child a cancerous stick of isolation and apathy has pretty much destroyed humanity already.

The US army also wants *all* American soldiers to have 24-hour internet access. It's essential for operations that they continue to be anaesthetised by porn and *Tekken*, even when being begged to stop throwing grenades at a school.

The much-anticipated game *Medal of Honor* came out but it's not realistic at all. You've actually got a chance of winning, and all the equipment works. The next one, however, promises to be just like the real thing. It takes 27 years to complete and, whenever your character dies, you get a crappy, badly spelt letter from the prime minister.

There was outrage because of plans to let you play as the Taliban. You can't ban a game that has fighters in it just because they kill British soldiers. What about all the ones with US troops in? I'm quite advanced at it. The thing to do is be the Taliban. Then, when you get to Stage 3, sneak off and hide in a British coffin. Next thing you know, you can be pumping bullets into the till girl at Somerfields in Wootton Bassett.

★

France and Britain signed a treaty to share aircraft carriers. One week we'll put nothing on them, then the next week France will put nothing on them. Having a military agreement with France feels like getting help with your school homework from Peter Andre. At a joint conference, French military chiefs told their UK counterparts they were looking forward to the cost-saving consolidation of their respective forces, and the English ones replied, 'Hello, my name John is what I'm called, and my hobby I am cinema watching.'

David Cameron insists budget cuts won't affect our fighting capabilities – we'll keep losing. The army has to lose 7,000 soldiers. Probably the best way to do this is to put them on joint military manoeuvres with the Americans. I'm just worried that with thousands of unemployed troops, and Simon Cowell with a spare £100 million, *The X Factor* will move into its sinister second phase.

More than a quarter of the civilian posts at the Ministry of Defence will be cut over the next five years, following the Strategic Defence Review. Which will make James Bond films less interesting. 'Ah, Miss Moneypenny ... has gone ... I keep forgetting she had to go off and retrain as a classroom assistant.' Part of the defence cuts is the withdrawal of forces from Germany ... Really? Do you think it's safe yet? Do you think there's a chance we could return them, only to have an 80-year-old Nazi try to destroy the tube network with a Doodlebug?

The British military are spending £8 million a year on parties. You can imagine how much they'll spend if we actually start winning any of these wars. And there's uproar that military bosses are travelling the country by helicopter. Why would they do that? I mean it's not as if they've made it awkward for themselves to travel by tube. One general flew a military plane to Wolverhampton. But I suppose the only way to happily approach Wolverhampton is when you're watching it through a missile-targeting system.

25 per cent cuts across the board for education, health, social services – yet only 20 per cent on defence? That's like a family skimping on buying medicine, books and clothes so they still have enough money to catapult shit into next door's garden. The army admits it's lost more than £6 billion worth of equipment. That's the problem when you cover everything with camouflage.

They've also scrapped HMS *Ark Royal*. What does it say about the safe future of our country when the first boat to be scrapped is the *Ark*? We're building two aircraft carriers that, eh, won't have any aircraft on them. Basically, we'll defend ourselves by threatening hostile nations with a giant floating ironing board. What are they going to use all that space for? Sailors' hornpipe practice or overflow parking? Why would you build an aircraft carrier if you had no aircraft to put on it? Probably for the same reason that my father built a sun room in Scotland. It's a very handy place to store bulky furniture. Two giant boats that impotently travel about the world attracting ridicule. How on earth did they decide on the names *Queen Elizabeth II* and *Prince Charles*? Everyone is asking what will become of the *Ark Royal*? It will operate in the same manner as it did before being decommissioned. As a floating gay bar. Only now it will be docked in the Thames instead of prowling around the Persian Gulf in the dark like an old queen looking for trade.

Defence cuts mean fewer weapons – so at least it's a break for Afghan wedding photographers. You've got to feel for them. Just setting up the tripod and in comes a NATO drone. You've got an 8 by 10 of shrapnel and body bits, and all you can think to put underneath is 'The bride's family'.

A beauty queen joined the RAF in Afghanistan. It's nice to see someone in modelling who wants to kill someone other than herself. She has realised that there's more to life than being beautiful. There's being appreciated for your brave humour as they graft your bum skin onto your charred skull. Jodie Millward was pictured in a red vest and her RAF uniform – and I must say she looks better in blue – so I hope for her sake she'll die in a gas attack rather than from shrapnel wounds. Most models hate bits of their bodies; Jodie will be able to have those bits shipped home ahead of her rehab.

Fears about women now being allowed to work on British submarines are just sexist – they are just as capable as men. And anyway, under the sea there isn't as much call for being able to reverse. In the US, women have previously been barred from their subs because it was thought an unborn foetus would be affected from living near nuclear weapons and fuel fumes. It's now realised that this child would still grow up to be a fully functioning American. Protocol is very different in the navy now. In the old days, a woman entered a submarine and all the sailors would stand. Now, for young male recruits, women being on board will mean they'll be able to sit down for the first time in months.

Afghanistan has had a massive effect on me personally. Those shares in coffins and Union Jacks have gone through the fucking roof. I could retire tomorrow. According to defence chiefs, we have just completed the 'first stage' of the war against the Taliban. First stage? We've been there for ten years! What is the second stage going to consist of? Waiting for the tectonic plates to move and change the borders organically? Why is everyone talking about this as if it's only just started? I've got news for the Ministry of Defence. If you thought you'd erased all our memories, it didn't quite take. You may have to flash us again.

Support for the war in Afghanistan is at an all-time low. A lot of Scottish people used to say that Afghanistan was the only war we really needed to fight. But now that the street price of heroin is so low, even they don't see the point.

Hamid Karzai won the corrupt election and now has sovereignty over, er, Kabul and a miniature golf course just outside Kabul. In fact, even the capital isn't secure – they're thinking about renaming it Kaboom. He beat Abdullah Abdullah, who was unfortunately baptised in a cave with an echo. Karzai's brother was shot dead by his personal bodyguard. Never mind training Afghan leaders in democracy, we should probably start with interview technique.

The US army had to apologise for photos showing their troops posing with the corpses of Afghan civilians. Generals have been quick to say they've insulted the dignity of the rest of the US army. Is that the dignity of pissing on a Koran in Abu Ghraib, or the dignity of dangling from a rope ladder off the last helicopter to leave the US embassy roof in Saigon while your illegitimate children scream beneath you?

The Taliban are finding it impossible to get hold of essential supplies, so at last we're fighting on equal terms. But let's not get complacent. Just because they're running out of bullets, we mustn't assume our boys won't get shot. Remember, US troops have still got plenty.

Children of troops killed in Afghanistan are going to have their university education paid for. Kind of ironic that some girls will get highly educated thanks to the Taliban.

The British forces have handed Sangin to US forces. Many middle-class liberals are asking how we can leave these vulnerable people in the care of poorly educated, poorly paid, selfishly driven rednecks? And then they pick up their children from the two 16-year-old work experience girls that staff the best local nursery.

To be fair, British generals do a difficult job. Usually very, very badly. The Taliban are holding us off with regular prayer, and guns they stole from the set of *Rambo III*. Still, good to see it's all spilling over into Pakistan. A whole load of nuclear missiles and a bunch of people with different ideas about what Mohammed said. What could possibly go wrong?

The other day I was reading a book about how the Israelis captured Adolf Eichmann (there's a thrilling intelligence operation to check his identity, then they hit him on the head and throw him in a bag) and realised how little I knew about the Holocaust. In the course of reading up on it I found a collection of pictures – taken at the camps – of people on their way to the gas chambers, which is really something you should be certain you want to see before looking at it. It will remain with you. These are the people fresh from the trains, tired and bewildered. Children sit exhausted at their mothers' feet as they unwittingly queue to become victims of this monstrous and inhuman crime.

It all seems so remarkably singular, and yet also you can see these sort of pictures every day – newspaper photos of refugee camps, of families in war zones, emergency rooms in Gaza, children from the dollar-a-day world. Some of these people are victims of dictators too, but most are victims of an economic theory, and of our affluence and indifference. Daily, you see pictures of people queuing for death and somehow the worst thing, the very worst thing, is that if you really tried you could do something about it.

'Aye, it fucking is him an all'

★★★★

Paul makes me a cup of tea - he's one of those people who always makes half a cup of tea - and I get my panic list up on email. It's the only group email list I've ever had, one I compiled to announce that my daughter had been born. It included anyone who might give me work. I'd just got home from the birth and knew I was so broke I didn't have the money to get a taxi the next day to bring her home.

I'm flush nowadays - my company just landed a big advertising contract for an anti-speeding campaign. On dangerous stretches of road we are putting up family photos (the ones you get done in a photographers where the kids have been distracted by bubbles) of the actual people who have died there, over the words DEAD NOW. It's a suggestion I made as a despairing joke after they hated our other ideas. Everybody loves it. It's like the fucking 'Glasgow Smiles Better' of the post-Apocalypse.

I drag my suitcase out of a cab at Glasgow Central and take my glasses off. I'm trying to buy the papers for the train but I can see fuck all, accidentally picking up the *Star*, which has a front page about a mystery Old Firm player being blackmailed. I queue and wonder what Lovecraftian practice could set this young pervert apart from his peers.

The woman at the counter goes, 'What's with the beard, Frankie?'

I honestly can't think of a single response. Eventually I say, 'When I stop shaving, hair grows out of my face,' and she laughs like I've made a joke.

I'm squinting up at the departures board looking for the London train. I'm normally OK without the glasses but some wee guys by the bank machine are nodding over at me. Eventually one of them walks over, stands about 18 inches away from me and blares, 'Aye, it fucking is him an all,' as dispassionately as if he's noting that it's raining.

On the train I'm trying to do some work on a pitch for tomorrow but every time I look at the screen I feel sick. There's a slight smell of sewage but that's normal on Virgin. My stomach pitches. The disabled-passenger alarm sounds continually. Someone thinks they are pressing the flush. I log onto the internet and check the BBC news. The top headline is 'Prince William is a really good bloke'.

I look through the ideas I'm pitching. I was just going to be doing these for my company, but now I'm desperately trying to think how I can host or be involved.

Celebrity Land of the Giants. *Eight of the UK's most recognisable celebrities have signed up for what they 'think' is a new game show. They are put up in a hotel and wake up the next day. What they don't know is that overnight our clever set designers have built everything from cars to hedges to paving slabs outside at 10x scale, giving the celebs the impression they've shrunk overnight! How will they cope as each week the least practical star is eaten by what they think is a giant spider?*

Unbelievably, that is idea number one. The other one is about a celebrity slave ship where young black rappers are made to live as slaves for a week. I can't focus on the screen without feeling nauseous. Maybe it's a psychosomatic reaction to this shit? Or the fucking roast-beef sandwich they gave me was so old it's like a fast-acting poison. I sit watery mouthed in denial for a bit, then run to the toilet and puke loudly. The disabled-passenger alarm is painted red, illustrated with a ringing bell and the word alarm is written on it in large letters.

The young guy across from me recognises me and tries to start a conversation.

'Feeling sick?'

'Yes, I just puked.'

The sort of conversation dogs would have if they could talk.

'Aren't you Frankie Boyle?'

I put my earphones on and stupidly plug them into the side of my shut laptop. He's reading a book called *Confidence: There are No Coincidences*. Confidence is only worth having if you're not a fucking idiot. Try speaking German using just confidence. Start skiing with confidence and break your fucking neck, you cunt. I wonder why there are so many idiots now and whether in the past the big wars used to thin them out. I wonder if the free coffees are winding me up, or the rapist, or the work.

I look at the 'War' chapter of the book. That end bit is maybe everything that's wrong with the world. Wanting to help but feeling it's all to do with 'you', the ego that thinks it can make a difference is the same ego that wants a new car, praise, pussy, immortality. Still, maybe I'm just being honest, and what I honestly am is an idiot.

★

In London, I have to go straight across town and into a script meeting. It's a voiceover thing I'm doing for a clip show, which is a pretty shit thing to be doing, but I get to write the jokes, so that's something.

I sign the visitors' book and walk wordlessly past the security guard. In the event of some terrorist atrocity they will have the guy's signature. There are whole floors of talented people beavering away making shit. An infinite number of Shakespeares producing the work of a monkey.

I'm met by Gary, a tall, spindly production runner who looks like a freakish wind chime or insect king. He leads me to the meeting room, where there's a pyramid of Diet Coke, and some fresh notepads and biros. During the awkward wait for the producer, Gary tells me at length about his new baby while I reflect that in the wild his mate would have eaten him now.

I sit down and start reading the stack of tabloids that's in any writing room, whether the show is topical or not. Alex Ferguson is playing mind games. If only he would - telling the opposition that there is a sniper in the stadium, or staging a coach crash then sending out players everybody thought were dead in a macabre piece of gamesmanship.

★
WORK! CONSUME! DIE!

The producer, Gerry, drifts in. He has the jovial air of a corrupt small-town cop. I've not seen him for years and, in the meantime, his face looks like it's had kids. I go through the intros for the show

Welcome to The Frankie Boyle Clip Show. *There's nothing like being on television. And let me tell you, reading out this shit, to you pricks, for this money, is nothing like being on television.*

Hello and welcome to the show that made the Crossbow Cannibal refuse to pay his licence fee. Feels good, doesn't it, knowing that cock is currently watching video tapes of Minder *wishing I had tits and he had a lifespan of 300 years.*

'I prefer the first one!' says Gerry, and I agree, having included the second one so I had something to give up. I launch into the rest at a pace calculated to delay discussion.

The show that masturbates to the Oscars' Obituary Montage.

The show that's laughing with you, not at you. Ahahahahaa! Oh no, wait a minute, it's at you.

The show of clips you could find for yourself on YouTube. If porn didn't exist.

The show that three of your personalities only agree to watch because they're scared of your dominant personality, a murderous lesbian midget.

*30 minutes that will leave you sweating like Peter Andre
on Countdown.*

*The show that eats your pussy with neither skill nor
enthusiasm.*

*The show that knows you felt a hand running up your leg
on a crowded bus. You grabbed the hand and held it up,
saying, 'Whose hand is this?' Only to find out that it was
your own.*

*Hey! Mongo! It's evening. The bright ball of wonder has
yet again left the sky, so take your hoof from out your
pants and once more suckle at my TV teats.*

*Hey, friendless! Yes, you! Wipe the dribble from your
fleece and once more feast on my distractions. Together
we can get you half an hour closer to the dawn of
another worthless day.*

'Ehhh …,' starts Gerry.
   'We only need six or something,' I interrupt. 'It's
just intros, we can come back to it …'
   We nod, both agreeing to different things.

★

The first clip we're doing is of some hugely misguided
children's show from the 80s, teaching yoga to little
kids. It's set on a farm and hosted by a real sandpit
haunter calling himself Yogie Okie Dokie. We see him
bending the kids into various positions.

*It's amazing how flexible kids are when they're drunk.
Yogi Okie Dokie is only his first name. His surname is
Pokey Chokey.*

'Now the lawyers are worried about that … we
can't actually imply that he's a paedophile …' Gerry
havers.

'The lawyers?' I ask. 'It's a joke. I don't think
anyone would really think his surname was Pokey Chokey.
Or that his first names are Yogie Okie Dokie …'

'You can't imply that he's a paedophile.'

'Fuck, look at the show. I mean … fuck!'

There's a clip of that wee toddler that smokes in
fucking Papua New Guinea or somewhere.

*Of course, he doesn't smoke any more. He's dead now. His
little brother uses his skull as an ashtray.*

'We can't say that,' murmurs Gerry.

'Why not?' I ask and open another Diet Coke because
maybe this would be easier if my brain were dead.

'He's not dead.' Gerry is getting exasperated. 'So
the lawyers say that we can't say that he is.'

'It's a joke. They're saying we can't say anything
that isn't the literal truth? He's going to sue? He's
out in the fucking jungle. He's hardly … getting driven
on a moped to a clearing where they all sit round and
watch fucking clip shows.'

We keep hitting bits the lawyers have vetoed. They
have suggested replacements, the lawyers have written
jokes. I have met lawyers and these are the sort of
jokes you would expect them to write. It's not immediately obvious that they are jokes.

The final clip is a terrible video about how to use the techniques of a magician to pull women. We type the last joke up in a way that it can be altered if there's a legal problem.

These are the techniques that Debbie McGee [an older magician's assistant] warns [a] young magician's assistant about, before heading home to another night of being sawn in half so Paul Daniels [a magician] can watch her [them] eat her [their] own arsehole.

I suggest that we start the show with me in an armchair, cradling a huge horn. I will explain that not all of the jokes are literally true and that when I say something not meant to be taken literally I will blow a note on my mighty horn. Perhaps we should change the title of the show to *The Horn of Balathor.*

'Where is Balathor?' says Gerry

'I thought of it as more of a what – *Balathor the Green. Balathor the Mighty.*'

Another producer comes in and this idea sort of catches fire. Yes, we could call it *The Horn of Balathor.* It's only a fucking clip show. Perhaps I could appear at the bottom of the screen when I blow the horn, like the guy on sign-language programmes. Maybe there could be different sizes of horn, depending on how offensive the joke is. There is a clip from the 70s that suggests black people can't swim. I suggest we do the line:

Of course it's a ridiculous racial stereotype to say black people can't swim. How do you think AIDS got to Europe?

And then I come on with one of those huge Alpine horns that rest on the ground and give a blast so loud it would actually blow the speakers on people's TVs. I'm thinking that will keep me in the papers long enough that my arse will remain un-raped. I maintain to the guys that it could work as a show. Fuck it, it could work as a show, or has my judgement just gone? Yes, my judgement has gone but perhaps I could be right by accident.

I look them both in the eye and beam, 'Comedy is tragedy plus laughter!'

But I know the fucking thing is not going to happen.

★ ★ ★ ★

The bright old day now dawns again; the cry runs through the land,
In England there shall be dear bread – in Ireland, sword and brand;
And poverty, and ignorance, shall swell the rich and grand,
So, rally round the rulers with the gentle iron hand,
Of the fine old English Tory days; Hail to the coming time!

Charles Dickens, *The Fine Old English Gentleman*

★ ★ ★ ★

02

Having travelled a wee bit, I'm convinced that Britain's sense of humour – the sheer scope and breadth and complexity of our piss-taking – is unique. That's what I hate about these various joke scandals. They have at their heart the idea that the public won't be able to decode what was meant by the joke; that even if *you* understand, other people might not, when everyone here has a PhD in wind-ups.

People are struggling with the whole idea of comedy at the moment. I think comedy is probably a descendant of shamanism. The comic is some guy or gal covered in shit who'd live out in the desert and come roaring into the settlement every so often to tell everybody what was up with how they perceived life. Of course, this made them a pariah.

Comedy is a fictional space. Some of the things the shaman says are true, even heartfelt. Sometimes she says things she doesn't mean; sometimes she says the opposite of what she means. And, admittedly, she isn't always good, but nobody is. Sometimes you end up watching Peter Kay, but sometimes it's Bill Hicks and sometimes it's Loki.

There are a few problems. One, you get the soul-grinding mill of television, which sees that it can use a few laughs to keep people dumb and distracted. It likes to employ shamans with their eyes poked out. Two, you get some well-meaning types who would like the status of the shaman without the whole pariah bit. They could maybe skip the drugs and keep the status – or even just the cash? Sorry, those are all false paths. The shaman knows that the route to enlightenment is to lose the ego and, what with one thing and another, she's going to get too much attention to get very far with that. So the joke is on her. The price the trickster pays for her existence is to be, ultimately, the butt of her own joke. Glad I managed to explain comedy to y'all before I died [tips hat].*

* *I don't believe any of this. The idea of the comedian as shaman is simply a different way for a practitioner to gather status and feed the ego. In man's original nomadic tribal state, the role of social critic would have been vital in deciding when to move on. Comedians are just the descendants of the guys and gals whose job it was to say, 'It's fucking shit here,' and moan until everybody upped sticks and headed west, into an ambush prepared by a rival tribe, or a barren wasteland.***

** *This is all bollocks. Comics are sort of the opposite of shamans really. Shamans, poets, priests are all people whose role is to power-up symbols. In our scientific reality tunnel a hallucination might be a manifestation of the unconscious mind. In a shamanic one it might be a fairie, in a religious one, an angel. The comedian is actually there to de-power the symbolic world. With Lenny Bruce, cancer goes from being this big demonic taboo to being, well, just cancer. The best comics are really trying to wake you up from the symbolic world; they're desentimentalisers, pointing out that those First World War soldiers who had a truce to play football at Christmas probably killed each other the next day, and not even remorsefully but muttering, 'That was never offside, you cunt.'****

*** *Of course, none of this is really what you would call accurate, but between these viewpoints there is something close to the truth. I think that by constantly undermining and subverting himself a comedian might be able to communicate quite profoundly, by a kind of triangulation. You can't really ever defend a joke because at the point it's getting dissected it's not a joke. Is a dead butterfly in a case still a butterfly? Even a mermaid wouldn't look too beautiful during an autopsy. This is as close as someone like me can ever get to explaining himself. Do you get it? [smiles hopefully with a brittle smile].*****

**** Look, it's not supposed to be analysed. You can't create a space that asks what would happen if we abandoned all the rules and then start saying things are outside of the rules. There aren't *any fucking rules. OK, here's something that should stop you dissecting comedy, something I could prove scientifically if I could be arsed. Do you know the main factor in whether you find something funny or not? The kind of day you've just had.*

So, the Tories are back. If you don't remember them, they were big in the 1980s – like dungarees and white people getting AIDS. The British people spoke, and they conclusively shrugged their shoulders and said, 'Whatever. I'm not bothered. Him. You. Or the other one. *Britain's Got Talent's* coming on, you sort it out. See you in five years.' So, we've got a new prime minister and, unlike Gordon Brown, this one was actually nearly elected. Obviously, Cameron got straight down to work while Samantha got all of his forehead polish into Number 10. Can Cameron really manage to create social cohesion? I mean, his head has only just managed to create some semblance of a face. Cameron is the youngest prime minister for nearly 200 years, which is odd, because he's also been alive for far too long.

People who say we shouldn't have royalty *and* an elected representative seem to be missing the fact that we have royalty as our elected representative – both David and Samantha Cameron have royal ancestors. In fact, now William is married to Kate Middleton, we actually have an elected first family that have more royal blood than our future king and queen. Do you get the feeling that Sam Cameron is one of the few PM's wives to consider Number 10 a step down on the property ladder? It comes to something when our prime minister regards his trip to Buckingham Palace as part of his gritty contact with working-class people. He's descended from King William IV and his mistress. Why did we vote for him? Even King William knew he didn't want to take him on permanently.

It was claimed that Cameron has a fortune estimated at £30 million. Do you really believe he really gives a flying fuck as to when your bins get emptied or where your rat-faced children go to school? Does he even know how to use public transport? I can see him now, queuing at his nearest helipad, clutching an Oyster card.

For a while, Cameron was on the board of the company that owns Tiger Tiger. This is his idea of how Britain should enjoy itself? Rows of spandex-clad women trying to work out which former reality TV star they are least terrified of accepting a drink from?

Not long after the election, David Cameron and Barack Obama had a historic meeting in Washington and Obama rolled out the red carpet for Cameron. A lovely gesture, but Cameron really should not have tipped him a dollar for doing so. It was a low-key welcome. I feel a bit sorry for the PM. It can't be good for your self-esteem, seeing a cabbie at JFK airport with a bit of cardboard with 'Mr Macaroon' written on it in marker pen. When Cameron first saw a black man standing in a white mansion he thought they were remaking *The Fresh Prince of Bel-Air*.

The PM met with the president face to face, after breaking free from the White House tour group when they passed the door to the Oval Office. Apparently, Obama and David Cameron 'swapped anecdotes'. That must have been fascinating for Obama. After telling David all about his rise to become the first black president of the most powerful nation on earth, he then had to listen to Dave tell a rather amusing story about going to Waitrose and buying chorizo instead of salami.

Reports also said the men were on 'Christian-name terms'. Dave calls him Obama and Obama calls him Nick. When David's in Obama's company he always has a very serious, concerned, concentrated face – like he's desperately trying not to fart, but knowing that only minutes ago he ate four catering-size tins of pickled cabbage. He flew to meet Obama on a standard BA flight, to save money. If he really wanted to save money, he should have flown Ryanair. During a recession, it would be inspiring to see the PM pissing into an empty Fanta can, just to save a quid.

Ah, the Big Society. Does Cameron really believe Britain would be a better place if it were run by the public? Have you seen the public? It's hard enough to get through the laboured and tedious process of getting a pair of trousers dry-cleaned by someone who has been in the dry-cleaning business for 20 years. How's it going to work when your lollypop man is in charge of a prison?

George Osborne said, 'Everyone in our society has had to make a contribution.' And Osborne's contribution is to destroy our society. Everyone's going to muck in. First, you can make up for the lack of police by doing a citizen's arrest, and then – due to the total lack of nurses – attempt to stitch your face back together.

If we really are genuinely all in it together they should disband all political parties and run the country in a true democratic manner. In the past the Greeks used to run their parliament in a similar style to jury duty. You were called up to serve and you did your time. There were no career politicians. It was part of your civic duty. And at least that way everyone in Britain would get one year to do their house up, employ their relatives, make some extra cash on expenses and find out what it's like to live like a fucking king.

Sir Michael Caine helped the Tories promote their National Citizenship Service, a plan to help youths experience being a citizen of the UK in a non-military national service. Kids don't need to have their own brown shirt to join, but the names, addresses and occupations of all friends and family are an essential.

The prime minister announced plans for private firms to run more public services. Clearly a good idea. You only have to look at Southern Cross care homes to see that. Thousands of OAPs may be kicked out onto the street after the care-home giant said it was closing. It's a really distressing thing and my heart goes out to all those unfortunate people who must be worrying that they'll have to let their parents move in with them. Staff said they've been kept in the dark. Something Southern Cross previously only did with residents, having them suckle a sedative paste until their direct debits ran out.

Cameron says he wants to give charities and community groups more power to run organisations such as youth clubs. Exactly how much power do you need to run a youth club? I'd have thought a Sony PlayStation and a box of biscuits, and you've pretty much covered all the bases.

Conservative MP and Education Secretary Michael Gove has announced that teachers will be allowed to discipline unruly pupils outside of school. This should allow teachers to be assaulted even when they're not at work. They'll end up getting their heads kicked in, and probably their assistant heads too.

More than 100 state schools failed to enter a single person for GCSE history in 2010. Which sounds like a shocking statistic, but bear in mind in just a few years' time it will have been completely forgotten. Along with the Holocaust and slavery. A report said there's one bad teacher in every school. Of course there is. They can't cut PE out of the curriculum altogether.

A teachers' strike hit over 5,000 schools. Gove wants teachers to work an extra eight years before they retire. But look on the bright side, teachers – you'll be on holiday for four of them. Maths lessons will be interesting with a teacher who's nearly

70. 'If there are two milk bottles on my doorstep and they are joined by another twelve milk bottles, how long have I been dead?'

Luckily, on the day of the strike they also shut the job centres and the courts, meaning Glaswegians could spend the day with their kids. Civil servants, court ushers and teachers – we couldn't have had more ineffectual strikes if the dead had decided to stop decomposing for a day. But it's nice for British teenagers to have the day off – watch some *Jeremy Kyle*, find out what all those girls who left at 16 are up to. The *Sun* interviewed a teenager from Gateshead who was worried that the teachers' strike would ruin his future. How will he sign on if he can't spell his name?

There's controversy over the ballot, with the government saying that many who voted for the strike were simply marking the fact that 'Yes' was spelt correctly. How can it be a 24-hour strike when these people only work until 3.30? Or did they also take the evening off when normally they'd have been getting drunk in the local pub while trying to grope ex-pupils?

Teachers don't have my complete sympathy. I remember turning up without my kit and saying, 'I suppose I have to do it in my pants?' and my PE teacher whispering, 'That was last time ... you've raised the stakes. This time you'll have to do it in *my* pants.' The cross-country run was much easier, but I confess the whole arrangement did make me feel a bit like a baby kangaroo.

That strike went against everything the Big Society is all about, which is 'work constantly for free until you die'. I love the way the media pretends that the erosion of workers' right to strike is some kind of advance. In the 1970s, we're told, strikes were the British disease. I guess we're supposed to be proud that it's changed to chlamydia. I still remember the last miners' strike, when a shortage of coal led to a terrifying winter of blind snowmen. Still, it's clearly ridiculous for teachers to go on strike for a better pension. A teenager will have stabbed them through the heart ages before they reach retirement. Some people defended the strike by saying that it was only one day. Unfortunately, it was the day all the private-school kids got taught how to run banking software and pass the Oxford entry exam.

★

The General Election was a surprising result for Nick Clegg – he was bounding around Parliament with the joy of a bullied child who'd just changed schools. His first action as deputy prime minister was to make sure Jeremy Beadle was still dead. Never has someone so mediocre been so fought over – he must feel like girl at a *Star Trek* convention.

The Lib Dems found it very hard to decide whether they were Labour or Tory supporters, mostly because they're Lib Dem supporters. I mean, had most of them agreed with one of the major parties they would probably have applied to join those parties, rather than spend their career standing at the back of town halls looking disappointed.

Clegg said he wants the British to experience a taste of the Lib Dems in government so that they will be confident to vote for a fully Lib Dem government. I know that reasoning. It's similar to when you bring home someone for a threesome who *smells* like a goat.

During the coalition a few compromises have been made. The Lib Dems have had to agree to Tory policies on taxation, immigration and policing – but they will be presented in a nice yellow folder. The Tories have dropped their cap on immigration, but have axed £150 million from the local government housing budget. You can't get rid of immigrants while you're cutting social housing – who will we blame? Horrible to see

Child Trust Funds have been scrapped. By the time they are 18 our current generation of babies will need that cash to forge their papers and bribe a Chinese camp official.

Of course, the Lib Dems didn't even get the voting reform that they sold their souls for. The problem with the Alternative Vote was that it wasn't a real alternative. They should just make the candidates do an *It's a Knockout*-style course with their last year's expenses in 2p pieces in a rucksack on their back. My idea of an alternative vote would be having the option of electing someone who isn't a cunt.

The coalition is also proposing to cut benefits to heroin addicts. Surely it would be better to send them to Afghanistan. If the Taliban are between them and those opium poppies we might just win. And when Al-Qaeda blows up the Olympics there won't be a TV left in the country for them to watch it on.

The Lib Dems aren't totally comfortable with a new deterrent being ordered. But in this new spirit of political cooperation they've been given some options by their coalition partners. They can either shut up or piss off.

The Lib Dems say they want to give everyone in Britain the chance to fulfil their potential. What potential does Britain have? If you're talking about young people, then it means they'd all get the opportunity to release a single, be on Page Three or finger Cheryl Cole. And when it comes to old people, think about your parents. What potential do they have to fulfil? As long as they get their two weeks in Lanzarote and can afford wafer-thin ham they wouldn't care if the country was run by a military junta of humanoid gorillas.

'It should be what you know, not who you know,' said David Cameron's mate, Nick Clegg. Mr Clegg admitted he feels 'quite miserable' that he does not see enough of his three kids. I suppose someone has to work to pay for them to get through university. He's also admitted he doesn't want his kids to see him smoking. Luckily it doesn't bother David Cameron at all. Apparently he's even put a little ashtray in Nick's hutch. David Cameron has suggested patches. But Clegg wants to stick with the name 'Nick'.

Clegg says he and Cameron wander into each other's offices to chat. Well, Cameron wanders into Clegg's to chat and Clegg wanders into Cameron's office to be greeted with a tuft of black hair bobbing behind a desk and some giggly shushing.

Nick Clegg's popularity's slumped to just 18 per cent, but David Cameron leapt to his defence, saying he's a great politician and work colleague. Good move, Dave – never slag off the guy who brings your coffee. Especially if you have froth on the top. Clegg's even been getting flak for doing the morning school run. I certainly take my lad to the school gates whenever I can. Then whisper in his ear, 'See all those laughing children? Improve your stitching around the instep and maybe you can join them.'

Energy Secretary Chris Huhne isn't faring any better in the popularity stakes after he allegedly tried to get off a speeding ban by claiming his ex-wife was driving. I guess he's got to switch to plan B – claiming that a bomb would've gone off in his Vauxhall Nova if he'd dropped below 80. I suspect he was just confused by events. As a Lib Dem Euro MP, when the camera flashed he would have had no idea what it was.

If Huhne really was the one behind the wheel then it could have a devastating effect on the country. Just imagine experiencing the uneasy feeling that maybe MPs can lie. If Chris Huhne deserves any points then surely it should be for dumping his wife for a bisexual woman ten years younger than him. Bisexuals are really attracted to senior Lib Dems – as they're both a man, and a great big pussy.

The cabinet performance of Vince Cable has definitely convinced me – to have my parents' euthanasia documentation rushed through. Only kidding. I'd vote for Vince Cable. I did at this year's EuroPorn Awards.

His speeches about Unions have been peppered with aggressive language, which is odd because he normally saves that sort of thing for his home help, who he thinks is stealing from him. Cable plans to sell off a portion of the Royal Mail but also to hand over a significant chunk of the service to employees. When he does hand it over I hope he does it in the style of a Royal Mail employee, by creeping up to the front door, pretending they're not in when they clearly are, quietly slipping a 'Sorry you were out' card through the letterbox and making them go down to the depot to collect it for themselves.

The business secretary said that by giving them 10 per cent of the company this would be the largest handover to employees attempted in the UK ever. Really? I'm sure almost every employee has stolen more than ten per cent of the business they work for. If the plan for privatisation goes ahead, postmen will get regular performance-related payouts. As opposed to the current system, when they only get a bonus if they hold a torch up to an envelope and can make out a tenner wedged in a birthday card.

The Post Office is launching an evening delivery service. So now there's a chance you'll be interrupted while you're trying to get drunk, as well as while you masturbate. It'll mean no more postie-leaving-parcels-with-a-neighbour. At a stroke trebling the cost of my Christmas shopping.

★

Is it too much to ask that we have a fucking opposition in this country? Ed Miliband against David Miliband was the most titanic battle between brothers since Wimbledon 2009, when Serena played Venus Williams. Ed's victory was wonderful news. We now have a choice of three interchangeable suited drones come 2015. With David and Ed being successful, I wonder if there's another Miliband brother to come out of the woodwork? Jethro Miliband – he's got an IQ of 70 and is defined by sexual jealousy, but Mummy Miliband insists he has a role in the shadow cabinet. What's the future of the party? The only thing we can say for sure is it's going to be a grim family Christmas round the Milibands. Bit like the one at the Minogues.

Ed Miliband looks like someone who's talking while having dental surgery. His cum face must look like a widow's vagina hitting G-force. There are a lot more cheap cracks that can be made about his appearance but I won't be making them. Not after the trouble the last Down's syndrome joke got me in.

It was announced that Ed had won and then the next day David made a speech, then the day after Ed's speech David held a press conference – this is basically the political version of repeating everything your little brother says in a mocking voice. David was the first politician to resign so he can spend less time with his family. He looks like Mathew Horne being slapped in the face with a hammer. As do most of my fantasies. Ed now faces the huge challenge of trying not to look smug in front of his brother. Which won't be easy, as it will mean having plastic surgery.

Diane Abbott said there was a plot to get rid of Ed Miliband, but I hardly think you can call the next election a plot. Miliband is now so invisible NATO wants to use his skin to cover stealth planes. Embarrassingly, he polled lower than Nick Clegg. That must be like your wife telling you she's leaving you for an occasional table. Miliband's approval rating would have been even lower if people had recognised his name.

★

The Scottish Nationalists had a huge result at the Holyrood elections. If we go independent all the beggars in London will have to be reclassified as refugees. The most persuasive argument for independence is that 'We've got all the oil.' Have you seen what happens to small countries that have oil? We might get independence but that will quickly be followed by pilotless US drones attacking Edinburgh Castle, being captured by the locals and reprogrammed to find Neil Lennon. Within six months, Alex Salmond will be hanging on a gibbet as David Cameron announces a plan to introduce democracy to Scotland.

We'll finally have our own customs officers to check that we haven't brought more than our personal allowance of 18,000 litres of alcohol into the country. Even if we did go independent, what's the biggest change going to be? There will still be dog shite in the streets. Scottish dog shite. Our pubs will still be full of pricks. Scottish pricks. The only difference I can envisage is that on Saturday nights we'll watch a TV show called *Scotland's Got Talent*. And the winner will be a lassie who can mark a bingo card while having a heart attack.

★

The population of Britain is projected to grow by almost half a million people every year until 2032. Most of them will be immigrants from Eastern Europe, and a good thing too, as I can't see anyone from here wanting to give me blanket baths and change my adult diapers for a few pounds an hour. Actually, I'm not talking about the future. That's just what I'm into.

Iain Duncan Smith gave a speech demanding British jobs for British people. Where did he deliver this speech? From a balcony in a sports stadium shortly before Jesse Owens ran the 100 metres. Asking employers to consider British people for British jobs contravenes EU human-rights laws. Which has upset many Tories. Listen, when your policies are the direct opposite of human rights, it might be time to take a long, hard look at your soul. I confess I sometimes employ foreign labour to write for me and they do a great job. OK, some of the references may be a little off, but if you don't like it, go whistle at the clay mountain, dragon shoes!

Theresa May says she's going to cut immigration by 5 per cent, by standing on the cliffs of Dover with no bra on. In future, applicants will have to have a degree, private health insurance and a sponsor, or be able to do at least 50 keepy uppies in front of officers at Heathrow. There will be no restrictions on highly skilled professionals who create wealth, such as entrepreneurs and employees of multinational companies. That's a weird one, isn't it? Entrepreneurs are allowed in, but teachers and nurses aren't. So, if you can work an X-ray machine, it's a 'no', but if you've got an idea for *Dragons' Den* about a biodegradable chair made out of cheddar, it's a 'yes'.

May is also cracking down on foreign students. Because we don't want intelligent immigrants coming here, just the ones willing to sell us chips and sex. She also hopes to have more police out on the streets. Bad news for muggers, car thieves and blokes not in the best of health who've had a few pints and are wandering past a march.

Every time I see Theresa May I can't help thinking that she looks like a woman going out on the town the first night after she has just finalised her divorce. She's made way too much of an effort and there's the very real sense that in two hours' time she's going to be crying in a toilet and wearing only one shoe. She admits that tackling immigration is her toughest challenge. Really? I'd have thought her toughest challenge was finding a foundation to match her skin tone that wasn't solely available for wholesale to funeral parlours.

The BNP have voted to allow non-whites to join. They now look set to have their first Sikh member. What's he going to do?

Move house because he doesn't want to live in a street with him on it? At least the turban will soften the blows to his head. He said that joining the BNP won't change him. Although he's stopped using the toilet and now craps into his own letterbox. Yes, I find myself forced to agree that 'There ain't no black in the Union Jack.' But to highlight the counter-argument for a moment, there aren't that many red or blue people.

I've finally worked out why Nick Griffin is so hated. It's not just his policies, it's his face. In particular, the big, mad eye. It makes him look evil. Like a bogus caller as viewed through a pensioner's security peephole. Simply put, Griffin permanently looks like he wants to steal your granny's pension and beat her to a pulp with a tin of soup. Look at him closely and you'll see that he wanders around as if he's gawping through an invisible magnifying glass – as if looking for clues that might lead him to an Asian's lair.

After his piss-poor appearance on *Question Time* I suspect he'll receive sack loads of hate mail, which will be delivered sometime around Easter. Host David Dimbleby tried to assure the audience it would 'not just be the Nick Griffin show'. Although I'd love to see *The Nick Griffin Show*. 'Tonight's guests are Carol Thatcher, Ron Atkinson and the restless spirit of Jade Goody.'

Griffin's political ideology is so confused I can't wait for the next party political broadcast. He associates so closely with Churchill but is far more in tune with Hitler. Picture the scene. Griffin is made up as Adolf but he screams his speech in a Cockney accent, while thousands of Chelsea pensioners goose-step down the Mall singing 'Knees Up Eva Braun'. There are Spitfires overhead, emblazoned with swastikas. Finally, we see Griffin, made up now as Churchill, talking to a young Jewish girl. Churchill takes a deep puff of his cigar and says with a terrible German accent, 'Madam, I might be drunk. But you are ugly. However, in the morning I'll be sober. You, however … will be dead.'

After Griffin compared Britain's military generals to Nazi war criminals, he said that the party's website attracted 77,000 unique visitors. Not that unique, I suspect. I'm willing to bet they all had a couple of things in common. Like the IQ of cat shit and a very scared black neighbour.

A British Muslim who wants to enter Miss Universe has received threats. Perhaps she could just compromise and ask if she can appear once in an evening dress, and once under a big pile of stones.

It turns out we're all eating Halal meat without realising it. Basically, the animal has its throat cut with a sharp knife. Either by a butcher or, if it lives in South London, it might just have popped out for fags. It can't be stunned, as followers of Islam are forbidden to consume blood. A revelation that's pissed off the *Daily Express*, just as they were about to run their 'Dracula Was a Muslim' headline. The advice seems to be if you're not sure about your meat's origins, ask supermarket staff. That'll work. 'Erm … I'm usually on bread … Mr Richards. Mr Richards! There's a man here don't like sausages or somefin'.'

It's also been revealed that chimpanzee meat is being sold in Britain to eat. Chimpanzees – could they get any more amazing? Are we to believe that they can add being delicious to their other qualities, like being funny and sexy? Before you ask, no, chimp meat doesn't taste like chicken. It tastes like bananas and tea. I could see this catching on – imagine at Christmas. Instead of arguing over who gets a drumstick, there'll be enough for everyone to have a finger.

Tesco plan to introduce the country's first drive-through supermarket. Actually, that's something Paul Gascoigne tried out when he lost control in the car park of Morrisons after knocking back a bargain bucket of Listerine.

Takeaways are to have their hygiene rating stuck on their doors in stars, from one to five. You put one star on a takeaway door – the rats will just think it's their dressing room.

The boss of Burger King reckons British women are ugly. I'd like to disagree, but he is an expert on disappointing lifeless baps. How can he say that? The guy's a clown. No, wait, that's the other lot isn't it? He also said the UK was terrible. Yes, some of it is. Burger King, for starters.

★

Last winter it got so cold that at one point a Geordie was spotted wearing a coat. It was later proven to be a hoax. It wasn't a coat; it was simply a tattoo of a coat. The freakish snow conditions came as a total surprise to the authorities, for the third year in a row. Philip Hammond, the UK transport secretary, said that he had learned some valuable lessons. Next time he'll just phone in and say he can't get to work 'cause of the snow.

There was total travel misery, with thousands of train passengers attempting to reach Scotland and succeeding. Norfolk proved impossible to get to, bad news for anyone needing to bury a body. If you are supposed to be visiting relatives this Christmas make sure you check conditions of the relevant roads. If they're clear you'll have to make up another excuse for not going.

People waiting for the Eurostar had to queue for eight hours in the freezing cold, treated with no respect or consideration. Making their planned holiday at Disneyland Paris unnecessary. The queue for the Eurostar stretched for over a mile round St Pancras. Some passengers eventually abandoned plans to go to Paris and had to fuck their secretary on the pavement. The Eurostar was cancelled? Doesn't it travel in a tunnel under the ground? Are the tunnels crowded with nomadic populations migrating from the new ice age?

Some people waiting for Eurostar became hysterical. How bad is the UK now when people cry because they can't get to Belgium? Stop bloody moaning. What is more true to the original story of Christmas than taking a highly difficult journey, which puts your wife and child's health at risk, and ends up with you having to sleep on a filthy floor because all the hotels are full?

Conditions at Heathrow were described as 'Third World'. 'Every day little Mr Alan Thomas has to walk 500 yards for water. Down to the gents past Tie Rack and Garfunkel's.' Can you imagine being one of those families stuck at Heathrow on Christmas Day? Waking up your 5-year-old to tell him that Santa has been, and he's brought a ploughman's sandwich and a pair of socks. Heathrow looked less like a Third World country and more like Heathrow airport exactly 12 months ago.

Apparently a flight to Newcastle was cancelled seven times – although that may've just been because the plane itself simply refused to go there. One passenger said it was 'absolute mayhem'. Weird – my idea of 'absolute mayhem' isn't a load of people sat around looking grumpy. It's an astronaut indiscriminately firing a custard gun in Debenhams. I was upset that all those flights were cancelled. Anything that slows down the approaching death of the planet is a tragedy in my opinion. The snow caused quite a few injuries round my way. Apologies, but if you will keep saying 'So much for global warming', I've got no choice but to punch you.

My favourite Christmas game is hide and seek – last year I was undiscovered until New Year's Eve. People worry about the elderly being lonely at Christmas, but the old woman next to me got loads of cards. They're piling up on her doorstep since the letterbox got full. People were unable to buy presents due to online stores shutting down delivery. Mainly because people confused 'some snow' with a deadly stream of radioactive lava preventing them from walking further than their own door.

It's definitely worth a deliveryman risking his life on treacherous roads so my missus can get *Sex and the City 2* on DVD. Royal Mail postmen did their best to clear the parcel backlog – helping themselves to a couple of packages whenever they knocked off a shift.

Why does everyone always say there's no grit? I saw loads of grit – granted, it was all in a van surrounded by bewildered council workers. They couldn't find enough salt in Scotland? Surely they could have flushed the inhabitants of the motorway services onto the roads and opened a few arteries? I'm pleased they haven't gritted the pavements; sliding into strangers is the only physical contact Glaswegians get.

A great-granddad nearly froze to death when passers-by ignored him after he slipped on ice and lay on a city street for nearly five hours. It's hard to believe he lay there all that time and nobody stole his shoes. Happily, he got back home, where he'll spend the next three months being ignored before freezing to death.

The head of British Gas said their profit margins are smaller than Marks & Spencer's. I think the difference that he fails to recognise is that thousands of old people don't die every year because they can't afford to shop at M&S. Despite making £2.2 billion in profit this year, British Gas executives say they have been forced to pass on to customers some of the rising costs of heating their country mansions.

★

So, farewell then, *News of the World*. 'Thank You & Goodbye' was the final headline. Apparently, 'You Can't Sue, We No Longer Exist!' wouldn't quite fit onto the front page. If Rupert Murdoch had been allowed to take full control of Sky, it would've been great. You could've pressed the red button and it'd have given you 24-hour coverage of Gordon Brown's bins. The whole Murdoch business reminds me of Grima Wormtongue from *The Lord of the Rings*. Formerly a tenacious-looking, sharp practitioner, whispering poison into the ear of power, suddenly this arch manipulator looks like a fucking Tequila worm.

The politicians, of course, are more like Denethor, whom Sauron drove to despair with images of his swelling armies. Looking deep into the *palantír* of the media, our leaders though it showed them reality, when it actually only showed what Murdoch and his like directed their gaze towards.

I'm so disgusted with News International that I refuse to read anything they print. Including my own column in the *Sun*, which is why I write it with my eyes closed. I say 'write' – I mean, I let my cat run across the keyboard and then clean it up with the spell check. If it's good enough for Dan Brown, it's good enough for me. Just to be on the safe side, I've never given the *Sun* my mobile number. In fact, every week I dictate the column onto the voicemail of a random victim of crime. Of course, it's easy to learn the precise details of people's mobile-phone messages. There's the high-tech procedure where you hack into their SIM account, and the lower-tech one where you somehow lure them into a giant imitation train carriage.

The hacking story took an explosive twist when it was alleged that the *News of the World* hacked into Milly Dowler's phone. The police are investigating – which shouldn't take too long. Officers, flick back your diaries to 2002 and see if any of the entries read 'Helped *News of the World* hack Milly Dowler's phone'. Some policemen were so sickened by the *News of the World* that they refuse to even line their budgie's cage with it. Instead, they are using used bills with non-sequential serial numbers.

Ford cars halted advertising with the *News of the World* when the Milly Dowler story broke. Nice showing solidarity by ceasing to advertise the one thing that kills the most UK teens every year. Orange and T-Mobile also pulled their advertising. Makes sense – the *News of the World* had shown their products to be a little flimsy, security wise. Mumsnet cancelled £30,000 worth of advertising with Sky. Money they raised by selling their collected bile to the Chinese medicine industry.

Glenn Mulcaire, who's accused of hacking Milly's phone, asked the press to leave his family alone. I'm guessing he then went to look up the word 'irony'.

Does anyone else think Rebekah Brooks looks like the exhumed Milly Dowler? It's so sad that the mobile phone of a murdered teenager was hacked into – a life cut short before her natural death from a radiation-induced brain tumour in her 30s. Listening to a murdered girl's messages. It's a new low. Whatever happened to the traditional methods of tabloid journalism? Nicking stories from regional papers and doing Select All/Copy/Paste from *Britain's Got Talent* press releases.

We celebs must take precautions. I urge any I meet to follow my example and make themselves a carrier-pigeon runway hat. The only tricky bit is training the mouse in the control tower. The *News of the World* hacked Lembit Öpik's phone messages – after six months of waiting, they rang him just to check he was still alive. Apparently, Chris Tarrant's phone messages aren't very interesting – it's mostly just people saying 'Sorry I was out. I don't know what the capital of Ecuador is.' At least I know the newspapers will never listen to my answerphone messages, as no one ever calls me.

Rupert Murdoch appeared at a parliamentary select committee and some very important questions got answered. Such as, how hard can a Chinese woman punch a man in the face? Rupert said he'd never felt more humble – which is saying something. He owns the TV channel that shows *Fat Families* and *Gladiators*.

The committee room was full of searching questions. Well, apart from 'Why are you carrying a plate of foam?' The amusing thing about the incident is that normally, if you want to see an old man, a younger Chinese woman and a cream pie, you'd have to turn to channel 973 on Sky TV.

After the fight, the MPs missed an opportunity by not asking Wendi what her surname was. She'd answer and then they should've asked her to repeat it. 'Deng. DENG!' And then Tom Watson could have shouted, 'Seconds out. Round two.' Shaving foam in the face. What's the big deal? If you read the side of the can, that's the manufacturer's exact recommendation. I could understand the outcry if it were toothpaste.

Before this incident the rest of the world only associated the Brits with Benny Hill. This won't have helped. We might as well have ended the proceedings with Murdoch pulling his trousers down and chasing his wife around the room while intermittently being slapped on the head by Tom Watson MP. Jonnie Marbles (which isn't even his real name by the way, it's Jonathan Marbles) said that he wanted to shove a pie in Murdoch's face, 'for all the people who couldn't'. Well, Jonnie, after your piss-poor attempt, you can now join the ranks of those people who couldn't.

Of course, Jonnie Marbles should've stayed perfectly still – Wendi's vision is based on movement, just like a *Tyrannosaurus rex*. After the attack it was difficult to tell if the white stuff on Jonnie Marbles's face was shaving foam or if Wendi had slashed all the way through to the bone. Everyone's lost interest in the hearing now and just want to see a UFC cage fight between Wendi and that other high-profile bodyguard, Sinitta.

I actually think Murdoch made quite a good impression. Of a garden gnome in a hospice. I'm starting to wonder if we're actually dealing with the ghost of Rupert Murdoch. In the select committee I expected to see him starting making a clay pot with Rebekah Brooks. Met police chiefs resigned and Rebekah Brooks was arrested over the allegations. Talk about the pigs and the vultures being thrown to the wolves.

Sir Paul Stephenson was Britain's most senior policeman – he's so important he even invented the phrase 'Evening all'. With Stephenson and Yates having quit, it means a dinner lady called Trisha is now the country's highest-ranking officer, outranking Rav Wilding and the guy who does the funny noises in *Police Academy*. In Sir Paul's defence, on his watch crime in London fell – well, apart from among policemen. After the stress of resigning, Sir Paul probably needs somewhere to relax for a few days. I hear Champneys Health Spa is quite good. What? Oh.

I liked former Assistant Commisioner Andy Hayman's reaction in the select committee when asked if he took money – 'I can't believe you've suggested that.' The fact that it came as a shock to him to be asked if he'd done something wrong gives us some insight into how the investigation might have fallen down. John Yates admitted that he didn't investigate thoroughly because he had a lot on. Come on, mate, you're not redecorating the back bedroom – it's a criminal investigation. Not exactly *Columbo* is it? Just one more thing – I can't be arsed to read all of that.

Surely the easiest way for the Met to prove they weren't being bribed by the tabloids is to point to all the newspaper sellers they've killed.

Strange times. If you can't trust the police, politicians and journalists, then who can you trust? Police officers have been resigning, politicians have been compromised and journalists are being arrested over the phone-hacking scandal. So it's reassuring to know that their conduct is being investigated by the police, parliamentary committees and the Press Complaints Commission. There really needs to be an inquiry by a less corruptible group, though, like FIFA. David Cameron said the hacking inquiry will widen – or in other words, he shouted, 'What's that over there?' and ran off.

Of course, let's not forget that Murdoch's decline will largely benefit the *Mail on Sunday* and the *Daily Mail*. Papers whose worldview could best be summed up as mentally ill. I also catch a slight air of monied celebrities and critics telling poor people what they should be interested in. Inequality in our country is so rampant that a big chunk of what was the *News of the World*'s circulation isn't literate enough to read a broadsheet. Also, broadsheets are partly about consumption. Who wants to read about box sets, holiday homes and beauty routines they can never afford? Much as the whole thing was hugely enjoyable, I feel a slight prickle on my scalp wondering who might replace Murdoch as an owner, and how many decent billionaires there are around.

It would be great if the tabloids went back to being investigative, campaigning papers, but I think that muckraking and perverse nosiness are actually part of their function. Maybe the tabloids are a kind of Jungian 'shadow' of intelligent inquiry, addressing the wearying and disappointing part of ourselves that wants to see who Rio Ferdinand is fucking. The newspaper proprietor William Randolph Hearst pursued a vendetta against Mae West because of the forthright sexual confidence of her work and because he was appalled by how much money she made. Meanwhile, he had affairs and built a business empire. Perhaps we just project hatred onto things we see as embodying what we hate about ourselves, and perhaps tabloids simply embody the worst of us.

'Haye punches his arm so hard that he falls over screaming'

★ ★ ★ ★

First thing I do when I get back to Glasgow is I phone this drug-dealer lassie and get some pretty hefty Valium and some acid. We walk round a park for a bit before she hands them over. I'd always felt guilty about the chit-chat with a dealer, trying to hide the fact that you'd just like to buy the drugs. For the first time I'm aware that she is doing the chit-chat but would just like to sell the drugs. I gub two in the local coffee house and everything, the fact I've left my bike on the other side of the park, the fact I've agreed to do *8 Out of 10 Cats*, the rapist, everything is OK. In a way they are all positive developments.

I'm trying to place some short stories I wrote ages ago. My agent is struggling to get me on anything ('They're scared'), and tidying them up is something to do. I get a big bag of Diet Cokes and chocolate at the newsagents on the high street.

'Some rain, eh? It looks crazy out there!' says the young assistant lassie and I switch into banter mode. A mere observation about the weather turning her from drone snack-parcel conduit into chatty fuck-target.

I sit in the kitchenette and go through the net-checking procrastination I always need to do before

work. Some guy has Facebooked me about *Tramadol Nights*.
His daughter is disabled, blah, blah, he's going to
kill me, blah, blah. Of course, I can't really say that
I think some people get sympathy and attention from
their link to a disabled person. That (like anything)
people laughing about it dilutes the horror but also
dilutes the attention those people get. That all the
disabled people I've met hate those people, blah, blah.
Instead, I befriend him on a page where I'm pretending
to be a woman and think listlessly about destroying his
marriage.

I understand but genuinely despair of people speaking up for the disabled. They have enough taken away
from them in our society without taking away their
voices as well. People like that sector of society to
be invisible. I had a lynch mob on my tail for making
a joke on tour that wasn't disablist in any way and
that nobody had heard. Luckily, I'm mature and sophis-
ticated enough to realise that being given a hard time
by the papers doesn't mean you're a bad person (I've
read a lot of *Spiderman*). Rather than feeling prejudice, I'm just someone who doesn't see why there's
anything that shouldn't be talked about. I was criticised by people who stereotyped the disabled as 'weak'
and 'vulnerable', something I would never do. People
with disabilities are people, just like anybody else
and, strangely, that is a real taboo.

We live in a culture where the only time you see
someone with a disability is on a freak-show documentary. *The Man with an Arse for a Hand and a Hand for an
Arse*, that kind of thing. Is that really where we're at
with this? Where the Victorians were? I'm generalising,
but disabled people are often more fully realised human

beings, in that they have been forced to think about the nature of existence a bit more. It's the 'average' person that should be in a freak show. *The Man Too Busy to Love His Kids*. Show that on Channel 5.

★

I get a cab down to BBC Scotland studios. It's brand new and at its centre is a big staircase with bits off it with couches, tables and so on. The idea being that people meet in a village-type way, sharing ideas and energising each other. There is no cunt there.

My company is making a game show for Scottish TV called *Dullion*. It's based on a dead-arm game from school. Contestants can win the opportunity to punch their opponent on the arm before they perform a manual-dexterity test.

Kevin Bridges is doing a fine job of hosting it. A gallus local DJ contestant is well in the lead until the other contestant plays her joker, which here is called *Hauners*. World boxing champion David Haye comes out to deliver the dullion. The DJ is not that bothered, clearly thinking it'll be a bit of a love tap for the cameras. Haye gets a big laugh by putting in a gumshield, then punches his arm so hard that he falls over screaming. We make the cunt try to play a game of Operation afterwards and it's hilarious.

★

I go home and try to have an early night but there are big scratches on the front door. I think someone tried to break in, so fuck, it's normal for the area. Then I go back a minute later and they look like animal-claw marks or something.

I take two Valium and try to sleep but downstairs is blasting out cheesy Top 40 pish. I will try to buy downstairs' flat off them in the morning. I go through to the stateroom and get the model of the guy downstairs and I think I'm cool about everything but I end up holding him up by his wee neck, this tiny wee man, and punching the fuck out of him against the wall.

I used to think that we live in a wedding rules society. Like the way that the playlist at a wedding will be a load of shit records that nobody really likes. Because, while everyone can be disappointed, not one person can be offended. Conversations at weddings have the same rules … conversations everywhere have the same rules. So we all go through the motions, while the DJ plays 'Born to Be Wild' and some shit from *The Commitments* soundtrack.

Sat on my bed feeling the actual throb of those records, the hum of that conversation, like a spider at the centre of a web of banality, it occurs to me that it's less than that. Most people don't give a fuck what records get played or what gets said, so long as they can get drunk and have some prospect in the future of fucking a stranger/the wife of a work colleague/a slit they have cut in an uncooked steak.

The guy puts on a Daniel Johnston record and I feel sorry for having hated him so intensely. I remember this old Daniel Johnston drawing of a guy choosing to put on his happy or sad mask for the day. I text a few of my pals and suggest that they come round tomorrow, and we scoff in the face of reality. Stewart texts back, 'You mean take acid?' Yes, now that I think about it, I do.

★

The guys come round and we have a cup of tea and watch Florence and Connell in this BBC Scotland sitcom about an unemployed former metal band called Bitches Buroo, and drop the microdots I scored. It starts as this philosophical, futuristic buzz and when the show ends Stewart goes over and puts Dr. Octagon on the stereo.

Paul has this completely asymmetrical face. He got a bad eye injury as a kid, which exaggerates it, but I start to think how it's expressive of him, the bit that wants to visit the 23rd dimension and the tense bit that wants to be normal. His face, it suddenly occurs to me as I come up, is a yin-yang symbol.

Stewart is talking about Terence McKenna, who he's got right into. He starts quoting this thing about how we can choose to enlarge our consciousness or remain brutish prisoners of matter.

'Yes!' I laugh, as the acid drips me that loose physical buzz. 'That's that quote I used for that HMV thing! They wanted a quote from someone who'd inspired you for a poster campaign at Christmas. I gave them *brutish prisoners of matter!*'

Stewart: 'That's cool man!'

Me: 'They didn't use it - they used someone quoting Ferris Bueller.' I'm overcome with the giggles.

Stewart is grinning. 'That's fucked … these fuckers are … brutish prisoners of matter!'

I shrug. 'I dunno, man. I think you can choose to be amused by the hopelessness of the world. Laugh at every … crass awful thing, it's like this fucking universal armour! You know that Buddhist thing where they say you can't choose what happens, but you can choose how you react to it? You can choose to just laugh.'

Paul is struggling badly to make a joint and looks up.

'"You can't choose what happens" sounds kind of apolitical … like, laugh at stuff instead of doing anything about it.'

'*I'd love to debate this further but I seem to be losing my mind,*' I interject in an English voice and lurch towards a porthole.

Sheets of rain are lashing down and I feel a surge of excitement. For some reason it looks like it all starts below us, like we're above the weather system. These flats sway a bit and we're all standing there, and I know we're all thinking it's like a ship.

'Haharr!' I turn round roaring like a pirate waving a rolled-up notebook as a cutlass, but they're laughing and giving me a look like *What the fuck?*

★

I'm still kind of high in the morning and go for a walk up the Necropolis. I meet this girl I know walking her dog, and we have a joint behind a gravestone and I start necking her. She starts wanking me off, her hand inside my tracksuit bottoms as I look out across Glasgow, breathing the cold morning air deep into my lungs. I stand up to get a better view and she just stays on her knees, reaching up. I feel like a post-millennial Tom Weir, my face proud and unreadable on a book jacket.

What I think about during the whole thing is Superman. He saw his whole planet die and became this force for good. Batman just saw his parents die and wanted revenge; it was all about him, his ego. Superman saw his whole world die and realised you need to transcend what you want, transcend the ego. Perhaps now, as our world dies, we will be forced to become good, to have perspective, to be Supermen even.

And I know it should feel sordid, this whole thing. But it doesn't. Even with the dog there, it feels tremendous.

★ ★ ★ ★

Capitalism only supports certain kinds of groups, the nuclear family for example, or 'the people I know at my job', because such groups are already self-alienated & hooked into the Work/Consume/Die structure.

Hakim Bey, *Immediatism*

From the moment of birth, when the Stone Age baby confronts the twentieth century mother, the baby is subjected to these forces of violence, called love. [...] By the time the new human being is fifteen or so, we are left with a being like ourselves. A half crazed creature, more or less adjusted to a mad world. This is normality in our present age.

R. D. Laing, *The Politics of Experience*

★ ★ ★ ★

03

The old cliché of men saying their partner 'doesn't understand them' comes about because we deliberately look for women who don't understand us, who don't understand what cunts we are. Women who have insight? Perceptive women who see through us? We run like hell from those women. No man wants to hear the truth. That after 40 nobody desires you – they put up with you because you remind them of their dad. Don't hate yourself for struggling in relationships, it's tough. Only being allowed to fuck one person – and that being the person whose farts you've listened to for the last ten years – is the sort of abject test that you would be set in hell.

We live in a society where women are demonised for having children in their teens when they are biologically meant to have them but there is no such stigma for women having children via IVF in their 40s. This is because what we see as the defining factor in bringing up a happy child is whether you have money, not whether you are still young enough to engage in play, or have the energy to love them properly. Still, you can use the money to hire some teenage girl. 'Tommy! We've hired someone who's fun, we've hired someone who likes you'; and she can play with them while you look on exhaustedly with a mug of tea.

On April Fools' Day I sat my kids down and told them they were adopted. You should have seen their faces! They were delighted. I find the best way to deal with the news on April the 1st is to consider it all lies. Which is only slightly different to how I approach the news on any other given day.

I read that one in four children eats their supper alone in their bedrooms. Of course, the alternative is having to listen to two adults talk about photocopying and bills while staring at you angrily, analysing every mouthful that doesn't have a carrot in it. Gazing at a cold dark wall is possibly preferable.

Social services say they want to stop kids eating themselves into an early grave. I agree. There's nothing sadder than a child's coffin. Especially one being carried by twelve men dripping with sweat. The Department of Health has promised new measures to cope with the fat-kid problem. For starters, a scheme where paedophiles can exchange sweets for bits of carrot and apple.

Experts say under-5s should be physically active for at least three hours a day to lower their risk of getting fat. Of course, there are some clever gadgets to help toddlers keep the weight off. For starters, you can put them in a launderette tumble dryer and it's like a hamster-style exercise wheel … and if he wets himself, it doesn't even matter. Just another 20p will sort it.

Bloody social services! The nerve of that Sharon Shoesmith! The Court of Appeal says she was unfairly dismissed, and she's off again, trying to pin the whole Baby P thing on the mother and boyfriend who tortured him to death. It makes my blood boil. When will these people realise it's their job to constantly oversee us raising our own children, and take responsibility should we kill them because they didn't stop us?

Apparently, what you call your son can have a huge effect on how their life turns out. You can't take chances, as I was saying just yesterday to my young lad, Doomcop Ace Rock. Studies have shown that you should name your son David, George or Michael if you want him to get into Parliament, and just the last two names together if you want him to arrive there by crashing through a window.

Top Gear's James May says men these days are losing their 'dad' skills. I disagree. We're just swapping them for new ones, like deleting our browser history and skipping pages of a bedtime story but having it still make sense. He says men can't put up shelves properly anymore. Nonsense! Not only have I put up loads recently, but they double as little slides for my son.

90 per cent of parents have admitted plonking toddlers in front of the TV to entertain them. Guilty. It's easy to wean a toddler off TV. Buy a cheap one, then put them to bed after the *Dr Who* monsters have been on for a minute. Then smash a hole in the screen and stick a note on it saying 'Free at last! Exterminate! Exterminate!' for when they come down in the morning.

I think outdoor activities should be encouraged. I was lucky, as our local priest cheerfully turned a blind eye to our scrumping. He'd just paint his nuts red and hide amongst the leaves.

There are fresh concerns over the safety of Facebook. I must say that I've always found Facebook perfectly safe and enjoyable, but then I'm a predatory sex attacker. The bespectacled pervert Peter Chapman had a photo of a 17-year-old hunk on his Facebook page to attract young women. You should get yourself on the telly, Peter. I have a photo of a bespectacled pervert on my Facebook page and I'm rolling in pussy.

There's a very simple way to check if you are being groomed for sex on Facebook Chat. Are you on Facebook Chat? Yes? You are being groomed for sex. Remember girls, that guy you're talking to might not be who he says he is. Often someone who pretends to be a teenager will actually play for England.

There have been calls for a law so we can check with police if partners we meet on the internet have a violent history. Let's not forget the happiness internet dating can bring. The simple joy of watching the restaurant with binoculars as they sit alone at the table waiting for you to arrive. These internet dating sites can lead to violence against men, too. Especially if you forget to delete your browser history before lending your partner your laptop. Call me a Luddite, but I miss the more traditional arts of dating. The impossible romance of sinking pint after pint in a nightclub to find the courage by five to two to slur nonsense into a girl's ear, in the hope she has sufficiently low self-esteem to be groped by a man so drunk he needs his spare hand to grip her coat for support.

Miley Cyrus said the internet is dangerous. That's true if your Miley Cyrus – even Tom from MySpace sexually harasses Hannah Montana. The dangers of children being online is overstated. After all, what inappropriate content could possibly breach the impenetrable fortress of security that is the 'Only press Enter if over 18' button?

Surely the genie's out of the bottle here. Let's face it. In 20 years' time, kids will so totally shop, date, chat, doze and interfere with themselves in front of a screen that the only skills they'll really need are moving their buttocks to prevent sores and learning how to suck sweet and savoury nutri-pastes from dangling rubber teats.

Apparently 40 per cent of teenagers see nothing wrong with posting topless pictures of themselves online. I wish they had more self-respect, so that maybe I could finally close my Bebo account. And a third of boys under 10 have watched internet porn. Sadly, the other two-thirds don't get quality time with their dads at all.

Basically, our kids are fucked. My daughter's primary school are teaching a 'pirates and mermaids' project to the kids this term. Not because they're fun kids' characters but because it's time to teach them to steal at gunpoint and live on plankton.

Of course, our children will never have 'nothing', because our capitalist, Thatcher-moulded hearts know no way of showing love to our kids other than through the medium of a Rapunzel Light-Up Tower. From the first time our child breaks from our embrace because he's spotted a Winnie the Pooh figurine, we know that – should we starve, should we owe the bank the roof over our head – our last vision, before death clouds our eyes and steals our breath, will be our child throwing a Kung Zhu Hamsters Battle Arena to one side while shouting, 'And what else have you got me?'

It's just hard to feel Christmassy when you're shopping online, isn't it? There are no garlands, no mistletoe … They need to decorate the internet. Maybe Jason Manford can put a Santa outfit on his cock. The *Sun* referred to shopping on 18 December as 'last-minute'! No … 'last-minute' is when you have to pump sedative gas into your kid's bedroom on Christmas morning as you hastily draw Snow White onto a packet of fags.

In my day, it was all hand-me-downs. One year I asked for an Action Man, and ended up getting my sister's old Barbie doll with the tits scraped off with a hot knife.

The top-selling children's toy this Christmas is expected to be a building kit with real wood and tools. It comes with a booklet of handy phrases like: 'Sorry I'm late, Mum, the traffic was murder,' 'What cowboy's done this? It looks like it was made by a 2-year-old,' and 'Get us a cup of Ribena please love, I'm parched.'

Lidl's selling reindeer meat. Critics say it'll destroy the magic of Christmas. Don't worry, *The X Factor*'s already got that one covered. I say they deserve it. Last Christmas Eve one did a shit when Santa flew over, and it froze on the way down and cracked two of my slates. So what if they're selling reindeer meat? We eat all kinds of animals, after all. I hear it tastes a bit like puppies or panda cubs.

Half of all British firms are cancelling their Christmas parties. In the current economic climate they can't afford to pay for the maternity leave in nine months' time.

The *Sun* has a phone line to deal with the stress of celebrating Christmas. It has the voice of Dear Deidre, but I'm campaigning to change it to me saying, 'There is no God, stay at home and masturbate into the sink.'

Of course Christmas is simply a corruption of old Pagan festivals celebrating bitter family arguments and lashing out drunkenly after finding a flirtatious text on your partner's phone. Domestic violence rates also soar during big football matches. Because of course it's your wife's fault that you have nothing in your life except football. If she'd only castrated you like she should've, you'd have been happily watching *Titanic* together.

The police in Scotland produced a leaflet about domestic violence that answers a few old questions about the issue, such as: Q. 'Why didn't she leave?' A. 'Her head and outer limbs were in a bag', and Q. 'Why don't we just leave the couple to sort it out between them?' A. 'Because her floating corpse will become a bio-hazard for the canal wildlife.'

Apparently Britain's mums do housework worth over 30 grand a year. It's made me look at my partner in a whole new light. I'm sure she could get twice that on the game. We could get a Lithuanian in to hoover and keep the difference.

A study shows that men judge women in a millisecond. Guilty. Sometimes it can be so quick the image hasn't even fully downloaded. Ladies, when are you going to realise that you don't need to endure all these stupid, expensive beauty therapies. We love you just the way you are. Unless you're a real pig, in which case go for it.

A survey revealed six out of ten women are happy to split the bill on a first date. Nice to know. After all, dry cleaning can be expensive. Never mind splitting the bill; I've been known to empower women even more by climbing out of a toilet window after coffee if it looks like they're not up for it.

Love is meant to produce the same results as cocaine. Certainly, whenever I make love it usually causes the death of an orphaned Colombian street-child. Women fake orgasms because they are riddled with insecurities and have a fear of intimacy, according to researchers. It's a shame that women feel they have to do that, especially when men couldn't care less if they have one or not.

Actually, 18 million people were injured having sex last year. No wonder, I sometimes get hurt when there's just three of us. The most common injuries people reported were pulled muscles. I bet that's because not many people reported accidents caused by shutting their laptop too quickly when someone came into the room unexpectedly. A third of us have had sex with someone at work. Guilty again. All part of being self-employed.

I was surprised by the hoo-ha about breastfeeding at work. I'd suggest just tattooing your breast with a megaphone and having the baby stand up for feeds. By playing selected recordings from the History Channel it will just look like a tiny Churchill addressing the troops.

★

A drinks company is funding a campaign to warn of the dangers of alcohol during pregnancy. Booze companies say they've always supported mothers, adding that without their products most mums wouldn't have got up the duff in the first place. Especially the mingers. The unborn child absorbs some of the mother's alcohol, which can cause premature births. Usually, when the placenta bumps into the foetus and the foetus says, 'Outside. Now!' If you drink while pregnant the foetus is basically addicted. Which means it's best to always wear tight-fitting knickers so it can't sneak out to the pub while you're asleep. In parts of Scotland the problem is so bad there's evidence that breasts are gradually evolving into optics.

A 3-year-old from the West Midlands became the country's youngest alcoholic. His parents have been giving him booze to keep him quiet for the past six months and he may now be taken into care. Mum and Dad are furious, as it's his round.

I'd never let my 3-year-old drink. Nike quality control send back too much of his work as it is. His first AA meetings are going to be weird: 'My name is Tyrone and I'm a cowboy.' There is something sad about seeing a baby unwilling to shake its rattle because it's got a splitting headache.

At least he learned to crawl. He just copied his parents. Apparently, this child displayed all the classic symptoms of alcoholism. He kept turning up at crime scenes with a fishing rod and picnic basket. His parents deny charges of neglect – they worked really hard to stretch the teat off the baby's bottle over the top of a can of Tennent's. Being an alcoholic is only really a problem when you have a job, a car and a family to look after. This is the perfect age to be an alcoholic. What's the worst that can happen to a 3-year-old alcoholic? He pukes on his mum's tits.

Asda are giving £1 million for schemes to dissuade kids from drinking. I'd suggest a good one might be having them dangle damp beer mats from the top of a stepladder and have Gazza dance barefoot on broken glass beneath, just in the hope of catching drips.

Nearly 40 teenagers are admitted to hospital daily due to alcohol. At least it's keeping class sizes down, and gives doctors a chance to check up on how their pregnancies are progressing.

A 50-year-old mum from Cambridge is teaching her 7-year-old daughter to pole dance. Her mother says she's teaching the child pole dancing to lay the groundwork for her future career, as one of England's biggest heroin addicts. Her mum says it's good fitness, but then so is being chased by Gary Glitter. The worrying thing is that when the little girl forgets to bring her kit she's made to pole dance in her vest, pants and junior nipple tassels. Seven years old? That breaks the golden rule: never sexualise a child small enough to fit under a cardinal's mitre. It's asking for trouble.

Parents of children at a school in Glasgow have been advised not to dress their kids in short skirts and tight trousers in order to deter paedophiles. From now on, if pupils don't go to school in baggy clothes they'll be made to attend classes in their vest and pants. Of course, it's Glasgow. Keep them on till 16 and many can't concentrate on their studies as they're wrapped up in a mid-life crisis.

The government plans to introduce legislation to ban inappropriately sexy clothing for kids. That's all very well, but what are kinky midgets supposed to do? Only morons would let their children wear padded bras. Which is why in this country they sold millions.

I refuse to put any of these sexualised clothes on my children; they look much hotter when they're naked. If they ban sexy T-shirts for children, how will we know which ones are going to grow up to be future porn stars? Unless we actually witness their dads violently beating them? Thing is, little girls will always want to dress like their mums, and a large proportion of British mums are 18-year-old slags.

SlutWalkers marched in London in their bras and pants. Unless they forgot them, in which case the organisers made them march in full PE kit. It's a wonderful message. I just think it might be lost on the men turning up to view all the sluts. I applaud the principle. I just can't help thinking the title could have had a little more gravitas. After all Gay Pride wouldn't have achieved so much if it had been called 'PoofMarch'. Those banners have important messages – let's hope they always hold them in front of their tits or no one will read them.

It's a shame, though. This pressured sexualisation of teenagers is not how I remember that beautiful flowering of girl-to-woman from my youth. Returning to school after the summer holidays to notice her new curves and flawless skin … every boy straining to revise for their highers as she effortlessly and unknowingly drew our eye … then her suddenly having to leave. Then Mr Clark the gym teacher going, too. Me returning home six or seven years later and catching a glimpse of her in the precinct at Cumbernauld, wheeling a triple-seat buggy, her once-bright complexion spent and grey, dropping her Lambert & Butlers as she slapped her toddler … Mr Clark shambling up and, as they exchanged resent-laden greetings … me catching in his eyes the desperate regret for the life-long price he must pay for following his urge that balmy autumn evening all those years ago … Still, it was nice to catch up with them.

A 25-year-old man on benefits in Tyne and Wear has been found to have ten kids by ten different mothers. Terrifying to think how many he'd have if he lived somewhere where the women were lookers. Because of Tory tax and benefit changes, families with three children have lost £1,700, though their houses are so messy it will probably turn up stuffed inside a Fisher-Price garage.

David Cameron's hit out at absent dads. He said his own left early and got back late every day to support his family. Dave, maybe that's just because you were as tedious as a kid as you are now. It's easy to generalise. Even in the toughest areas here in Glasgow, most absent dads will visit their kids at least once a week. Sometimes more if they forget what day the child benefit arrives.

Cameron has said families shouldn't have children if they can't afford to maintain them. Cameron just started a war he can't afford to maintain! There's no more child benefit for people earning more than 40 grand. Which I find a little upsetting. These last few years I've become quite attached to my little boy. But ... if he can't pay his way ... A single mother will be worse off than a couple with these new rules. Of course, single mothers can make up their missing child-benefit payments, as the paedophiles that start dating them usually bring lots of presents.

Thousands of school kids are to be given £10 in a *Dragons' Den*-style drive to create Britain's next generation of entrepreneurs. Some have already doubled their money, using a system called bullying. News surely greeted by the weary sighs of parents country-wide as they realise they're going to have to pay out for some shit their kids bring home. It sounds like a way of shifting the blame for our failing economy to the next generation. In a decade's time, I can just see bitter families forced to work fighting giant rats in the sewers while Dad shouts at his 20-year-old son, 'Yeah, well maybe we wouldn't have to do this if you'd shifted a few million more of your stupid popcorn necklaces.'

If you have no condoms, remember this – it takes an hour and half to talk her into anal and 18 years to raise a fucking kid. Kids have got so expensive now that, if it wasn't for my basement sweatshop, it would be barely worth having them.

On Mother's Day I wanted to show my mother how much she means to me, so I did nothing. I'm joking, of course. I planned something really special. I took the phone off the hook and watched a box set of *The Sopranos*. Mother's Day is the day when children everywhere show their appreciation for their mothers by saying, 'What, it's *this* Sunday? Oh shit, I'd better hope the garage hasn't sold out of flowers or she'll be getting a box of Jaffa Cakes again.'

Canoe fraudster Anne Darwin's sons say they forgave their mother once their wives got pregnant – there's nothing like the fear of having to pay for babysitters to cure family rifts. Wait till they find out the whole trial and prison sentence was just one more elaborate hoax and Dad has been living in the DVD cabinet for three years laughing at them – hahahahahahaha!

J. G. Ballard had this idea that we had built up a deliberately unsustainable world because we wanted it to fuck up. Our little shoebox homes destroyed and our careful, rectangular lawns on fire, so that in the rubble we can go back to being our primal selves, enjoying the struggle for survival. And perhaps the domestic unit is that idea in microcosm – mother, father and children can't possibly provide complete stimulation for each other and we know that one day soon we can relax as the kids finally run away and we get sympathy handjobs from our co-workers.

I think it's more likely that we just enjoy struggle and heroic failure. Struggle, because it's where we came from, and failure, because it's our inevitable destination. In Glasgow, junkies used to take Temazepam (jellies), a powerful sedative, and the whole joy was to fight against the sleep urge, putting yourself in an exciting place of struggle. Relationships are maybe that too, a fight against powerful odds, anaesthetising and enervating.

'Enya is playing under the water'

★ ★ ★ ★

I'm on the train back to London eating a panini. That's capitalism for you. Nobody likes paninis, nobody ever says they could murder a panini, yet we all end up eating fucking paninis and they burn the fucking roofs of our cunting mouths. I restlessly try to focus on the fleeing fields of sheep. Eventually I feel a little better and watch a movie Paul has put on the laptop for me: *Source Code* with Jake Gyllenhaal. After trying to hold onto my optimism for half an hour, my mind starts to spasm. A train blew up and they went and searched the wreckage for some teacher's brain? If this is the signal from a dying brain then all the people on the train are only what he would imagine them to be. Why doesn't the conductor ever check the woman's ticket? Why doesn't he ever CHECK HER FUCKING TICKET? People like this movie. WHAT THE FUCK IS WRONG WITH EVERYBODY? WHAT IS THIS?

'Beleaguered Castle'; that's how Americans see themselves. There hasn't been a bombing in a decade. The US spends that decade bombing other people. It's not that hard to make a bomb. One conclusion is that terrorists aren't that keen on bombing civilians any more. The US government fucking loves it.

There's a story that the band Slayer were always trying to get the bass at their gigs tuned so they could deliver some mythical note so deep that it would make everybody shit themselves. Hollywood is pretty much the same: the naked manipulation, the swelling minor-key music, the actor's eyes filling in the sudden close-up.

I arrive at my hotel in London, where everyone is ridiculously nice. If I ever tried to leave without paying, if I was even a pound short, they would call the police. Perhaps they even have special staff there that would beat me, but I enjoy the enthusiasm they put into the illusion of friendship. The staff always remember me, as Mr Boyd. I have a long swim in an empty spa. It's a businesspersons' hotel and they never have time to use the pool but they like the idea of it. Enya is playing under the water.

I automatically stick the TV on in my room and find myself wanking in a half-hearted fashion to what might be *The One Show*. Monkeys in captivity will start to masturbate after months of boredom, and TV is so concentratedly boring it immediately induces the level of ennui associated with a long period of loneliness and abuse. Someone is on because he's got into the *Guinness Book of Records*, the place where we celebrate obsessive-compulsive disorders. Some cunt will have the record for counting to the highest number, I think numbly. It'll be fucking millions.

My agent has left a message. Looks like I'm going to get to pitch my idea for an Adam Sandler movie to Adam Sandler's people! The highest I've felt for weeks and a new low.

I watch *Frank Skinner's Opinionated*. He asks the audience what they want to talk about. The first punter says, 'Integrating paedophiles into the community,' and

Frank says, 'Two words, mate. Comedy show.' The second punter wants to talk about the nuclear-reactor problems in Japan. The panel laugh it off and go straight into their scheduled items. People who wear glasses and how to be happy. Tonight the TV is not even pretending to care what we think, like a bored magician pulling rabbits from a clear Perspex top hat. Is this really what people want? Nothing? Do people want to just die out without a fight? We can't let them, I decide, before watching an hour of porn on my hard drive.

The film is titled *Fuck It You Japanese Fuck*. Titles on porn are often badly spelled or totally illiterate. Porn addiction is like being addicted to food when the only restaurant is McDonald's. I think I look at Japanese stuff because the cultural difference makes it hard to tell how bad the acting is. Unexpectedly, a bunch of extra guys run in at the end of the scene and the woman ends up looking like a candlestick from a Hammer Horror movie. Who's into this? There should be a wide-ranging reclassification of what it means to be gay.

In bed I check the BBC News page. The most popular story is 'Spanish gym offers naked workouts', ahead of 'US flies armed drones over Libya'. I write a story for my son. A proud feeling warms me like a whisky that I'm doing this instead of working. He likes to hear little stupid events from his life so I have started writing this thing called 'Funny Stories' in a big black notebook. Tonight's is:

When you were three we took a shower together. I came out of the shower and stood staring at myself in the mirror. I asked you why I always looked better when I came out of the shower than when I had put my clothes on. You said, 'It's because you're not wearing your glasses.'

★ ★ ★ ★

'Are we gonna kill the kid?' Peter asks, looking jumpy and
nervous, rubbing his arms, his eyes wide, a huge belly
sticking out beneath a **BRYAN METRO** T-shirt and he's
sitting in a ripped-up green armchair in front of the **TV**,
watching cartoons.

Bret Easton Ellis, *The Informers*

★ ★ ★ ★

04

Television wants to get the biggest audiences possible, so it ends up being pretty crass. The things about people that make them interesting – hopefully, you yourself are into Jack Kirby comics or practising Chinese spear forms – are quite varied. The things that people have in common are basic and dull, really. If you want 11 million viewers on a Saturday night you'd better have some morons kick a ball between two sticks or a muscular guy outrun a fireball or hold a fucking karaoke competition. That's just the socially acceptable options. You could stick a porno on and it would out-rate *EastEnders*.

Television is just a distraction, really, a jangling set of keys hoisted nightly in front of our stupid, drooling faces. Marshall McLuhan said, 'The medium is the message,' meaning that the way TV makes us think – the shorter attention span, the dullness to sensation – is more important than its content. Railways changed the Wild West and it didn't really matter if the trains were carrying wood or marshmallows. We don't even retain the information. Think about how many TV shows you've seen in your life about Ancient Egypt. Now think about what you actually know about Ancient Egypt. Fuck all.

Don't go away thinking that you're not part of the herd because you don't watch *The X Factor*. There's distraction for all, it's just got different reading ages. Did watching *The Wire* really help you understand inner-city life? More than having a conversation with someone who lives in your own inner city?

In comedy, you might have Michael McIntyre talking about all-inclusive holidays* for the lower-middle classes but, if you feel above all that, you can watch Stewart Lee talk about Chris Moyles's autobiography not being very good, or Adrian Chiles being ugly or whatever. A rule of thumb for recognising a critically successful show is the same as the one for a commercially successful show. You can watch the whole series without knowing there's a war on.

I think punk was the last time they let anything happen. After that, they decided to tighten the fuck up with what was allowed into the culture. Maybe if you work in some marginal area, like comics or sci-fi or dance, maybe you are doing something interesting, but the mainstream of culture has got a whole lot more policed.

Take *The X Factor*, TV's very own tumour – it just keeps on growing. When *The X Factor* comes back, I thank God. I get tired of re-creating its effect by bending over in front of a mirror and pulling out the cork I'd wedged between my buttocks the week before. Every year the show has dozens of acts who all have something to prove. That modern psychiatry doesn't work.

The only moment on that show that ever had any resonance for me was when the contestants had a drunken brawl and destroyed Cowell's villa. Their drunken antics woke Simon up from his sleep. Champagne corks kept bouncing off his coffin lid. Cowell was furious. As we know, he won't stand for anyone on the show behaving like actual rock musicians. It was

---

* I tried to watch some of his act to get an example of something he actually does, but my brain made me hold my breath in an attempt to suffocate itself.

unprecedented – there was no drunken violence with Jedward, unless you count their conception.

Astounding. How could a group of teenagers go to someone's house and treat that person with no respect? It's almost like they've grown up watching some sort of programme where the ugly and mentally infirm are publicly ridiculed for money. Of course, the reason this violent behaviour has never happened before is that *The X Factor* has now auditioned everyone in the whole country and is having to rely solely on entrants that were in prison during the last six series.

ITV has a contract for three more years of *The X Factor*. I'll believe it when I see it. They said the First World War would be over by Christmas. But without that show, there's a real danger that in a dozen or so years' time a jaded karaoke-level singer might not return to their tatty, windowless cruise-ship cabin after straining their way through the Motown back catalogue, and curse the day they were plucked from blissful obscurity before washing down 62 paracetamol with a half bottle of Scotch and slipping out of consciousness to the sound of a propeller shaft spinning but yards below their sweat-stained acrylic pillow.

Sometimes when I watch that programme I feel a connection with a darker Frankie, and can momentarily understand how one might feel distinct from humanity, that they are all but ants, doing nothing more than occupying space and converting food into shit … that it would mean nothing to cleanse the streets by smashing a claw hammer into their gormless faces. Maybe I shouldn't watch it in future, and perhaps I'll switch to decaffeinated coffee. At least on Saturdays.

There were claims that the last series of *The X Factor* was faked and set up. Why, it's almost as if TV and music executives want to make their own decisions about whom they sign and not leave the future of their industry to the amoebas who watch Saturday-night television.

This year, Cowell turned up on *Britain's Got Talent* with a left eye that wouldn't open properly. Looks like he made the mistake of blacking up to give Cheryl the bad news about America. Cheryl was sacked from the US *X Factor* because nobody in the US could understand her. They must have been playing her miming tape too fast. People were asking how *The X Factor* could possibly replace Cheryl with Nicole Scherzinger. Apparently, it's a straightforward procedure. They just replace the face panel and make minor adjustments to the processor.

Nicole's new job means the Pussycat Dolls have lost two of their members. I expect to see a tattered photocopy of their faces taped to a lamp post with the offer of a £10 reward. Hopefully, they'll be found safe and well, but in all likelihood they're currently in some maniac's cellar having a banger shoved up their arse.

The fiasco with Cheryl can't be allowed to happen next year. Some viewers even threatened to boycott *The X Factor*. Well, what they actually said was, 'Me angry. Me no watch sing song show.' There needs to be some better way of picking the judges, like a competition where a panel of judges are auditioned by a panel of judges and then the audience can vote for the best judges.

My television announced that Simon is back in the country and my newspaper announced that Cheryl is back in the country. What about Gamu? Is she still in the country? Or have the Zimbabwean horse militia beheaded her yet? Anyone care?

This year Cowell gave us a whole finals week of *Britain's Got Talent*. I cannot be sure. I suspect possibly I just experienced a week of hallucinogens being pumped into my living room at around 8.30pm. Cowell ... Holden ... McIntyre ... An amazing line-up. I didn't think it was possible for David

Hasselhoff take part in a show and not be the biggest arsehole on it.

Hasselhoff claims that he has mystical healing powers and has brought someone out of a coma – by leaving the room. During an interview he said, 'The upside of being in showbiz is being able to hold the hand of a kid who is dying.' Indeed. Unfortunately, the downside of having childhood leukaemia is having to hold the hand of some tactless, delusional spastic.

Simon Cowell gets a bit of stick, but he is patron of several major charities and has committed to donating £100 million in trust to children and animal welfare charities upon his death. So, if you like animals and you like children and you like killing, you know what you have to do.

The *Sun* interviewed Simon Cowell's mother. Well, if you can call throwing a burning axe at the heads of a howling sea monster an 'interview'. She's worried about his health and wants him to slow down. What the hell is going to happen to him? All he does is sit in a chair, pulling faces. All he has to fear is the wind changing. You've really got to look at yourself when the fact that your mother loves you is headline news. Simon's mother has worried about him ever since she dreamt of the next-door neighbour wearing a bull's head on the night of his conception. His mum is begging Simon to listen to her – unfortunately her back story isn't interesting enough for his assistants to let her calls through. I'd hate to see Simon have a heart attack. Paramedics rushing into the studio having to unzip his flies so they can defibrillate his chest.

It must really be a strain having to think up a new way to have four low-rent celebrities watch people singing. Cowell has five new shows. Well, actually, it's one show with slightly different titles. He deserves his place at the top of the entertainment ladder with that amazing talent for sometimes putting the word 'America' into those titles. Slow down? How can a man who sits still, smirking, slow down? The only option would be for him to leave a longer pause between 'You know what?' and 'I like you.'

Who's Cowell to say who'd look right on a TV show? This is a man who allows himself to appear in front of millions with his shirt open to the waist exposing his man-breasts like a pair of sagging, toad-skin saddlebags. Let's hope that soon Simon will have enough money to stop having his hair cut by a topiary expert into a rhomboid.

I'm staggered that the judges kept criticising the singer's images. After all, Cheryl had the horrific gaze of a woman being held hostage by her hair; Louis, like he'd won his suit in a colouring-in competition; and Simon looked like he was wearing the tightened carcass of a Colombian road sweeper who went missing in 2002.

Dannii was voted the most popular judge last year. I didn't realise necrophiliacs were such a core demographic. I suppose Simon gets all of his mates to watch. But that didn't save her, as Dannii was axed! 'Anger', 'surprise' and 'sadness' were just some of the words she managed to blink out in Morse code. *The X Factor* replaced her with Kelly Rowland, who I must say scrubs up nice compared with his 'Come On Eileen' days.

Dannii's departure is a blow to the West Midlands, as Amalgamated Plastics were banking on getting her refurbishment contract for the new series. Dannii was understandably frustrated at losing the job, telling friends it means she'll have to spend more time with that shouty little thing that came out of her vagina last year. Fans of the show are furious, with many resorting to angrily breaking wind into their sofa cushions as they lean over to shout, 'Juss fold it in half and push it froo the letterbox, push it froo the fuckin letterbox!' to bemused pizza-delivery boys outside their front doors. At least Dannii's too high profile to go the way of previous contestants, encased in silk spun from a gland by Simon's cloaca so that he may feast on their still-warm organs at his leisure.

Simon says he wanted fresh blood, a sinister insight into his true motives. I'm saying nothing more, but I went to a bash round his and I have to say the hearth rug bore an uncanny resemblance to Steve Brookstein. But he couldn't replace Louis. Who could ever replace Louis? Except for a baby concentrating on doing a poo while someone waves a teddy at him.

So, the new line up on *The X Factor* is Tulisa, Kelly, Gary and Louis. When the Bible mentioned the coming of the Horsemen of the Apocalypse I didn't envisage them being named by a teenage mother on a council estate. Tulisa Contostavlos, from hip-hop group N-Dubz, was the one on *Buzzcocks* who didn't know what a kestrel was. If I were Cheryl Cole I'd send Tulisa a welcoming gift of a hat made of dead mice and suggest that we meet up in a cornfield to discuss the handover. Poor Tulisa wouldn't know what hit her. As Cheryl Cole's army of hungry kestrels viciously pecked out Tulisa's kidneys she'd be thinking, 'What is this. Literally, what is this?' N-Dubz. That's the sound Americans hear when Cheryl says, 'Any jobs?'

The X Factor is now allowed to show product placements. That's powerful advertising. Last series I realised that looking at the judges alone had made me subconsciously buy a gnome, a scrag end of mutton, a vacuous mannequin and a suspected gay. Product placements, downloads, text and phone votes, pre-Christmas launch, mimed live shows. The only way Cowell could be extracting more from us is by breaking into our houses at night and clamping milking machines to our tits and tadgers.

I, for one, will be joining the campaign to remove unwanted technology from *The X Factor*. Let's start with the cameras and the microphones. It's amazing how Auto-Tune changes a vocal performance. We hear pitch-perfect songs on a Saturday evening when what the contestants really produce are the desperate screams of a dying civilisation. In fact, if we are going to ban Auto-Tune we need to ban other things that make the singers sound better – singing lessons, emotions, facial bones, lungs, evolution … I'm sure the baying public would be much happier watching a programme where Dermot O'Leary brought on endless buckets of fleshy slop and told us which one of their relatives had recently died.

There've been calls to make sure dancing by guests on this year's *X Factor* isn't as sexy as on the last series. I'm all for sexy dancing. At least it gives me a fighting chance of covering the screen if I can't reach the remote. Rihanna, whose wholesome performance last year kicked things off, clearly has sad events in her past that she's battling. Hopefully, enough to keep the self-loathing, semi-naked writhing going for another six or seven years. I'm hoping Rihanna isn't into dominance, 'cos, as a female pop singer, about the only choice she'll have in her life is whether to chew off her own tongue. I once had a sexual fantasy about Rihanna but my girlfriend ruined it for me, by cuming.

Rihanna has said she doesn't want to appeal to kids. She should produce songs with a more complex chord structure than 'Baa, Baa, Black Sheep', then. Rihanna says she wants people to stop expecting her to be a parent. Don't worry, baby, I don't expect you to be a parent. Not a decent one who gets custody of her kids, anyway. Rihanna's latest video shows her being assaulted – well, opening that umbrella indoors in her first video was always going to bring bad luck.

Parents are told to censor the TV themselves, but it's tricky when you are expecting a show to be family-friendly. Watching *Britain's Got Talent* with your children was like trying to watch a dancing dog while someone throws a bucketful of tits at you. There's a relentless sexuality across our whole culture now; I saw a photo of Iggy Pop and I'm ashamed to say that I was flushing the hanky down the toilet before I realised it wasn't Madonna.

South Africa is hosting an *X Factor*-style competition for porn stars. It'll be unusual for South Africans to see people having sex who haven't been dragged from a car. There are lots of parallels with *The X Factor*, like when they ask contestants if they've had any professional training and they reply they've just been practising in front of the mirror with a hairbrush. Given the massive AIDS epidemic, the elimination rounds will be slightly more literal than usual. To be honest, if I wanted to see someone fuck reality TV stars in a sad pathetic quest for fame I'd watch *Katie* on Sky Living.

Apparently, more people have now voted on *The X Factor* than did in the last election. Luckily, I've thought of something we can do about that … we can all kill ourselves. 12.6 million of us watched *The X Factor* last year. That makes me despair. Whatever happened to the traditional British Saturday night? Necking 2 for 1 blue drinks on an empty stomach, then trying to finger a partially conscious bride-to-be behind a giant, reeking bin.

How did all this happen? Bring back the innocent days of *Stars in Their Eyes*, when we'd have laugh at a bin man from Stoke pretending to be Louis Armstrong, then just get on with our lives. And they'd just be happy to shake Matthew's hand and muck up the role of Buttons at a local theatre before slipping back into obscurity with a new tedious anecdote.

You know, if you really want a better culture, just stop watching this fucking thing. Do as the expression says and 'vote with your feet'. Christ knows, most of you can drink a cup of tea with them. Try a walk, or a drive in the country. If that feels a bit poofy, just combine it with some fly-tipping. My *X Factor* tip: Not only don't bother watching it on Saturday night. Record it, then delete it without watching it too. It's great.

Again, this critique feels kind of futile. *The X Factor* was created and commissioned by individuals who think that most people are morons with fairly bland tastes. It's very difficult to lay into *The X Factor*, or even just describe it and its popularity, without broadly suggesting that people are indeed morons and don't like complex ideas. It's important to remember that this is the result of a bland general culture that's been forced on us for decades now. If you grew up without serious TV drama, with largely anodyne TV comedy, with the Top 40 as your idea of what music was, *The X Factor* is a natural end point.

I was once asked to pick a couple of records for an interview I was doing on Radio 2. I picked one by Will Oldham and one by Joanna Newsome. Someone on the production phoned me to say that I couldn't have either record because they were 'too alternative' and could I just pick two from their playlist. Now, personally, I think Radio 2's listeners would dig both Joanna Newsome and Will Oldham if they heard their records, and that the fact they don't get to hear them contributes to the cultural wasteland we live in. I told them that I'd been to see Joanna Newsome in the Albert Hall a couple of weeks before and it had been sold out. How could she be 'too alternative'? I asked if *Desert Island Discs* was chosen from a playlist, and they told me it was, but maybe they were fucking with me.

'Alternative' and 'mainstream' aren't strictly to do with whether things are popular or minority interest. They are ideological labels. Someone like Joe Pasquale would be called 'mainstream' and regularly pops up on TV, but would play the smaller end of the touring-theatre circuit. If Joanna Newsome can sell out the Albert Hall, why can't she get played on Radio

2? I would argue that it's because her work is too layered, challenging and interesting. Think about that. What you get to hear about is filtered, and not filtered to get rid of useless cunts like Joe Pasquale, but of things that might enrich your life.

The last rung above hell are these new fictional documentaries. First was the Gary Glitter execution, and now Prince Harry's been captured by the Taliban. I'd like to see lots more of these shows made. Who wouldn't watch the heart-warming story of when Rolf Harris discovered the cure for AIDS? How about one showing what would happen if Konnie Huq went on a gun rampage on the planet of Pandora? These fictional documentaries are so good, I bet if they put enough time and effort into the script, casting and performances they could even make a convincing one that successfully depicts John Leslie as a rapist.

The producer of *Midsomer Murders* was suspended after saying he'd banned non-white actors from the show. The show's production company denied they had a ban on minorities, adding they'd only just finished an episode where John Nettles defeats a gypsy army with a helicopter gunship. The producer says he's only avoided using ethnic actors in order to create a more timeless version of the British village, one of cricket on the green, warm beer, and sinister swingers and sacrifices to appease the horned god of the apple harvest. There are plenty of ethnic minorities in *Midsomer*, they just don't bother investigating their deaths.

People who watch *Midsomer* don't want to see realism. What they desperately want is to see their grandchildren. We can't have the core audience of *Midsomer Murders* being scared that ethnic minorities will kill them – it will make it difficult for them to bond with their care worker in the hospice. Anyway, there are plenty of shows where you can see black people being murdered. News programmes.

I had my tea in front of the apprentice on Tuesday. He just sat there saying, 'Meester Boyle, whenaa you gonna letta mee drive ze tractor?' Then I noticed there was a show of the same name on TV where a dozen power-dressed fools get told by the lion from *The Wizard of Oz* 'they're fired', even though he's not yet employed them.

For those of you who haven't watched *The Apprentice*. Basically, 16 arseholes attempt to impress one massive arsehole while a couple of other arseholes with clipboards tut. The biggest arseholes never win but nor do people who don't act like enough of an arsehole. Instead of a search for 'an Apprentice', the show is a search for a medium-sized arsehole. Apparently, next series they're introducing a few things to keep the format fresh. Celebrity mentors, higher-risk tasks and, in the final, Lord Sugar will fight to the death with his nemesis, the evil Professor Insulin.

We've had so many series of this show now, but one question still remains unanswered – does Nick Hewer actually have eyes? If you were working with Nick you'd constantly be saying, 'Sorry, is this lamp too bright?'

Alan Sugar admits using his name to jump the queue for a plastic surgeon. If he'd used his face he'd have got in even quicker. Sugar went to the school of 'hard knocks' – and it looks like he's taken most of them to the face. He looks like someone has sexually assaulted Yoda's corpse.

Gordon Ramsay is also rumoured to have had plastic surgery. He looks horrendous, so there's certainly been an improvement. Ramsay says he's had a hair transplant. How can you see a face looking like a side of pork that a Peckham teenager uses for stabbing practice, and think it's the hair that's the problem? Ramsay's face looks like a photo of a middle-aged man that a ballpoint-wielding toddler has discovered on your desk. If you had a face like that, would you worry about your hair? That would be almost as ridiculous as a news team speculating over who ate a murder victim's pizza.

He's had a year of plastic surgery now but, let's be honest, he still looks like he should be on a poster for a seatbelt campaign. If you had Gordon Ramsay's face, where would you even start when talking to a plastic surgeon? His entire face looks like the treads on a pair of kid's trainers.

Gordon's rival, Jamie Oliver – a Moomin-faced circus freak who by rights belongs in an Aphex Twin video – made £106 million last year. Perhaps next time he goes to 'save' an impoverished town he should 'pass on' a bit more than a meatball recipe. In these days of digital technology it's good to see a man making money from good old-fashioned exploitation of the poor. People have named Oliver as their ideal neighbour. Of course, one chat over the garden fence a week and you wouldn't have to buy a garden sprinkler. He'd be my ideal neighbour too, if he lived in Palestine and I owned a bulldozer.

★

It's the same story every year. How much should the licence fee be? They need a logical formula that pleases everyone. I suggest it's based on how many 2p pieces can be inserted into James Corden's back passage before his sphincter gives out like a fruit machine. Granted, that may mean a rise from the current £145.50.

Countryfile's Miriam O'Reilly has won her BBC ageism claim. The BBC say they are now interested in working with her again. She's already been offered *Grumpy Old Women*, *Walking with Dinosaurs* and *Ready, Steady, Die*.

Cutbacks will be affecting all programming. Huw Edwards will tell you the news personally in a restaurant round the corner from his house, and a relaunched *Tomorrow's*

World will be showing us how to make fire by using our dead skin.

The plans to close 6 Music would have been a blow to a lot of 30-something males. What would we have had to talk to student girls about? I know – the morning-after pill. 6 Music has been criticised for its lack of female presenters; much like the Jo Whiley show on Radio 1.

There'll be no cutbacks at BBC Scotland. Scottish TV programmes often cost less than the television sets they are shown on. Not every programme will have its own website. For instance, if you go online seeking more information on *The One Show*, you will be redirected to the Samaritans helpline. The *Dr Who* website will simply redirect you to a video of your family begging you to communicate with them. The *Holby City* website will just redirect fans to a picture of a cake with a submissive man's face drawn on it. That should keep the core fan base distracted until school pick-up time.

They are also getting rid of chat rooms that aren't directly related to a BBC programme. I am taking this as a personal challenge to see whether I can instigate an internet sex session simply through references to *Cash in the Attic*.

'I would pay far more than the £30 offered to clear out your back passage, and I'd love a stab at your antique cherry workspace.'

BBC websites will no longer be local. That means my hate-mail to the *River City* cast will have to be posted. Which is a problem, as Glasgow has dozens of homeless shelters.

The last episode of *Last of the Summer Wine* was broadcast 37 years after it was first shown. It was basically the same storyline repeated over and over again. Luckily, all the actors had Alzheimer's and it kept the performances fresh. And the audience's Alzheimer's made them feel as if they were watching it for the first time. It's a shame that the show couldn't have had a more realistic portrayal of ageing, where they just died of neglect and malnutrition in an NHS hospital.

If you're worried about missing the Formula 1 now the BBC don't want it, just ask your neighbour to flymo his lawn while you look at something utterly pointless. The plan is to stop screening Formula 1 so they can keep BBC Four. Radio 5 Live has already worked out a back-up plan – trapping two wasps in an upturned paper cup.

But despite the cutbacks, the *Blue Peter* garden has been saved. It'll be moved to a rooftop garden at the BBC's new home in Salford. Spare a thought for the poor runner whose first job in television will be to dig up Shep and Goldie, and post their bones to Manchester. And then spare a thought for whoever has an office on the top floor of the building, where they are putting the rooftop garden. To conform with local bylaws, the famous dogs must be buried six feet underground, which means they'll have to be kept on the desk of a researcher on the top floor who'll probably use their bones as paperweights and Bonnie's skull as an ashtray.

The BBC revealed how many of its stars earn more than £500,000. They say 'earn'. I suppose in most cases they actually mean 'get'. Chris Moyles gets £600,000. People slag him off but maybe he's just not yet found the right vehicle for his talents. I'd suggest a hearse. ITV's *The Marriage Ref* got stuffed in the ratings. I can't imagine why. The idea of couples in relationship trouble getting guidance from celebrities – how could that *not* work?

The Only Way Is Essex star Amy Childs got her own beauty slot on ITV's *This Morning*. I can't see much vajazzling going on. Broadcasting rules mean the only cunt they can show at that time is Adrian Chiles. It's easy to criticise, but there is an easy way to raise the quality of what appears on your TV. Simply wipe damp slices of bread across a toilet floor and stick them to your screen. The emerging mould patterns can be pretty BAFTA-winning.

There's a James Kelman essay in which he talks about why he doesn't write for television anymore. That it's asking the writer to describe the lives of people using language different from the language they use themselves. I find it hard to get away from that, that even words themselves are censored, and that this goes all the way up through the process, to the concepts, situations and set designs. Exerting control over language is classic colonial behaviour, and that of course is what television is, herald of a colonising ideology, bringing us new terms that are actually ideas like benefit cheat, reality television, celebrity chef, worthy cause.

I picked my daughter up from school one day and she had a poem to deliver at a recital. It was the Scots poem 'Twa Craws Sat upon a Wa', but they'd taught her it as 'Two Crows Sat upon a Wall'. Even though 'crow' doesn't rhyme with 'wall'. That's what so much of television seems to me. Two crows sat upon a wall.

'The line-up is strictly Justice League Europe'

★★★★

I shave my beard off for the show. The first big patch I shave out of it reminds me of when you see a cat that's had an operation.

I turn up early to rehearse in the dressing room. I ask a runner to bring me a chicken sandwich and he brings me a chicken sandwich and a Red Bull. Why aren't there tests of this shit that have killed rats? Probably because it smashed them through Time. Then killed them. I wonder blankly about a time machine that would only transport the severely disabled. A guy with cerebral palsy being trained to stop the Kennedy assassination, with a finale where he tries to wiggle up the stairs to the book depository. Writing this idea down I am struck by my desperation.

It's a panel show called *It Was the Best of Weeks, It Was the Worst of Weeks*. It's a pilot for BBC Two, hosted by Mark Watson. He's stopped pretending to be Welsh but is still pretending to be a hunchback. Hosting some BBC Four pish, he knows his name is on the list. I can almost see it myself, double underlined and surrounded by doodles, maybe notes about his movements. His hands shake every time he raises a cue card and, after his opening monologue, he just gives a laugh so hysterical I'm afraid he's going to start crying, openly sobbing like a child.

The idea is that one side says, 'This is the worst of weeks because …', and lists three terrible things that have happened on this week in history. The line-up is strictly *Justice League Europe*, with the other team captained by some cunt I've never heard of doing an Essex wide-boy character in a baseball cap. Their actual opener is that this is the worst week because it was the week of the 7/7 London tube bombings. The Essex dude takes the angle that now you can't get on a plane without hassle anymore and does a load of shit about air travel. I share a look with Watson that says 'This idiot will get us both raped.'

Of course, we question the other team about their shit. I go low and start saying that this is indeed the worst of weeks because it's the week this show was piloted. Things are already so dismal that this gets big yuks. I'm losing interest so I crack the Red Bull they always leave under your desk. It's the only way we can all look interested. I surf an overwhelming caffeine rush and prepare to talk myself into the edit of a show that will never be shown.

Our team say, 'Ah, no, this is the best of weeks because …', and we all give some light-hearted reason. Josie Long is on my team doing her 'Hello trees, hello sky' retard thing. She does some bit about how this is a great week because it's the week that *Tiswas* started. Drifting off, I imagine pretending to be her long-lost brother, drugging her parents on a cruise and making them actually *believe* it in the freebasing MK-ULTRA camp I'd turn their cabin into. A couple of years later, when Josie had come to terms with this seemingly unbelievable news and noticed all these little similarities between us, I would start coming on to her. She'd become an alcoholic and fall face first onto a three-bar fire on Christmas Day. Weeks later, she would be found with a blackened stump of a face on top of a homemade T-shirt saying 'Use Your Local Library!'

At the morgue her autopsy would be performed by a third-generation descendant of Dr Josef Mengele. He would be a key figure in some underground Nazi New World Order. He'd remove her brain and she would awake in a cage in the body of a tiny monkey, her brain stitched in painfully and amateurishly. Sharing the cage would be the monkey host that Mengele had used to save the brain of his Führer. For a long time Josie's life would consist of being fucked endlessly by this shrieking and insane Monkey Hitler. Members of the Nazi hierarchy would turn up to masturbate over the scene. There would be an amateurish sign scrawled on A4 and sellotaped to the side of the cage. Reading would be difficult for Monkey Josie - especially back-wards - but eventually she would decipher the words 'CAREFULNESS! JISM ON EXPOSED BRAINES (sic) CAN CAUSE AIDS.'

The other occupant of the lab, naked in a cage no bigger than a large suitcase, would be Dr David Kelly. Eventually he and Monkey Josie would escape into a nearby wood. Never understanding that Monkey Josie was able to speak because she was a scientific chimera, Dr David Kelly would think he had developed a magical ability to talk to animals. This would lead to him being badly gored in the groin by a bull. Monkey Josie would die from a mixture of exposure and depression.

Dr David Kelly would eat her, unaware that the chemicals used to bind her brain to her monkey body made her flesh highly toxic. He would die, poisoned on the self-same spot where he was once said to have committed suicide. The tiny skeleton of Monkey Josie clutched to his breast, the proud Iraq War whistleblower would thereafter be remembered as a cannibalistic paedophile. As they both die, they would see primitive computer lettering floating in front of them saying 'YOU HAVE MASTERED 3% OF THIS ADVENTURE.'

Is this really me? Is this the Red Bull? I dimly wonder if I might be gay. Then I think about how this woman used to be a little kid, and it makes me sad enough to laugh and clap when she finishes.

The second round is straightforward celebrity bashing, where Watson will ask a question like, 'Who had a bad week sexually?' And we guess it, then do some shit off the back of it. I guess Colonel Gaddafi on that one, but am quickly closed down.

I can see that I am going to have nothing in the edit of this whole round. Watson makes some quip about how it's supposed to be a light-hearted comedy show and I do the story about being in the shower with my son.

Watson says, 'You should tell more stories, it humanises you.'

I reply, 'I have never felt less human,' which gets a good laugh, and will probably go in.

★

The green room has the relaxed atmosphere of a failure. Watson is having a beer and spluttering something about some fucking charity gig he's doing. It's televised on Channel 4, but I doubt the two minutes of 'What's all

that about?' they'll cut him down to will save his
arsehole. He's terrified that I'll mention the rapist
and gabbles on about how he's wheat intolerant. Why is
it that these self-diagnosers never read an article
that makes them think that they're an attention-hungry
bullshit artist?

In the corner of the room, all the researchers and
runners are watching *The Game*. The Essex character guy
is trying to engage some of the females in the group
but they're holding him off like a tightly drilled herd
of buffalo. One of them glares at him and snaps, 'Don't
you watch *The Game*?'

I wonder whether some people have no embarrassment,
or if they are simply aware that in terms of human
degradation there is a long way to fall. Someone somewhere will have fucked a snowman. Definitely they have.
Hopefully drunkenly they will have tried to look for
some glimmer of response in its stone eyes, perhaps
have wet its makeshift vagina so they could slide
against ice, their child's scarf being blown up into
their eyes like a final plea from some despairing God.
It's not the moment of ejaculation that I pity, but the
first time that they do something normal afterwards. How
do you eat a mince pie or make a phone call or shave
after having fucked a snowman?

As always at these things there's the weirdly sexual
atmosphere of a journalists' hotel bar in a war zone.
There are some young and attractive people around. A
tall black girl is listening to one of the comics. He's
still high from the show and blowing it. Thank God I am
38 and now invisible to women. If I were to approach
one of these girls it would be like a piece of furniture had started talking, like a trestle table had

turned round and said, 'Hey, do you work on the show?'

I am drawn into *The Game* and sit with the group who are watching in silence as the people behind us gradually leave. It's a one-off episode, featuring a guy called Adam living the perfect suburban life. He has a beautiful wife and a beautiful little boy, and he's throwing a ball around with the boy when he notices puncture marks on his own wrists. At home his wife finds him sitting on the end of the bed and we know he's staring at these brown, rusty marks. She misunderstands and massages his neck, trying not to show she's a little upset. 'Are you happy, Adam?' she asks, and then we see that he's really hooked up to a drip in a cellar somewhere. A doctor with a moustache leans over him while a man in a suit stands in the shadows.

'It's not enough for him!' the doctor exclaims, shocked. 'Then give him more,' murmurs the shadow.

Adam is back in his wonderful life, enjoying days out in the park with his family, but now he has a mistress. We see him experiment with drugs and open up sexually. One night he comes home and checks in on his sleeping boy, kissing him gently on the forehead. Then he checks himself for bites and scratches in the bathroom mirror and sees the big brown punctures on his chest, on his neck, on his wrists. As he looks in the mirror there is a slight distort, like the film is playing at the wrong speed.

The doctor is panicking now. 'It's still not enough!' he shrieks. The body on the trolley is convulsing with wet, gasping noises. The suit in the shadows says, 'He can take it, give him more.'

We see Adam sitting on a table at a conference. He has a beard now and everyone seems in awe of him. From the questions he fields we learn that he has written a book, now a film, that hints at the unreality of the world, that makes people question the robotic nature of their actions.

We see him in his palatial hotel room with a groupie. She's sitting in bed smoking a joint, enthusing about a comic book she's read but the camera gradually closes on Adam's face.

'Didn't you think it was brilliant?'

'Somebody waking up from a dream? It's the worst cliché in storytelling.'

'Did you enjoy it?'

'Yes, you're right. It was genius.'

He smiles, but the actor is really good and you can tell he's hiding a bitter rage. We start to lose her dialogue as he turns inward.

He works hard, we see his wife, older now but still beautiful, and you feel somehow she knows and forgives everything about him. His new books are as big as *Harry Potter*. They're about two little Viking boys taken as hostages by a rival clan. As they grow up, one assimilates into his new life, the other pretends to, but always plans his revenge and tries to keep his brother mindful of their lost family.

By the last book, Adam is drained and jaded by success. The world anticipates the final instalment but as he knocks it out, he knows that, written while negotiating the talk-show circuit, book tours and status-based friendships, it can only be a brutal disappointment. As he writes he starts to get into the alienation of the book. The younger boy realises he can never break the spell their new life has cast on his brother and flees. The brother, happy in his position at the Viking court, is summarily executed to secure a trade agreement. We realise gradually that the ship the other little Viking has stowed away on belongs to sexual slavers, bound for Haiti. The final scene is of an archaeologist from our time digging up the boy's trademark throat chain beside some wall manacles and a huge floor-mounted dildo.

★

Someone we recognise as Neil visits Adam and tells him that he can't publish the book; there is too much expectation in the culture and this is not something that can happen. To illustrate his point he places three photographs in front of Adam and says they are 'from the future'. We assume this is some kind of threat, and Adam seems distraught.

The final shots are of Adam in his vest watching TV late at night. He says, 'I rewrote the book to make it as unrealistically, satirically happy as possible. What I wrote didn't even make sense. And yet everybody was happy.' He opens a can of beer and continues watching numbly. 'Now that I've done that, I wonder how many other people that young man showed his photos to, because I see that everywhere.' We see the TV light washing brightly across his face as we hear some canned laughter. 'I see it everywhere.'

On the trolley, the body has ceased to struggle. The torturer looks relieved. 'Disappointment, angst, that'll keep them under when nothing else will,' the voice in the shadows intones. An uneasy look passes over the torturer's face, and we see him surreptitiously check his own arms for marks. 'Everyone's a bit disappointed …,' he offers.

Suddenly, we see the torturer from the shadow's point of view. Looking through the shadow's eyes we see that the torturer is covered in rusty brown marks on his arms, his hands, his temples. A drip we've been unaware of connects from above to his neck, and the trolley is empty. 'Yes,' agrees the shadow, chuckling. 'I like that.'

★

I have a car to take me back to the hotel. My driver is Turkish and explains that he killed two people during his military service, then went insane. 'One of them I kill with electricity.' It seems he was sent to some re-education centre, where they told him this was OK. He's in his mid-20s. He asks me what I've been doing and I have a go at explaining the concept of the panel show to him. Eventually, there is a big enough silence for me to put my earphones in.

When I get back to my room I go to the living-room bit and there's an empty beer bottle on the table. I can hear music. I go through to the bedroom and there on the bed a figure has been made from my clothes. A jumper stuffed with blankets, a yellow balloon for my head. My jeans are hitched down to reveal two white pillow buttocks. There are traces on them of what looks like dried blood, or possibly jam. I pick the balloon up and it has a sad face drawn on the underside. A CD is playing in the music centre. It takes me a moment to identify the theme tune from A *Question of Sport*.

★ ★ ★ ★

In many North American indigenous cultures, generosity is a central behaviour in a broader social and economic system. One anecdotal account examined what happened when boys from white and Lakota communities received a pair of lollipops each. The white boys put the second one in their pockets, while the Native American boys presented it to the nearest boy who didn't have one.

Raj Patel, *The Value of Nothing*

★ ★ ★ ★

05

Capitalism is a religion. Acolytes believe in its principles even when these are proved wrong. Business people, in case you haven't noticed, dress in costume, go off on retreats together, and speak with the same glassy-eyed passion about their orthodoxy as Christians.

The market is our new God. It's everywhere. It can turn into a bull and it can turn into a bear. Sometimes its priests will tell us it's 'expectant', other times it's 'gloomy'. We quiver in our huts and wait to see what it will do. When the market is angry, 'sacrifices' have to be made. Market research is the new confessional, a perverse quantifying of desire. You could view Jesus attacking the money changers in the Temple as the Judeo-Christian God having a fairly astute idea of who the competition was going to be. Likewise, it's no coincidence that Muslims have strong views on the lending of money at interest. Any religion looking at money must have seen in its wing mirrors a hungry new deity.

Of course, we might ask ourselves what kind of God it is. A God that thinks you shouldn't receive medical treatment unless you can afford it; that tells us patent profits in the developing world are more important than affordable medicines. Go to your nearest scheme, look at the lives of the kids there, and tell me that it doesn't demand child sacrifices.

It will be interesting to see how it fares against the Chinese pantheon. The Soviet Union was bought off with promises of jeans and cars and cheap stereos. It'll be difficult to sell the same mirage to China, because they make all that shit.

The amazing achievement by the coalition government is to have laid the blame for the financial collapse on people claiming benefits for invalidity, local councils and single-parent families. As spins go, it's amazingly bold, like blaming 9/11 on Duffy.

Recently, I saw the headline, 'Bankers threaten to leave Britain'. And thought, what's the rest of that sentence? 'Poorer than Somalia'? We gave billions to the banks to try to get credit flowing and they just stuck it in their balance sheets. For a while, the only available source of credit was *Dragons' Den*. Of course, the government should have given it all back to the taxpayers. It was their money anyway, and they'd have got things moving, the economy buoyed by a sudden spike in sales of plasma TVs, decking and nachos. We'd have spent every penny and had the satisfaction of seeing the *Ten O'Clock News* reporting on Sony being taken over by Primark.

Life is, in a way, pretty difficult for rich people. Money alienates you from your community and commodifies your relationships. The rich never correlate being cut off from other people (often physically behind gates and security cameras, in case somebody tries to take their money!) with their lack of affection for them. Also, rich people tend to be cunts.

The *Sunday Times Rich List* could sell a lot more copies if it called itself *The Kidnapper's Bible*. Comedy is represented on the *Rich List*, with Ricky Gervais doing well. How galling is that if you're a temp? You work in an office and get six quid an hour. Gervais pretends to work in an office and gets £32 million. The obvious response is, next time you go to the office just pretend you work there. Will it get you £32 million? Probably not. But if your employer is a council, there's a good chance that you'll get a promotion.

★

There are fears that Britain could be facing a double-dip recession, or worse still, a double-dip with misery sprinkles and fuck-where's-my-job-sauce. We're teetering on the edge of recession, just like the small-business owners teetering on the edge of Beachy Head. Let's hope the recession catches a patch of daisies out of the corner of his tear-reddened eyes as well, or we're in the shit.

GDP is growing, but that doesn't mean we're out of recession. It just means you'll be eating dog food along with your dog, rather than selling your dog to pay for it. The economy has grown by 0.8 per cent, which has the depressing joy to it of a 13-year-old boy who measures his cock every day.

George Osborne revealed his emergency budget. The word 'emergency' makes it sound a lot more dramatic than it actually was. At the very least, Osborne could have run into the chamber in flames, while screaming, 'Head for the lifeboats, we're doomed, we're all doomed.' And exited while being chased by a rhino. But, sadly, that was all in the subtext.

If your children ask you what a budget is, you should explain that what happens is that every year an evil millionaire tells the poor people how much they need to pay for a pint of beer. And it's always a lot more than the poor people want to pay, so they get sad and angry. And you're probably wondering how this evil man gets his power? We vote him in. And when we do that we get sad and angry, so every four years we choose a different millionaire, who likes a different colour to the one we already have. It goes red, blue, red, blue. And we do that every five years until we get so sad and so angry that we die. And what little money we might have left isn't even given to our relatives. The evil millionaire takes some, and then it all starts again.

Air-travel duty didn't go up as expected. So, good news. You will still pay the same to sit in an airport lounge being filmed by Sky News.

The education budget was cut by a quarter. At least classrooms are now so overcrowded the kids can keep warm. Families with three children have lost £1,700 a year. Though I doubt they'll notice it through the blind hatred they have for each other. There are complaints over a proposed 20 per cent cut to the armed services. After all, if we're cutting education by 25 per cent, the army will soon find itself overwhelmed by applicants.

Of course, the biggest industry that lost out with VAT going from 17.5 per cent to 20 per cent is calculator manufacturers. If people aren't shopping, raising VAT is about as useful as Adrian Chiles washing his cock.

There are some great bargains to be had on the high street right now, particularly if you want to buy a shop. HMV are going bankrupt. If you look closely, you'll see that little dog has chewed off his own foot. Primark warned that high-street sales are dropping. Customers realised they can save a fiver or two by going through the cardboard box of forgotten clothes down the launderette. One exec actually said, 'It's ugly out there.' He just needs to get out of the shop more. I blame their latest refit, which included more reflective surfaces. Primark – I don't know who to feel most sorry for: the girls squeezing into something that makes them look like James Corden at a fetish club, or the kids in the Far East knocking the stuff up for less than the price of the pasty crumbs in their average customer's cleavage.

800,000 low-paid workers will no longer pay income tax, which will be a great comfort to them when their brothers are killed by a mental patient whose social worker was busy doing some photocopying. Everyone's pleased that the low paid won't pay tax on their earnings, as soon the only money they'll earn will be thrown into a paper cup in a doorway. There were some further tax breaks for the poor, or there would have been if any of them still had a job and weren't trying to claim benefits that no longer existed.

Maybe one solution to unemployment's not just to give redundancy money. Offer a hibernation option, as well. Then, when things pick up, the boss can open your straw-filled box, wipe your eyes clean with damp cotton wool, and it's back to five days a week of Facebooking with a hangover.

The government plans to boost the confidence of the long-term unemployed by making them do community jobs. I shouldn't knock the idea. There's nothing like trudging round a park picking up dog shit for a quid an hour to restore your self-esteem. There's a performance-related element too. The harder they work, the more re-smokeable fag butts they get.

Job hunters can have ugly tattoos removed at the tax payer's expense. Fair enough. I mean, who's going to employ someone with a spider's web on their face? They're much more likely to want someone with raw pink scarring in the shape of a spider's web.

Thousands of us face new bills for outstanding tax. There's no point complaining; the government needs our money. Those Afghan weddings won't accidentally bomb themselves. There are worries that fraudsters might start sending out fake demands. My tip – if it says, 'Make it out to Terry', don't.

The government's been told its benefits changes could leave 40,000 more people homeless. It's easy to underestimate the homeless. There's a guy who's always curled up in his sleeping bag in a doorway near me. Then, when I passed the other evening, he suddenly burst out with the most beautiful pair of powder blue wings. Sad to see him knocked down trying to reach that streetlight.

Watching the coalition front bench, you can't help but feel that if someone chucked a stake through Cameron's heart all the Lib Dems' shackles would magically melt away and they could be mermaids again.

Cameron condemned the North-East for being overly reliant on the public sector. It's almost as if, when you shut down all the industries in a particular area, 20 years on, those families seem quite keen to use social services. The area least affected by the cuts was Cheshire, where George Osborne has his constituency. The message is, stop voting Labour, or by the end of this government the only public service your areas will have is the weekly cart to carry away your dead.

The public were consulted by the government regarding the forthcoming planned cuts. And, overwhelmingly, they said, 'I vote for the dancing dog. Or the old woman.' The public? Does London have a mosque big enough for a Ministry of Racism? Did you contribute? No? Well, our country is now run by the same nutters who email newspapers to ask how long you can keep tea in the fridge. Expect VAT to rise on everything except cat food and night-vision goggles.

This wasn't George Osborne's first plan. Plan A was to spread the debt across his wife's credit cards. Plan B was to feign mental illness. He went with Plan B. Luckily, he was helped out by Danny Alexander, who looks like the Honey Monster's shaved to get gay sex on the internet. You can't ask the general public to cut the public sector. Most of us aren't even sure what the public sector is. 'OK, general public. Let's go … What is too expensive and needs cutting? What's that? Phone voting for ITV shows, multipack crisps and having to put a pound coin in a shopping trolley even though you get it back? There we go, deficit sorted. Now, on to crime and justice – death penalty for cyclists, anyone?'

The Comprehensive Spending Review showed that close to 500,000 jobs will be lost in the public sector. The government expect that, in the main, this number will be achieved by voluntary redundancy and grizzly suicides.

Vince Cable, a bald eagle with radiation sickness, also cut public-sector pay. Not cutting expenditure on weapons or telling the banks to sod off. No, it's those greedy council workers with their wretched jobs. Looks like council admin workers are becoming the biggest economic scapegoats since the Jews in Nazi Germany. At least we don't have to make them wear armbands. We can just start throwing stones at anyone we see with a laminated ID pass on a neckband.

The head of Suffolk County Council is paid £220,000 a year. Seems high, but she has to deal with the stress of finding bin men willing to deal with rubbish, recycling and the seasonal dead-virgin collection each harvest. If we knew how to run the country ourselves, we wouldn't bother having a government. The only reason we put up with this charade every five years is we know that, no matter how idiotic the cabinet is, they are still not as stupid as us. To revive the economy we should make a lot of cuts in public spending, reinvest the money in the war on drugs – then change sides.

A Tory MP said the disabled should be prepared to work for less money! If anything, they should get more money because it's more difficult for them to get to work. There are quite a few steps down to my sex dungeon.

By targeting the rich, Osborne has been accused of turning against his own. That's not true. He's yet to tax shedding your skin or the construction of Daleks. Osborne introduced measures to help first-time buyers, though. Good. They've as much right as anyone to have a house repossessed.

He announced there would be 21 Enterprise Zones coming to the most deprived parts of England. Those areas are delighted. At least there will be some decent computers to steal soon. The chancellor also announced the creation of a state pension of £140 a week. Which sounds generous, until you realise the state you need to be in to collect it is dead. Osborne laid out plans to change the age of retirement in line with life expectancy. Great news for Scots, who'll now be collecting their pensions on their 35th birthday. The crisis in pensions means millions of kids face having to support their parents in retirement. We owe it to them to make it easier. I've already got mine wiping my bottom for me so it's less of a shock when it happens.

Osborne said his budget would create jobs. I certainly see a vacancy coming up for Mad Max. The police force is facing spending cuts of 20 per cent. Such stringent cutbacks mean that from now on they're legally only allowed to greet members of the public with two 'Hellos'. And many innocent people will now have to run for their train without getting shot.

Greater Manchester Police is to shrink by a quarter because of these budget cuts. It's bad news as it means if you have your house broken into, there might not be anyone to turn up and say, 'They'll be miles away now. Nothing we can do really.'

Three per cent of people think their jobs will now be safer. This consists of non-homosexual cabinet ministers, Amanda Holden's team of psychiatrists and the staff at Britain's largest bailiffs. People in the future will look back on this time and wonder why we bankrupted ourselves for a new tumble dryer, then crawl inside a house made of tumble dryers to die of radiation sickness.

Ed Balls lecturing Osborne on his handling of the economy is like a Catholic priest tutting during a former altar boy's confession. In fact, Ed Balls blasting Osborne for his handling of the economy is like us bombing Gaddafi for using the weapons we sold him … oh.

It's only now the books have been checked that the money wastage has come to light. In retrospect, Labour's ladder to Mars, the elite Chihuahua military attack squad and Alistair Darling's street-dance team look expensive. The Queen had to deliver a speech that will outline how the government plans to save £6 billion. If I were her, I'd have been worried that the plan involved wiring up her throne to the mains. It's a strange world where a woman wearing an ermine cape and a golden crown worth £20 million gives a speech ordering us to turn the lights out when we're not in the room.

The protests against the public spending cuts were around a third of the size of the massive Stop the War march. Still, if it's just a third as effective as that, then … well, never mind. The protestors felt that we should never have elected these people. And that we didn't. Not to worry, several Arab countries have offered to back the protesters in toppling this corrupt regime. The crowds in Trafalgar Square were so raucous with all the jostling and hitting, at one point they actually started the Olympic clock. Fortnum & Mason was occupied – I salute that, having often felt that the proletariat was being held back by gourmet jams. Protestors smashed up an Ann Summers shop. Police beat protestors back with rubber batons. I think they were rubber batons, but I could have sworn that one of then had a fist on the end. Theresa May, the home secretary, wants to give the police powers to remove balaclavas from protesters. An easy way round this would be to have your face painted. Can you imagine the PR nightmare if the police started clubbing a group of people wearing clown make-up? Or when there was a YouTube clip of the moment a rubber bullet brain-damaged Spiderman? David Cameron was shaken by the protests and was working hard behind the scenes to have *The X Factor* brought forward.

The true extent of public debt was revealed as £7.9 trillion. If that worries you, just think of it as, £7.9 oooooooooooo! I doubt this country could have got itself into more of a mess if our PM and chancellor were a cardboard cut-out of Fireman Sam and an ironing board. Or what about something like a hostess trolley? Prime Minister Hostess Trolley. You can imagine it being wheeled out to meet Obama and him getting his photo taken, smiling and tasting some roast potatoes. Everyone would love Britain again. Until after two terms in office that damned hostess trolley is jaded, tired and corrupt and, instead of its compartments being filled with delicious roast chickens and gravy, it's just full of oil, shepherds' heads and foreign blood. But, give it it's due, warm foreign blood.

★

It looks like customers are to pay for new bank reforms with higher charges. Before you say, 'There's nothing we can do,' remember most cashpoints will happily swallow at least three After Eight mints. Some banks have already modified their customer-service lines to suit: press 1 for mortgages, 2 for current accounts and 3 for an impotent saliva-spitting rant at a minimum wager in Bangalore, who has to get clearance from a supervisor to even go for a piss.

Many Lloyds banks are being closed. I wonder if they will use the branches to house the homeless? It would be cool to get your *Big Issue* pushed at you through a cashpoint. Just as banks were told they could keep ripping people off with overdraft charges, it was revealed that the government made secret £62 billion loans to HBOS and RBS. I knew that RBS was close to collapse when I went to the cashpoint to withdraw a tenner and out popped a scratch card.

£62 million is twice Britain's defence budget. Think about that for a second. The RBS and HBOS could have joined forces, raised an army and defeated Britain. Twice. Or, alternatively, they could have used the money to win the war in Afghanistan by the year 2346. All banks are now required to reveal how many staff earn over a £1 million. It's basically a staff list with the janitor's name covered in Tippex.

The government lent £62 billion and there are approximately 62 million people in Britain. See what I'm saying? No, not that we should all get £1,000 each. I mean, the government should have used the money to cull at least 30 million British people. Suddenly, there would be prosperity and jobs for all. Admittedly, on the job front it would involve us all becoming grave diggers for the next 40 generations, but work is work.

Councils have cranked up burial costs as a way of pulling in a few extra quid. Tell me about it. When my granddad passed away I had to pay not just a burial fee, but a fine for putting him in the wrong coloured bin. A bloke round my way's offering a cut-price alternative. For 50 quid he'll respectfully douse your late loved one in unleaded, then an hour or so later snort him up using a Henry Hoover with the face of Christ drawn on in marker pen.

★

Andrew Lansley is reforming the NHS, in a similar sense to when they re-form beef to make it into dog food. They're desperate to introduce much more patient choice. Presumably along the lines of, 'So what's it to be? *C. difficile* or MRSA?' A report claims that the NHS is offering worse value than ever. Because of my regular volunteer work as a visitor, I feel I'm in a position to disagree. I've not paid for a loo roll in six years.

GPs are going to get control of their own budgets, leaving them free to do what they do best: playing golf and molesting patients under anaesthetic. Sacking managers, that's the key, apparently. Though I seem to remember when I worked at McDonald's as a student and the manager didn't turn up, me and the other plebs just ended up playing Russian roulette with a bucket of McNuggets, one of which was actually half a deep-fried tampon in breadcrumbs. Half of GPs think it's acceptable to have a sexual relationship with a patient. I really think it depends on certain factors, such as how long the queue is in the waiting room.

David Cameron says they'll be keeping patient choice at the heart of the revised health reforms. He says everyone should be free to decide which hospital they want to be neglected in. It's been suggested to charge drunks £50 if they go to A&E. That's not fair. How will they then afford a ticket to my show?

The NHS is under pressure to withdraw pornography from patients who need to give sperm samples. I think it's a terrible idea to remove pornography from hospitals. It's pretty much the only reason I visited Dad after his bypass operation.

Wales is to introduce presumed consent for organ donation. This should greatly improve patient survival rates … as doctors there offer still-beating hearts as gifts to call upon the healing powers of their many gods. And a hospital in Cardiff gave its elderly patients tambourines and maracas to summon medical help. Not sure that'll work. Bez from the Happy Mondays has been trying it for years.

It's sad, as we consistently undervalue the contribution the old can make to society. For example, stick a load of jigsaws in your loft and you can't keep them out – and with all those coats their insulation value is triple that of fibreglass.

★

A proposed rise in university tuition fees could leave students with debts of over £100,000. Forget going to university. If you want to make some money, start a university. If students have to pay these fees, then watching *Countdown* in your pants will become a more expensive experience than space tourism. Apparently, some hard-up students have turned to prostitution. If you meet a fellow student in this situation, then remember – you should get a 10 per cent discount with your NUS card. The only people who can afford to go to university will be the massively wealthy and the girls who're putting themselves through by stripping. If they marry, we'll have a whole generation with no chins and massive tits. Some universities may even close. The University of Bedfordshire in Luton has already said it might go back to being a bus depot. The good news is students now won't have to start paying their loans back till they earn more than £21,000 a year. Which means if you choose media studies, it's basically free.

Travelodge are offering school leavers a chance to manage a hotel rather than go to university. When you're standing in a tiny room at 3 am looking at an unchanging computer screen while you suspect people all around you are having sex, you'll find it's much the same as university. And you'll learn all you need to know about adult working life from watching strangers in suits desperate for sleep try to ignore human contact.

★

Ireland is in such a crisis that 25 per cent of its population is in the gutter. It harks back to the glory days at the height of its economic boom when 100 per cent of the population was in the gutter. Osborne pledged £10 billion to help bail out Ireland. I just hope they don't do anything risky with the money, like put it in a bank. Osborne is heir to the Baronetcy of Ballentaylor, County Tipperary. Do you think he will be giving Ireland the money by bank transfer or by his family's traditional method of a sackcloth bag of pennies and a lump of coal being handed to each farm worker at the back door on Boxing Day? Osborne has said he can't name City fat-cat bankers – mainly because he only knows them as Bunty, Slasher and Bulldog.

Ireland being criticised by Britain is like a man dying of kidney failure being slagged off by the blokes on dialysis. There's a lot of British money in Ireland – as well as a lot of our illegitimate children, stolen land and murder victims. Of course we want to help the only country we share a border with, but if we really wanted to help, we possibly could have resisted putting that border there in the first place.

How can the Irish have *nothing*? An Irish firm are building the Olympic village. Can't we just move the whole country into there? Come 2012, we can post them outside every tube station for a couple of weeks. After all, that's the only way tourists are going to get a warm welcome to London.

It's now suggested that we also give money to Portugal. We have a similar relationship to Portugal as we do to Ireland, except in Ireland's case it was us who abducted their children.

And Greece needs another bailout. The Greek protest movement is called Aganaktismenoi, meaning 'outrage'. It's unclear whether most of the anger is directed towards the police or the bloke who shouts 'Give us an A.' The austerity measures are so harsh, many people are already living off tinned taramosalata or moussaka on toast. David Cameron said he would fight to ensure UK money isn't used in the bailout. So, rest assured, UK money will definitely be used in the bailout. But if we lend them more, will they bother repaying? Let's face it, most of their decent collateral's in the British Museum. If Greece doesn't get the bailout it'll be unable to pay public employees' wages. Which means when you say, 'Excuse me, the ferry's going in five minutes, *please* could you sell me a ticket,' there might be nobody in the booth to nod dismissively and go off into the back office for a smoke.

Of course, 'bailout' is a complete misnomer. Banks lend the money to Greece at a rate of interest. Greece then has to decide how much of its public services to privatise in order to pay interest on these loans. The banks are largely French and German. Many are insured in the UK, so we do alright, too. Greece is being asked to live through a decade of austerity so that French and German banks make profits, money that they then lend out to things like German manufacturers, who make large amounts of goods that get bought in places that don't manufacture much, like Greece.

Obviously, with the whole system being weighted towards large, wealthy economies such as Germany, the Greeces of this world will occasionally go tits up. Lending to Greece is not a 'bailout'. It's the equivalent of a company subbing their toilet cleaner a week's wages so they don't fuck off and get another job.

Soon Italy might need to be bailed out, too. An out-of-control, morally bankrupt, multi-millionaire media baron having so much influence on government? Makes you glad to live in the UK, doesn't it?

★

The Tories are proposing that people earn recycling points that can be spent on the high street. Yeah, that's just what I need – more nebulous points to keep track of. I'm looking forward to lots of council admin workers being made redundant, as then I can employ some to keep track of all my fucking points and pay them in meals at Beefeater.

And motorists are to get bigger fines for littering. Of course, littering's not always as it seems. Just the other night I was out driving … nothing on the road apart from one car, a little way in front. Suddenly, out the passenger window came a bag of crisps. Normally, I'd let it go, but for some reason I thought, 'Not tonight'. So I put my foot down and overtook. But when I drew alongside and looked over, in the front seats were two giant bags of crisps and one was screaming, 'John! John! The baby's fallen out of the window!'

There was a lot of talk about fuel duty in the last budget. I thought 'fuel duty' was how to describe the time spent by anyone in the British military who's seen active service in Iraq or Libya. Truckers are furious about the record high price of diesel. Thousands may lose their jobs. Which is a serious worry, as most only have fat reserves to last a couple of months. It's the biggest crisis for long-distance lorry drivers since the 1970s, when they took industrial action to stop their wives continually answering the door in their negligees to randy, buck-toothed milkmen. The only region coping well with petrol price rises is the North-East, where you can squeeze an acceptable high-octane substitute from out of Paul Gascoigne's nipples for the price of a Wagon Wheel and a whisky miniature.

Protesters tried a 'go slow' on the Dartford Crossing – though they were disappointed at not being able to reach the hoped-for 8 mph. They're considering measures to help truckers, dropping duty on Yorkie bars, Razzle and those big knives for dismembering hitchhikers.

With petrol prices soaring and the VAT rise putting up the price of booze, people are now going to have to choose between drinking and driving. We'll feel it the most come the summer when we won't be able to afford enough petrol to get the barbecue going. The AA's warned that the jump in petrol prices will keep the poor off the roads. Nonsense. People will always need their windscreens washed at traffic lights.

It's a timely reminder of how much of what we use comes from such a long way away … That we could all source more locally. I get everything from the big Tesco on the ring road, so I'm covered.

I have a tremendous hope for the future of mankind, because what other way is there to go? Yes, it will be difficult breaking free from our reliance on fossil fuels. You know what'd be more difficult? Breathing without any fucking oxygen. Yes, it will be difficult turning our back on war. You know what'd be more difficult? Teaching your child to survive by showing them how to deliver the perfect blowjob onto the forked penis of a Chinese warlord.

Of course, it'll be a hard path to paradise. In a few years' time, we'll go through a phase where the news stories that fill us with horror now will be used as mood lightening items at the end of a news bulletin. '… And finally, a man went berserk in Birmingham today, killing 20 people with an automatic rifle. And now over to the weather from Hannah, and her rapist.'

What strikes me about the state of the world is the bullshit idea we used to hear that people were doing everything for their kids. Now, at least we know they drive about in their 4x4s and fly to their pointless meetings and vote for their sham governments for themselves. We're not trying to build a future for our kids; we're trying to build status and wealth for ourselves. The only thing we'll be leaving our kids is a dying fucking world. You travelled into your kid's future, and used the fuel and bulldozed the trees and poisoned the sea. You choked him with your skiing holidays, your iPhones and your lifestyle supplements. When your child was born, you straddled a grave and shat him into it. Did I just write that? Glad I got out of comedy when I did …

★

The international banking system thinks of itself as the pinnacle of human achievement. The markets are so intricate and complicated and yet, when you look at it, all they're doing is trading shiny beads and feathers. They might trade 100 tonnes of gold for $5 billion. But all that's happening is they're swapping some soft yellow metal for some neatly cut sheets of paper. It's no different to a kid on the beach swapping a handful of sea shells for a crab shell. Except the kids on the beach at least know it's just a game.

It's bizarre that humans have decided that gold is the most valuable thing in our society. A metal that, until recently, had very few useful functions whatsoever. You'd have thought bread, or bricks, or ceramics would be far more valuable. But we all decided on gold, because of its rarity. It could have been very different. We could have chosen literally any other substance in the universe. Right now, underneath the Bank of England, there could be huge reserves of the skeletons of conjoined twins.

The commodities market includes the buying and selling of diamonds, gold, silver and orange juice. Orange juice? Trading in orange juice? What is this, a fucking tuck shop? Are there guys in champagne bars boasting to their mates, 'Yeah, just made a million trading Pokémon cards for Coca-Cola bottles'? I suspect the trade in orange juice is at its peak from about 9 am to noon, and then demand falls away.

Perhaps, some day, people will look at the metal and paper in their pockets and realise it means nothing, and if they all agreed to agree that it meant nothing, we could all just head to the beach and watch the waves come in.

'Garlic bread? Garlic bread? We're fighting three fucking wars here, mate!'

★ ★ ★ ★

I have to write up sketches for what I thought was going to be a pilot for Channel 4. Then it turns out it's going to be a 'taster tape'. Then it's actually just one sketch they want. I get really fucking wound up about this, even though I haven't got any sketches. I get a bunch of Diet Cokes from the wee shop at the bottom of the building and try to write, sitting in the ledge bit of one of the stateroom portholes.

It's sunny outside, which always makes working difficult. I slide down off the ledge and sit in the glowing circle the sunshine has made on the carpet, like an ant under a magnifying glass. I take the wax model of the scheme down onto the floor and lie there, moving people into unlikely scenarios - wee shopkeepers forming drinking gangs outside the houses of teenagers, all the heroin addicts going down the swimming baths en masse to baptise each other into a new religion, the toddlers gathering in the boozer underneath me.

My sketch idea is about Peter Kay taking a heroic dose of magic mushrooms and becoming a politically conscious comedian. He then has to do his stand-up to huge stadiums of folk expecting jokes about the types of biscuits your nan buys, but feels compelled to deliver groundbreaking anarchist routines. He berates Cameron for Libya.

'No fly zone? We're targeting people who clearly can't fly and blowing them 15 feet into the air!' he yells with trademark camp exasperation. The punters get bored and heckle helpfully with stuff like:

'Garlic bread, Peter! Come on, pal! Garlic bread!'

'Garlic bread? Garlic bread? We're fighting three fucking wars here, mate!'

Peter persuades Michael McIntyre to take acid with him after the Royal Variety Performance and McIntyre starts 'noticing' more things than ever before. 'Have you noticed … the control matrix of our society with the media at its core?' he will ask Graham Norton during an ill-fated interview.

We finish with the video for Peter's Christmas single, a nine-minute hymn to frontal-lobe epilepsy. The lyrics are a verbal Jackson Pollock, a heap of broken images, with themes of sexual totalitarianism and prosthesis, and always ending with the refrain: 'MY SPINE FLIES PETROL AND ALSO GOES BEYOND ME. SPIIINE.'

Animal-faced dancers in peach military uniforms with medals for racism chipped from anthracite stamp across the melting screen like the pernicious progress of a virus. What at first seems to be a conventional tap-dance sequence becomes the majestic depiction of a semantic war between the months of the Gregorian calendar; all-conquering January vowing to set Time against Numbers as he leaps from a shattered altar into an episode of *Miami Vice*. A pair of ballerinas jerk like machine-gunned marionettes, leaving the viewer believing they're watching a porn mpeg called *Gay Interview and Fuck 1* while running flatfooted through their own childhood.

There's a moment of silence when we see Peter in a 1970s classroom filled with pupils of sculpted garbage. He turns directly to the camera and gives the knowing and amateurish smile of a porn star as his head opens slowly like a meat flower and out of it dance the sports stars of an unknown race. The 'ball' in all their games is a half-sized and particularly haunted-looking Harvey Keitel. In the bottom left of the picture, former Dundee United and Scotland forward Paul Sturrock tries to communicate the song in sign language, despite having no knowledge of sign language. What he actually signs is, 'I have been chosen to play the Chinese Dr Who. As Hu is a common family name in China, the show there is a fairly conventional medical drama.'

We see a baffled, very old Tony Christie, with a bruised and bleeding face, buried up to his neck in the ground, while an enormous, villainous carrot screams obscenities at him in some unknowable language. He mumbles that he thought they were going to be doing 'It's Not Unusual' before singing the words 'BITTER STASIS' in the powerful and beautiful voice of a German woman, while Peter Kay, reading aloud from a grotesquely sexualised and inaccurate novelisation of *Ghostbusters*, his face swollen with rage, spins and leaps impossibly across the set of *Newsnight* like the choreographer of William Burroughs's Nuremberg. We are aware that on *Newsnight* David Cameron is speaking firmly to Jeremy Paxman.

'I tell you right now,' he asserts with a clipped hand gesture, 'that I could hold open my arsehole and out would pour a Tarot of bestial imagery.'

It ends with Peter saying, 'Welcome to the Culture Wars!' over a picture of a can of John Smith's bitter.

★

I have my boy that night and he's supposed to go to bed at half seven but the Man U game's on and it's a European semi-final. I tell him he can watch the first half. He's sitting there in his pyjamas really excited and, as the whistle goes, he asks me which side we're controlling. He's only ever seen football on the PlayStation (he played once - he scored and shouted, 'I boofed it!'). Any time there's a shot on goal he asks if he did that or if I did that. I take him to bed at half-time but he comes back through at the start of the second half. He's got a dragon puppet that for some reason I always have to make sing about its day – a long, improvised song in a Welsh accent. We miss every goal, laughing. Eventually he tells me to stop and he sings a wee song about his day, going from nursery right up until now. 'And I heard the people yelling on the telly and I just came through!' he trills.

After I get him to sleep I try to look at porn but can't get interested. I only like it when the actress is really into it, so it's hard to find anything nowadays. I have another Facebook threat from the same goober. In his profile picture he has his arm round an impatient-looking Noel Gallagher. I'm also friends with him on the page where I'm pretending to be Alan Hansen, the former Liverpool player. He's a Man U fan, but after a few direct messages from Hansen he's cravenly admitting his admiration for Liverpool's European glory days and bemoaning United's ability to shut up shop in the same fashion as those boring bastards did. He's sent Alan Hansen a message just after he's threatened to run me over:

Not sure I fancy your chances against the big boys! You going to the game or are they making you pay these days, you tight Scottish c**t?

I shouldn't imagine he generally asterisks swear-words, but he has some corrupted idea of what passes for politeness when addressing Alan Hansen. I look at the BBC website and see that this is a reference to Liverpool playing Chelsea on Saturday. I reply:

Can't talk now, mate. It's not good here.

I check the rest of Alan Hansen's inbox. He has two new women wanting him, not great ones. I imagine meeting Hansen and slipping him this password. Getting FA Cup tickets anonymously through the post because he's delighted to be up to his nuts in Grade D muff.

That guy has responded with:

What's up chief??!!

I type *I have cancer*, and go to bed.

★ ★ ★ ★

Arizona talked about some of her experiences with the Queen Mother: 'The Queen Mother was cold, cold, cold, a nasty person. None of her cohorts even trusted her. They have named an altar (mind-control program) after her. They call it the Black Queen. I have seen her sacrifice people. I remember her pushing a knife into someone's rectum the night the two boys were sacrificed. One was 13 and the other 18. You need to forget that the Queen Mother appears to be a frail woman. When she shape-shifts into a reptilian, she becomes very tall and strong. Some of them are so strong they can rip out a heart and they all grow by several feet when they shape-shift. I have seen (Prince Charles) shape-shift into a reptilian and do all of the things the Queen does. I have seen him sacrifice children. There is a lot of rivalry between them for who gets to eat what part of the body and who gets to absorb the victim's last breath and steal their soul. I have seen Andrew participate and I have seen Prince Philip and Charles' sister (Anne) at the rituals, but they didn't participate when I was there. When Andrew shape-shifts, he looks more like one of the lizards. The royals are some of the worst. OK, as far as enjoying the killing, enjoying the sacrifice, and eating the flesh, they are some of the worst of all of them. They don't care if you see it. Who are you going to tell, who is going to believe you? They feel that it is their birthright and they love it. They love it.'

David Icke, *Children of the Matrix*

★ ★ ★ ★

06

The House of Windsor is the stage name of a troupe of petty German nobles. It was founded by King George V during the First World War in 1917, when he decided to alter his family's name from the German Sachsen-Coburg und Gotha to the English Windsor, so as not to provoke anti-German sentiment towards his family at a time when the Gotha G.IV was actually the name of a type of German aircraft bombing London. That's on the Queen's side, obviously. Prince Philip changed to Mountbatten from the House of Schleswig-Holstein-Sonderburg-Glücksburg.

Like many actors, it was the name change that signalled their entry into show-business proper. Our royals realise they are playing a publicity game and, when it gradually emerged that the media were fascinated by their sexual misadventures, their petty rivalries, their boorishness and their racism, they must have been secretly delighted knowing deep down that *they have fuck all else to offer.*

Of course, like all jaded entertainers they can't really raise their game because they don't need to. Their gaffes, their almost ironic smiles, their sheer duffness – if you're trying to put your finger on what makes you uneasy about their manner, it's the air of a children's magician who can't believe how well this shit is going down. Commentators said that the recent royal wedding was a tonic for the whole nation. That's like telling the homeless to go and stand outside Buckingham Palace and admire it. Just looking at the many rooms, the comfortable furniture and the warmth radiating from the building is sure to make everything better. A starving person has always been cheered up by watching another man eat.

In the *Financial Times*, Simon Schama wrote that the First World War swept away autocrats in Germany and Russia, which meant that in order for European monarchs to survive, their focus had to change from 'ruling to reigning; from the exercise of power to incarnations of historical memory.' This transition, Schama goes on to argue, was aided by the fact that the masses craved this 'mystique', memories of the horrors of WWI and the influx of mass-produced entertainment and goods being contributing factors to this desire. As a result, royal events – such as weddings, coronations and burials – became increasingly grand and elaborate. Schama's right, it's all a marketing strategy and their power was diluted to preserve the one thing they valued more: their wealth. It's interesting that no such opinions made the tabloids. The media can be propagandist, but let's not forget that elites are quite happy to tell the truth to each other when they think no plebs are listening.

The Early Learning Centre was selling three-inch-high figurines of the royal couple. I bought the Katie one. I've combined it with my boy's Scalextric to show him what might well happen if she doesn't toe the line.

The wedding meant that people got a day off work, which isn't much when compared with the 50 years off work that William and Kate are getting. Ironically, I didn't get a day off as I work part time as an Al-Qaeda sniper.

The royal couple said they wanted to share the wedding with the nation. The £5 million security bill suggested otherwise. They wanted to share their wedding with the nation in the same way they want to share their palaces, cars and jewels. From behind a 12-foot barrier 100 metres away, with a sharp-shooter aiming at your chest.

If you wanted to hold a street party for the royal wedding all you had to do was fill out one form. Which I suspect was the stumbling block for many. If you are the kind of person who wants to hold a party to celebrate the wedding of two people you don't know, and who hold you in contempt, then I imagine you'll find revolving doors and Velcro a challenge. A simple form from the council? They may as well be asking you for a PhD thesis on chemical grafting of antibacterial copolymers onto biomaterial surfaces.

The papers said there were no street parties in Glasgow. Bullshit. Every day in Glasgow is a street party. And Cameron suggested you make your own bunting! Just collect all your neighbours' eviction orders and redundancy notices, paint them red, white and blue, then see if there's any rope left in the corner shop after the owner tried to hang himself!

William and Kate's relationship was made into a film in the US. The biggest surprise is that something to do with the royal wedding that is so poorly made and exploitative wasn't produced by Kate Middleton's parents. It's a cheesy American film – I hope they don't add a car chase. I think that would be in poor taste.

Traditionally, at weddings you have your brother as best man. So William had to choose between Harry and an Arabic-looking foetus in a jar of formaldehyde. Prince Harry recently met some children who'd been blown up by landmines. 'How do you cope with being legless every day?' the kids asked Harry.

On the day of the wedding, Prince William's RAF pals staged a special fly-past. William must be used to that by now as they fly past him all the time, whenever they are sent off to a war zone without him.

Looks like William has made good on his promise to protect his wife from the tabloids. By marrying a woman with a far more attractive sister. It's great they've provided something from the royal wedding everyone can wank over. With the last one we had to wait till the summer of 1997. Pippa Middleton. Attractive to people who find Kate's face distressingly 3D. She's the only woman who tans by slotting her face into a toaster. Soon after the wedding, Pippa dumped her boyfriend, being upset that – in order to last longer in the bedroom – he would picture her face instead of her arse.

If William's marriage is half as happy as his mum and dad's then Kate might as well cut her own brake cables now. Hopefully, they'll remain faithful to each other. William's dad, of course, had an affair with Camilla, and his mum slept with Englishmen, Americans and an Egyptian before finally being fucked by that Frenchman.

It's said that Kate Middleton is from the lower classes, but her ancestry can be traced all the way back to the Duke of Norfolk. Her grandparents shagged on the pool table in there. If the British royal family keep marrying outside the aristocracy it won't be long before they'll hardly have any German blood left in them.

Obviously there will be a lot of pressure on Kate – although, in fairness, unless she shits on a war memorial she'll always be more highly regarded than Fergie.

Remember what happened with William's parents, though. Charles broke Diana's heart. Ten years before a steering column mashed what was left of it. Let's not forget that night. We all know where we were when Diana died. I, for one, was weaving around Paris in a white Fiat.

Prince Charles gets praise in the *Daily Mail* for the way he's brought up William and Harry since the death of Diana. Eh? For years a single parent living mainly on state handouts? Has the

Mail gone nuts? I don't think Charles should become king. His youngest brother should get a go, just so the Archbishop of Canterbury could say, 'I crown you King Edward,' put a huge nob of butter on his head, cut him open and stuff him full of tuna.

★

The Queen made a historic visit to the Republic of Ireland. Large crowds turned out to welcome her. It must have been a cold day as they were all wearing balaclavas. Sales of Union Jacks there have gone through the roof. Along with sales of paraffin and disposable lighters.

It was the first trip there by a British monarch since her granddad, George V, popped over there a hundred years ago for a shooting weekend and bagged four navvies and a priest. Don't know what he did for them not to be allowed back for so long. Maybe he got one of the Nolans pregnant. An abandoned suitcase was found near the Queen's route but the police kept the public at a safe distance, just by putting a *Big Issue* seller next to it. Royals remain highly vulnerable to bombs, especially Camilla, who might stampede.

Bombs in Ireland are, of course, reminiscent of the 1980s, but everything else was much different back then. There were loads of cuts, Colonel Gaddafi was our enemy and you wouldn't trust the government as far as you could throw a soggy mattress up a spiral staircase. Security was very tight yet, despite this, Prince Philip still managed to slip his minder and ask a passer-by how much they'd charge to tarmac his driveway. Ireland is really struggling with the recession. In fact, things have got so hard it's now the only place in the world that doesn't have an Irish bar. Ah well, what's 800 years of exploitation between friends? Especially when she wore such a lovely hat.

★

Prince Andrew is an ambassador for International Trade and Investment for the UK. In the current climate, that means he shakes a collection tin as tourists pass through Heathrow. He refused to quit, despite his links with a convicted paedophile. A member of the royal family shouldn't be making us look stupid overseas. That's clearly the job of the SAS, the MOD and Jordan. I find the reports about this billionaire paedophile highly upsetting. To think I got palmed off with lousy fruit pastilles.

The *Sun* referred to Jeffrey Epstein as the 'Paedophile Billionaire'. Is that like a new version of that Channel 4 show, 'The Secret Millionaire'? Every episode ends with a guy saying, 'I have to reveal I'm not really a binman. I'm a billionaire and I'd like to offer you this cheque – in exchange for your kids.' It reminds me of the old children's rhyme. *Ohhhh ... The grand old Duke of York, he had ten thousand friends. Not one of them what you might consider babysitting material.* Perhaps all paedophiles should be forced to have celebrity friends. It'd be an end to them being able to loiter anonymously around school gates. 'Get in the car, kids, quick! I don't like the look of that man playing conkers with Bono!'

Of course, it's all Fergie's fault. It's Andrew's friend, but everything must be Fergie's fault. I had a rather uncomfortable bowel movement on Wednesday. I'm thinking of making her apologise for it on *The Oprah Winfrey Show*. Fergie took £15,000 pounds from Epstein. How many people would turn down 15 grand, no strings attached, because it came from a child abuser? I mean, many people give more than that every year to clothing companies who tie 6-year-olds to sewing machines. Fergie said, 'I would throw myself under a bus for Andrew.' He'd be very touched, if he knew what a bus was.

What was Prince Andrew thinking? How can a man who had little contact or affection from his parents, who grew up with no purpose other than to be compulsorily placed in military school, who has no contact with normal humanity except when being paid to shoot at it … enjoy the company of someone like a paedophile? It just doesn't make any sense.

Andrew's a man you could meet by attaching a £5 note to a length of string and leaving it outside Buckingham Palace. This sort of thing runs in the family. Beatrice is selling access to her mother for one of those giant bags of Maltesers. £500,000 to get access to Prince Andrew? Prince Edward is a little easier to get hold of. Here's how. Step 1. Cut a 3-inch circular hole in a public toilet door. Step 2. Wait.

Still, Prince Andrew is used to handling embarrassment. After all, he married Fergie. Fergie said she hates grown-ups and loves children. As you can get a lot more for kids on the black market. One journalist claims that she might have drunk more than was good for her. I'd love to see the offers she was making after a few more drinks. Three quarters of a million, sex with a corgi. Two million, sex with Diana. Fergie said she was embarrassed – well, that's okay then. I'm not a solicitor, but I'm fairly sure that the penalty for lying for money and fraud is blushing. Why did people keep falling for the 'fake sheikh'? Don't celebrities read the papers? I'm going to throw on a tea towel, biro on a beard and see if I can't get Holly Willoughby to dress up as Little Red Riding Hood so I can pump her in my wolf costume.

Andrew also met with Saif Gaddafi. A man who lives in a palace while his people struggle in poverty. God knows why Saif Gaddafi agreed to meet him. Luckily, the Queen was warned of developments before they hit the papers, allowing Prince Philip to be extensively restrained with cable ties before being read the *Daily Telegraph*. Actually, the Queen's been surprisingly supportive. I hear she's even offering to pay for a stress-busting mini-break for Andy and Fergie at the Paris Ritz, inclusive of a driver.

Apparently Prince Philip's keen to buy iPads for all at the palace. After hearing about the manufacturing process, he's realised it's the most effective way of making Chinamen suffer. The Queen is actually a lot more technologically savvy than people give her credit for. Apparently, she knows her way not just round an iPad and iPod, but also the computerised braking system of a top-of-the-range Mercedes.

The Queen's also on Facebook. Members of the public won't be able to poke the Queen, which is only fair as members of the royal family are not allowed to poke members of the public, not unless they want to die in a car crash. How are you supposed to know if it's the real Queen and not someone that's pretending to be her? For all we know, her profile could have been set up by some family of German and Greek impostors.

She'd better watch she doesn't post on Facebook when she's next having a garden party. Buckingham Palace could end up being gatecrashed by 5,000 ambassadors and heads of state that she hadn't invited. They'll be drinking all her booze, drawing moustaches on all the portraits and having sex on her bed under a big pile of robes.

Despite being on Facebook, you cannot be the Queen's friend. That's because you are a fucking idiot who works in a factory for the minimum wage. Even the people who you work with, de-beaking chickens 18 hours a day, don't want to be your friend.

Whether or not she uses it, the Queen is apparently well aware of Facebook. I bet she thinks six postage stamps are a Facebook.

The Queen's staying on the stamps. Thank God. They're just the right size for my boy to stick on each side of his hamster's head so we can play our new game, 'Justice and revenge', by taping a picture of Diana's head onto the cat. Does it matter? If she wants to stay popular surely she just needs to try a little harder, perhaps taking her inspiration from the insect world. I'm sure we'd all have a little more respect for monarchy if a tour of Buck House included feeding her syrup as she relentlessly pumped babies out of her giant, distended, translucent abdomen.

We're told the Queen costs us all 62p a year. I don't begrudge her it but, to be honest, usually when I give someone 62p I expect them to at least do a silly dance and try to sword-swallow two-thirds of their *Big Issue*. Is it just me or do you reckon she could get it down to 58p if she went on the game? I know 62p isn't much, but I'd still like to offer the job out to tender. Who knows – we might find the Tarasewicz family from Warsaw are willing to do the job for 50p. And the value of Buckingham Palace would go up from them building an extension and laying a patio.

The Windsors claim to have got their expenditure down by a couple of million. It's going to be a hell of a shock for them when that 26 grand limit for families living off the state kicks in. The Queen has embraced the economic downturn and made dramatic cuts to the royal travel budget. If things get much worse, they could be forced to travel in first class. The government are making cutbacks on health services, and yet we are still funding the royal family? Soon, you'll go to the doctor's to be told, 'You have a choice of treatments for your daughter's leukaemia ... Prince Charles can make her a nice cup of fennel tea, or the Queen can put her out of her misery by breaking her neck.' The royals should be given out to old people who don't have a family of their own – like rescue cats. 'I'm looking after the Queen, you know. Sometimes I look in her eyes and it's almost like she's human.'

They're printing a lot of new fivers. If they want to encourage people to save, they could make the Queen's image just a bit different on each one. Then they'd be collectable. And if you had a load you could make them into a flicker book. Maybe she could end up naked. No, let's not be crude; just one tit out.

Of course, many people nowadays view joking about the royals as a bit passé. Indeed, the whole idea of republicanism seems vaguely historical. It's one of many areas where leftist hipsters actually converge with *Telegraph* and *Daily Mail* readers. Sometimes I feel like saying to those people, 'You know we've still got a monarchy, don't you?' It's been a neat trick on the part of the Windsors to harness a sense of their own irrelevance to reinforce their position. 'You do know that in a supposed democracy we don't elect a head of state and devote an incredible amount of resources to some of the worst people in our society? You do know how much this country defines itself by that irrational act?' For the Windsors, as for any corporation or billionaire, disinterest is a perfectly acceptable form of deference. Fuck yes, it's great to be a hipster, but the world we pretend to live in is not the one we actually live in. Although, with just a little re-imagining, we could make them the same. I know it's easier to pretend that it doesn't matter who owns our land, whom our taxes fund, that you'd rather collect vinyl and original comic-book artwork and pretend that was reality. I really am very sorry but if you want things to get better, you're going to need to wake up now.

'He hates life … It's pretty much autobiographical at the start'

★ ★ ★ ★

I get up when the air conditioning gives an other-
worldly groan and spend five minutes sitting looking out
the window trying to think what the fuck I'm doing back
in London. I'm nearly dressed by the time I remember
I'm meeting Adam Sandler's production company and
pitching a fucking movie. When you can't find your pants
that seems a ridiculous and alienating thing to be
doing.

At breakfast Mr Boyd reads the obituary pages in the
Guardian. Inspiring people, viewed at the moment of
their complete obsolescence as a kind of graph of their
commercial viability. I always like that they put them
beside the wee box of famous people's birthdays, an
added dig for the relatives to see that Richard Madeley
is still alive. Today has Kenickie from *Grease*, Jeff
Conaway, his life dealt with in the most harshly mercan-
tile terms.

In the late 1970s and early 80s, Taxi was one of the
best American sitcoms. It won 18 Emmy awards and its
stars, among them Jeff Conaway, who has died in hospital
aged 60, became household names. Conaway played the
narcissistic, 'resting' actor Bobby Wheeler, one of the

characters working for the Sunshine cab company, all hoping for better jobs to turn up. In a way, the role mirrored Conaway's own struggle for greater recognition as an actor which was not helped by his having been addicted to alcohol, cocaine and analgesics since he was a teenager.

In Taxi, the handsome Conaway, sporting the feathered hairstyle popular in the 1970s, had to compete with more fascinating characters in the avuncular Alex Reiger (Judd Hirsh), obnoxious Louie De Palma (Danny DeVito), sexy divorcee Elaine Nardo (Marilu Henner), unvictorious boxer Tony Banta (Tony Danza) and English impaired immigrant Latka Gravas (Andy Kaufman). Most of the cast of the popular show went on to bigger things, while Conaway's one moment of glory in the cinema was already in his past.

I can't remember him in *Taxi* so I google it and there's a photo of him looking fairly fucked, but a lot happier than I've ever seen John Travolta or Danny DeVito.

★

We meet in my agent's office in Covent Garden. Her four staff are working in utter silence, with the demeanour of being under hypnosis. It's the sort of place where in a movie you'd expect a distinguished old Frenchman to wander in and explain to everyone that they were all dead.

'Basically, it's about this guy who is just too critical, he can't enjoy anything. He goes to the movies and just can't get into what his friends enjoy … He hates life … It's pretty much autobiographical at the start.'

There is one of those polite laughs that end really suddenly. I have a big gulp of coffee.

'So it's funny, he rants about Twitter, he rants about Will Smith …'

They're nodding.

'And then he walks right in front of a fucking car. He gets a brain injury and when he wakes up his IQ has gone down by 20 points.'

'It's a brain-injury comedy,' notes guy with the beard. He's chuckling but being serious.

'I know, but it's upbeat, because now he starts to fit in. He goes to the new Will Smith movie with his girlfriend and loves it. His stupid ideas make great adverts, because they're just the sort of shit people could almost think of for themselves. He goes to an Adam Sandler movie and he loves it! We pick a really bad one, any of them will do!'

This goes over surprisingly well.

'Or maybe we do one specially for the film. Then, of course, his intellect starts going back up, his brain starts getting better. But he loves his new life so he keeps running out of meetings to smash his head in with a cupboard door or bang it on the floor. Eventually he gets smarter and smarter until he encounters this big alien consciousness that watches over us.'

'Could it be God?' asks Ron, suddenly all business.

'Yes, call it God if you want. It tells him that it's been waiting for a human to reach this level of consciousness and offers him the opportunity to change one thing about reality.'

'One wish. Well, that's different,' says Clay.

'He thinks about it. World peace would just break down. Heal the environment and mankind will just expand its bad ideas across the galaxy, destroying the universe in a consumerist jihad. Then he realises the value of stupidity and that his dumbass buddy Keith would be as likely to have a good idea as he would. He gives the wish to Keith.'

This seems to be going over OK, so I breeze into the finish.

'This consciousness, eh, God says that this will hurt a little and smacks him heavily on the head with a mallet. He wakes up in hospital and he's his old self but the world is completely different. It's a paradise where everybody is relaxed and helpful, people care about the planet and they care about each other. He tracks down Keith and he finds that he used the wish to create a sort of Viagra gel called 'FUCK WITH IMPUNITY'. It makes you hard for hours but removes your memory of the sexual encounter. Humanity is getting what it always needed - it's getting laid without all the guilt and bullshit.'

I sit back and spread my hands in what looks like a parody of someone who has just made a pitch.

'Ron's making Will Smith's new movie,' Clay stage-whispers, and we're all laughing. They are surprisingly decent old cunts. Clearly they wouldn't lend you ten pence for a cup of tea, or even let you make a call from their mobile in a medical emergency but they seem nicer than British show-business types. Cultural confidence of the US maybe. Probably they are horrible to someone who brings them a bad idea, like a fickle classical deity. Well, an unprofitable idea. They like this one.

On the way out Clay puts his hand on my shoulder and says that Catholics and Jews have had Shaolin training in guilt.

★
WORK! CONSUME! DIE!

'You know how in a movie, a Kung Fu guy will have forgotten he's been trained and kick someone's ass without realising it? That's what we're like with guilt. You're minding your own business and then you're like, *whoa where did that come from?*'

I feel glad that I've struck a nerve with this guy, for the sake of the movie getting made, and immediately feel guilty.

★

I run into a Scottish lassie in Forbidden Planet who recognises me. She's normal looking, ordinary, which is very much my thing. We go for a drink and I stagger through some attempts at flirtation. After a few misfires we talk movies, thank fuck, but even then the breadth of my negativity clearly spooks her. If it weren't for my panel-show profile she'd probably think I was a murderer. She looks innocent but from some hints she drops about her gap year, her fanny has seen more wear and tear than the space shuttle.

At the hotel we are kissing on the sofa and I ask her to whisper her sexual fantasy into my ear.

'Well … I'm in a butcher's shop … and I'm asking for some mince and there's a queue of people behind me …'

'Uh-huh …'

'But the butcher just comes out from behind the counter and he pushes me down on the floor and he gets on top of me and everybody is watching …'

'In the butcher's shop?'

'Yes! And I'm saying I just want my mince but he's got my knickers off and he sticks his cock in me and everybody is watching, and I say just give me my mince but he just keeps pushing and pushing himself into me …'

'This is your fantasy? Really?'

'Yes! And he just keeps pushing and pushing …'

There's just something in the way she keeps saying 'pushing', and I start to get into it.

After she goes I'm too hot and I can't sleep. The internet dude has messaged Alan Hansen about his cancer.

'Your joking? Alan, I am so, so fucking sorry. Is there anything I can do?'

I picture Hansen introducing his distraught family to this random who is going to help him through his illness, perhaps announcing the illness through him and having this guy deal with everybody for him, some mad cunt from Manchester.

I have friended this same roaster, Gary O'Donnell, on a page where I'm pretending to be a woman called Amanda. I've got photos from my pal Lyndsay in return for quite a lot of Valium. It's a nice spread including some of those shots women often have where they're messing about in a wig or a hat but they know they look fucking amazing. I'm disturbed to see that O'Donnell has messaged Amanda immediately after Alan Hansen ('Hi! How's it all going with you?'). Clumsy, Gary. Poor stuff. Amanda replies that she was trying to friend someone else with the same name, but there's a wee edge of flirtation. I end with *tee hee*. I find myself trying not to judge Gary for trying to pull some stranger just after he hears that I, Alan Hansen, have fucking cancer. But it's hard not to judge.

Alan Hansen messages Gary.

I am not joking Gary, it's been a hard couple of weeks. Thanks for your kind words. By the way, it's You're, not Your. You are, rather than the possessive your.

Alan

When you think of the long and gloomy history of man, you will find more hideous crimes have been committed in the name of obedience than have ever been committed in the name of rebellion.

C. P. Snow

07

I read an incredible article in the *Guardian* describing the summer rioting in Belfast as 'a marketing disaster' for a city hoping to encourage golf tourism. But how could these young people, from an area of chronic unemployment and lack of opportunity, actually benefit from golf tourism? They could get minimum-wage jobs changing the sheets at hotels, hold that 'Golf Sale' sign in the high street or become prostitutes. I mean it – those are the options. Kevin Costner caused a stramash at a Scottish golfing hotel by apparently trying to get a masseuse to touch his cock. Because it's the Third World to him and that's what these places do. They invite you over to some golf tournament and they touch your cock.

It's 'a marketing disaster' for hoteliers, investors and the middle classes. For the people involved it's a human disaster, one that is ignored. The effect the rioting has on their lives is not discussed. They are an inconvenience to capital.

Criminals are the Other that nobody gives a fuck about. And 'criminal' is cultural shorthand for 'working class'. In fact, 'working class' is virtually cultural shorthand for 'criminal'. Cultural contempt for the working classes is largely a projection of guilt. In slave societies you always had these myths of black men raping white women, because white slave owners raped black women a lot. So in our society rich people brand the poor as thieves, because the rich are busy stealing from the poor.

While you're at it, look at some of the other stereotypes of the underclass and see if they are projections:

- That they are unintelligent. Uh-huh? You're watching a Swedish detective series instead of *The X Factor* and you're throwing judgement around. Really?
- That they don't raise their children properly. No, they tend to have to get a sub-minimum wage raising your fucking children properly.
- That the underclass is hedonistic. Actually, I've seen a lot of the English middle classes and let me tell you that you are, collectively, pissed.

I loved that campaign in England a few years ago where they tried to point out the moral problems of cocaine use. The chain of misery involved in producing and transporting the drug. That might be the most misguided thing that ever happened – trying to appeal to the conscience of the biggest cunts on earth. Explaining that their habit will lead to peasant farmers being shot, to people who would really quite like to watch.

Look, here is a fairly basic rule of life; it's really obvious and caveman-y but everybody seems to be missing it. Cunts will always try to take all the cool stuff. You look at those pictures of Israeli settlers using these beautiful bathing places on occupied land with this incredible jade-coloured water and caves, and sure, there are lots of historical factors at play there, but basically they are just cunts who took something because it was cool.

It's the same culturally. Middle-class people grew up watching Hawkwind and Bowie play Glastonburys full of hippies getting high on acid and they thought, 'That looks cool, let's take it.' Now they all go to Glastonbury and watch Coldplay and U2 and have picnics and be cunts. And how do you take something culturally? Well, you use money, because you have it and they don't and now it's probably hundreds of pounds a ticket. I mean I can't even be fucked checking but it will be and that's how they'll have fucking done it.

Look at the culture and most things are that. Stand-up comedy (huge generalisation) was pioneered into its current form by some extremely damaged examples of what might now be called the underclass. Billy Connolly and Richard Pryor were from unenviably abusive backgrounds. The middle classes saw that and they took it because it was cool. How did they take it? Money. You can't be a successful comic now without going through the Edinburgh Festival system. On average that will take you five years and every year you will lose seven grand. So I don't know if you've noticed, but your comics aren't talking about the shipyards or being raised in brothels anymore.

Of course, one of the main reasons for criminal behaviour is the narrow conformity that we are asked to adapt to. The last Labour government created hundreds of new offences and, naturally, the stated reasons for police powers (the right to disperse gangs of teenage loiterers, for example) are often a smokescreen for what they will actually be used for (the right to disperse peaceful protests). For all the talk of getting away from big government, people sit in meeting rooms drafting legislation to stop you having a fag in your car.

Banning smoking in cars is going to affect one group in particular – the dogging community. What's a woman supposed do instead of a cigarette once she's finished pleasuring five strangers in the car park outside Carpetwise in Bolton? Listen to Radio 3? Two-thirds of people say they've had sex in a car. I'm in that group. Still failed the test though. Meanwhile, people who drink on buses will be barred from using them again. All very good in theory, but they'll run out of drivers.

Owners of dangerous dogs will have to take out insurance. It will be interesting seeing how the adverts change to capture this new market. Churchill the dog nodding in the back of a car will be replaced with Churchill the dog bleeding to death in the basement of a boxing club. 'You challenged Churchill to cheaper dog insurance. He's sorry he said "no" now, isn't he?'

And discrimination against vegans is to be outlawed. It's about time that that something was done to stop people from making cruel and unjustified comments about these twitching middle-class hippies with their ungodly farts and pasty-faced brittle-boned children.

Shoplifters cost every family in Britain £180 a year. Shocking news – I need to nick at least another 30 quid's worth just to be in credit.

Ken Clarke is annoyed at the suggestion he's softening his stance on knife crime and says, 'Anyone who thinks so is welcome to taste my steel.' Of course, a complete knife ban wouldn't work. Give it a fortnight and it'd be 'Sarge, there's been a spooning on the Cockcroft Estate, the poor sod's 'ed's caved in like Humpty Faaking Dumpty.'

Clarke suggested shorter jail sentences for 'less serious rapes'. So remember, if you're a serial sex offender, always carry a whoopee cushion. I agree with him; some rapes really are more serious than others. Melvyn Bragg being raped by Martin Amis? That's far more serious than, say, Joe Pasquale being gang-raped by Wallace and Gromit. Margaret from *The Apprentice* being raped by Sir Ben Kingsley? Very serious.

Ken Clarke actually faced a rape victim, but unfortunately not in a mirror. Surely it should be the rapists that meet with

Ken? Once they've got his image in their heads it should be so much easier for them to exhibit this restraint that the Tories keep saying is so impossible. Ken felt the meeting was a triumph of tact, in that she was an attractive woman and he somehow managed not to fuck her against her will.

Critics of Clarke's recent proposals said it was ridiculous to give violent and abusive offenders an easy way to cut sentences. Maybe, but if they're out sooner it would mean they could plug employment gaps in the care-home industry. Tucked into the revised proposals are plans to criminalise squatting. It's just common sense. Forcing people from empty buildings so they have to claim housing benefit to pay a landlord, how can that *not* save money?

Apparently, DNA matches help to solve a tiny amount of crimes. That's a relief, as I can stop carrying around my neighbour's fingernail clippings whenever I go for a night out.

A criminal who suffered horrific burns while breaking into an electricity sub-station has warned of the dangers of stealing copper cabling. On the plus side, if he hadn't done this he'd never have found out just how delicious he smells. He didn't manage to steal any copper but did manage to take about ten quid's worth of electricity to the face.

A French prisoner suffocated and killed his cellmate before eating his lung. Following an autopsy the coroner described the deceased as delicious. He always wanted to escape – now he can, through the toilet.

There are plans to make prisoners work full time so they're more employable on release. Then they can be told there are no jobs for them, as prisoners are doing it for half the price.

Prisoners having sex changes in UK jails will be allowed to buy padded bras and make-up. And why not? Who doesn't want to look their best as they're slopping out or being savagely beaten with a sock filled with snooker balls? No matter how feminine they look, I can't help feeling the fact they're in a male prison is a bit of a giveaway.

Young male prisoners are converting to Islam at an alarming rate, almost as alarming as the rate at which we are converting young Muslim men into prisoners. It's a great idea. They're going to be on their hands and knees five times a day anyway, so why not incorporate prayer? When they die they get bummed in heaven by 72 first-time offenders.

Convicts are getting methadone in prison. No wonder – the last thing I want to feel in a gangbang is my nerve endings. It's felt that these prisoners could not cope with life on the outside without drugs, which means their prison term was a success and they are ready to integrate perfectly into our society.

Dealers could avoid jail if they're carrying up to 50 wraps of heroin, an amount commonly known in Scotland as a 'dowry'. The judges say they want to be tougher on the people who produce or grow the drugs, but we're already at war with Afghanistan so how much tougher can we get? A recent survey revealed that half of all Scots know a junkie. While the other half have no contact with their father at all.

★

A Democratic member of Congress was shot through the head. Ironically, with a large part of her brain missing, she's still a keen supporter of the gun lobby. Everyone knows that guns should have no place in any democratic process, except *The X Factor* finals. Obama asked for a minute's silence. Doesn't sound like much but, remember, these people are Americans – that equals about 15 minutes for us.

And what about Norway? A nation consumed with grief, sorrow and endless tears. Then the shooting began. You know a news story is truly tragic when five minutes after it breaks the jokes in your inbox are still only in single figures. The shooter was a racist who hated Muslims. Our news programmes went one further by being so racist they assumed that he was a Muslim.

A devout Christian, Anders Behring Breivik saved 2,000 euros to spend on a top-class hooker. All I want to know is – where can I get a copy of this guy's Bible? I don't believe he's as ruthlessly intelligent as they claim. Look at the evidence of his white-supremacist plan for saving Norway's white population. Step one: kill loads of white people.

Experts said there were some signs that he might be insane. What would they be? The cruel and heartless way he took the lives of 80 people? Or something more obvious, like writing his death diary in green ink?

Breivik wanted to appear in military clothing at his trial, but the judge explained you can only legitimately wear the uniform of a European army when shooting young people if you're somewhere in the Middle East. Breivik expects he'll die in prison. Probably. I'm guessing, the day they let him out of solitary.

Meanwhile in Britain, with three shootings Raoul Moat made himself the twelfth-most dangerous man in Gateshead. Goes to show, there's one thing more depressing than living in Scotland, and that's living downwind of Scotland. Moat said he wanted to shoot his ex so she would never look good in a bikini again. He needn't have shot her; he could have just waited for her to turn 40. Actually, have you seen her? He could have just bought her a bikini. Why did she leave him? Because he looked like a hulked out Jimmy Somerville, with a face like a furious bun. Moat had vowed he would kill his ex, and yet the police ignored this. After all, a lot of men say this ... but how many actually go on to do it? Only two a week.

The prison service was baffled as to why Northumbria police did nothing when they were told Moat was going to shoot his girlfriend. Didn't they realise that if they really wanted him arrested they should have said he was a Muslim teenager who tried to hire a meeting room? There is something about Moat I admire … he vowed to be a cop killer and that's what he was until the day he died. Unlike Ice-T, who vowed to be a cop killer until he landed a part as a kangaroo in a Hollywood film. The *Sun*'s handwriting expert said that Moat had 'abandoned general rules of convention' – amazing how she could tell that by the fact that he writes in capitals, and had just shot three people at point-blank range.

Why couldn't they locate him? Look at the size of the fucker – couldn't they just have found the tree stump that the curries were getting delivered to? The policeman Moat shot says he bears him no malice – although in fairness, he does have a shotgun cartridge lodged in the part of the brain that deals with malice.

Gazza brought a can of lager, chicken, a fishing rod, a mobile phone and a dressing gown. What a generous man, to offer Moat his entire divorce settlement. That was a 20-mile drive – if Gazza arrived with one can of lager how many must he have set off with? It could have worked, though. Anyone's problems are going to be put into perspective if Gazza turns up in his Y-fronts clutching a bag of potatoes and wearing a tea cosy on his head. This incident captured Britain's imagination so much I think the BBC should consider it as the replacement to *Desert Island Discs*; a programme where Kirsty Wark asks faded 90s footballers which five items they would take to cheer up a homicidal maniac. 'So, Gary Pallister, for your packaged meat I see you have chosen breaded ham. What exactly is it about Peter Sutcliffe that made you think of pork?'

Ian Huntley had his throat slashed by another con. Looking on the bright side, he can now wear his tongue as a tie to parole hearings. Prison staff and surgeons did everything they could, but Huntley still survived the attack. Doctors weren't sure whether to stitch his throat up or fill him with sweets and use him as a Pez dispenser. To prevent Huntley from using his neck to smuggle contraband, surgeons have made it easier to search him. If a warden steps on his foot, then his head flips open like a pedal bin. The man who attacked him was very angry. You know how these environmentalists get with people who choose to fill their baths instead of using a shower. Let's hope this action doesn't make his attacker a folk hero. After all, if he has one thing to teach us it's that persistent drug use really affects your aim. Ian Huntley claims putting him to work in the kitchens was a dangerous move by the prison warders. No, Ian, surely it would be more dangerous to put you to work in the bathroom?

Rose West complained that the actress playing her in a TV drama was 'too dowdy'. Yes, it must be awful seeing yourself on the small screen hammering a child to death in a beige cardigan. To be fair, being a female sex-crazed serial killer and staying glamorous can't be easy. It must be a nightmare getting brain and skull fragments out of a vejazzle.

The Yorkshire Ripper is so mentally ill that he must be given a chance of parole. How does that work? If he's sane he'll spend the rest of his life behind bars but if he believes he is half vampire, half panther, he'll be put in a bedsit and be checked up on by a social worker once a month. He plans to tell the court he's been cured of his schizophrenia, before calling himself to the stand for cross-examination.

Peter Sutcliffe will be a low-risk inmate if he takes his medication. We're expecting a lot from a man who couldn't remember not to kill women. I'm not saying he's rehabilitated but he has learned some new skills in Broadmoor – apparently he's retrained and now uses his eye socket as a penholder. Of course, if he ever did get released they'd have to give him a new identity. How about Jon Venables or Robert Thompson?

We don't need to worry about Robert Thompson. After Jon Venables cocked it all up, the only freedom Thompson will see is a Stonehenge screensaver during his half-hour monitored internet session.

Chris Jeffries, the landlord of murdered Jo Yeates, was released without charge. I always thought he was innocent … he just doesn't look like the kind of bloke that eats pizza; shags dead women? Yes. But pizza? Never. Well, maybe ham and pineapple. He aroused suspicion when he was seen in his car outside the flat he lived in. If you look so weird that people think you're a murderer just by watching you park your car, it's time to get a fucking haircut. He was in a car? Outside his house? He may not have killed anyone but the country still despises him for being able to park so close to his front door.

I feel sorry for Cumbrian gunman Derrick Bird – constantly arguing with people about the spelling of your first name must drive you mental. Normally, the countryside is a place where you can leave your door unlocked, as the police are always looking for a fresh place to hide. If Bird had been caught he would have got a life sentence … and a 3,000 score on Grand Theft Auto.

It's been suggested that policemen having tattoos could be a great 'icebreaker'. As in, 'Hey, Winston, have you seen my lovely swastika?' Why do the police need an icebreaker? So that people on a protest march will feel like they've just been hit across the back of their legs by someone they'd like to get to know better? Why not go further – policemen's tattoos could be sponsored. That way we'd be able to all see which newspapers are currently paying them. It could be interesting though. It'd be the first time I'd have been wrestled to the ground by a heavily tattooed man in the police outfit without having had to pay up-front.

A teenage boy from Essex allegedly hacked into a government computer, causing chaos. It's like something out of a

1980s film. As is visiting Essex. Following the hack, Nintendo beefed up security – they put up another couple of walls and told Donkey Kong to throw the barrels more quickly. That'll now be the excuse teenage boys up and down the country are using: 'Mum, don't come in here, I'm hacking a website.' He's an agoraphobic who can't bear to go outside. It's a pretty common condition in Essex. A fear of open spaces probably won't be a problem where he'll be spending the next 25 years.

★

The police had plenty of warning that the riots were going to happen. The Kaiser Chiefs predicted them back in 2004. After three days of pillaging and looting, London suddenly became much quieter. Understandable. Why would you want to be out on the streets risking getting your new trainers dirty when you can stay at home watching a recently acquired 52-inch TV?

Cameron came back from his holiday. A couple of days with the family and any excuse to come back will do. His decision to take full control was probably due to Samantha suggesting that they visit a water park. He flew back to chair an emergency meeting of COBRA. David, do you ever sit there, chairing a meeting of COBRA and wonder if you're the bad guy? Meanwhile, Michael Gove argued that it was 'an insult' to the hard-working majority 'to somehow link poverty and criminality'. Which is why the riots seemed to contain a fair proportion of gentlemen cat-thieves and caddish bounders. Nick Clegg was booed by the public when he visited Birmingham, so much so that he accidentally blurted out, 'Hello, conference ...'

Teenagers were so sick of the police treating them like criminals that they decided to protest against it through a mixture of arson, theft and violence. They were trying to smash the system. The system of earning money to pay for stuff. The demands of the people have been put into a manifesto – the Argos catalogue. But it's not all bad news. Now that we have a population of violent teenagers with new TVs there's a good chance that I'll get another series.

The *Sun* ran a campaign called 'Shop a Moron'. Which coincidentally is Asda's new advertising slogan. Rapper Plan B wrote an amazing column about the riots for the *Sun*. He asked the looters, 'Would they like to live in a world where everybody was poor and everybody was on crack and everybody's mums were on crack?' Er, thanks for your contribution to the debate. I think Plan A was to read some books and go on a diet.

A community leader in Hackney said he'd warned the police there could be trouble. Then again, he says that every week. These riots have put smaller boroughs like Wood Green on the map – and then burnt them off again.

There have been some sickening sights, though. Like all these Twitter users trying to clean up their communities. You live in London, you idiots. You don't have a community. I don't know what the most used sentence will have been at those events – 'We've got more brooms than Hogwarts!' or 'I'm not a racist, but …' If I were a rioter I'd probably enjoy seeing the white middle classes having to clean up after an ethnic minority for a change. Hundreds of volunteers came out across Liverpool to help with the clean-up. They'd been working for several hours before they were told the riots took place on the other side of town.

Actually, the real question here is 'How shit is the telly at the minute?' These are people who happily sat slack-jawed through 15 weeks of *Britain's Got Talent*, and yet *Show Me the Funny* comes on and they have to run screaming into the street and throw a burning bin through the window of Halfords. I can only think that things will get worse, now that they have to watch *8 Out of 10 Cats* on an HD plasma.

It's not easy as a parent, explaining the harrowing news footage to your child. Luckily, I dodged that job as he nipped out that weekend and wasn't back till the worst was over. Many of the rioters were just 10 to 15 years old, making some of the coverage look like a black *Bugsy Malone*. The real tragedy here is that we have people whose life prospects are so poor they'd happily swap them for a pair of trainers. These riots have been an indication of young people's lack of hope, ambition and aspiration. This was demonstrated when they decided to loot Aldi. Go in with a fiver and you still feel like you're looting the place. I bet the manager of Comet was devastated when he discovered that every electrical item in his shop had been stolen and he hadn't taken out the anti-looting warranty.

Amazingly, Spurs' match against Everton was postponed. As if they were going to riot at the match and steal Gareth Bale. And England had to cancel a friendly with the Netherlands, which avoided a great deal of national embarrassment. Though you will still have to play them at some point.

Rioters communicated by encrypted BlackBerry messages. Where's Glenn Mulcaire when you need him? Police reckon they can trace the messages. Although something tells me a lot of these people might have new phones by now ... The riots revealed the awesome power of social networking. Never mind bringing down Middle Eastern governments, it can also get enough people together to force the shutters at JJB Sports.

Many people have called for the reintroduction of National Service. I agree. It'll be a lot more entertaining if next time this happens everybody has had some serious weapons training.

But what can the police do? Well, I suppose for starters they could try arresting people without shooting them. There's talk of police using rubber bullets. Doesn't sound scary, does it? A bit like threatening to hang someone with elastic. Rubber bullets have never been fired on the streets of London, a statistic of which we can all be proud. I'm sure Mark Duggan is pleased that he was blown away with red-hot, garlic-coated dumdums, rather than have us break our duck.

★

Crime is inevitable in an unequal society. John Maynard Keynes said, 'Nothing corrupts a society more than to disconnect effort and reward.' Thomas Geoghegan expands on this in his book *The Law in Shambles*:

> That's what did it in the old Soviet Union: no matter how hard people worked, they could not get ahead of those who did not work at all. Here, if people don't work, they would end up being homeless. Though if they do work they may still end up being homeless. And all the while they hear about dot-com riches and stock market winnings being showered on people who haven't really done much of anything … So, quietly and to themselves, people start to wonder, as the country becomes fabulously wealthy: *Why play by the rules?*

We live in a climate where big companies have a criminal outlook and often employ criminal methods. Where the City of London treats criminal money as indistinguishable from legitimate funds, acts as a tax haven and launders money. Meanwhile, people are told that more and more of their actions are illegal, as more of human experience is assessed and judged. Some people grow up to be a bank robber because their daddy was a bank robber. What do we raise the next generation to be in a country run by thieves?

*'The first time I ever played FIFA he beat me 6–0. Every goal was greeted
with screams of triumph'*

★★★★

Back in Glasgow I have to pick up my son almost as soon as my train gets in. I don't really like him coming to the high-rise so we usually go swimming or to the park. We have lunch and play 'I-Spy-Wee-Man-Live-or-Die'. Wee-Man features in lot of games; he's a relentlessly optimistic tap-dancer played by my middle and index fingers. The idea in this one is that if we fail to guess the I-Spy he will be executed. My son's only 3 years old, so I never let Wee-Man die, although I do some- times have to touch the object I'm spying or even wave it under his face.

In the pool we play a game where he throws his T-Rex dinosaur toy into the deep end and I have to catch it before it hits the bottom. I tell myself that if I ever let it hit the bottom I will be raped, and dive franti- cally at every throw, catching some while they are still in the air. There's a kind of cold Jacuzzi with a waterfall that he wants to go in. As I get out of the pool I throw him the dinosaur but it rebounds back into the water. I dive down but it has already hit the bottom. I notice for the first time what a malicious face it has, what hateful little eyes. As I'm drying him off, I ask him if he had a nickname what would it be. He says 'Nick'.

His mum picks him up in her car and I go straight back in to do my laps. I've been swimming every day because Don Draper started doing that in *Mad Men*. I looked at his body and thought that I'd like to look more like that. I know the actor will have got to look like that with weights and dieting. I take a pretty intensive chlorine poisoning every day and reflect that this - trying to be more like someone who doesn't exist by doing something they probably don't do - is one of the few times I'm behaving like other people.

★

Murphy and Stewart are coming round. I try not to have another joint because I know I'll be pish company but I actually end up taking some acid. There's a Chinese family killer on the loose. Channel 5's news does that slow zoom onto his photo and I'm afraid that he's going to turn into a lizard.

We used to all go round to Murphy's when we were teenagers. There was me, Marshy, Stewart, our friend Ian and a guy called Chris Murray. Chris was an Irvine Welsh character, a prototype of venal brutality. The first time I ever played *FIFA* he beat me 6-0. Every goal was greeted with screams of triumph, sometimes on his knees like a player. He was last sighted by Stewart with another villain and what appeared to be a school-girl. They were about to collect a Crisis Loan at the DSS so they could all go fuck at a Travelodge. His Bukowskiesque existence seemed to suit him, and he was described as fit and upbeat.

We'd often said we should all go back to Murphy's again but I was the one that really meant it. He still lives in the same flat. One day we all got in a cab and turned up on his doorstep with a PlayStation 3. He gave me that look that stoners sometimes have like I've stepped out of their TV. He told us to come in for a beer but there was a tremendous awkwardness hanging over the little kitchen table that now held a huge bag from Gamestation. Murphy's doing well for himself these days with some limo business and was wearing two different kinds of machine-frayed denim.

There was an awkward moment of maybe this wasn't a good idea, but eventually his wife and kids fucked off and we all ended up playing a big tournament of two players each team, which is always brilliant for getting everybody shouting at each other. I hadn't seen him in 20 years.

Stewart was in unbeatable form that night, and eventually we packed it up and watched this blaxploitation zombie flick of Murphy's called *Nigger Mortis*. It was really funny, and even interesting because we were all really stoned. Grass can be like salt for the mind. Paul told me he ran into someone who knew me through somebody I went out with when I went to uni. Paul reports the verdict.

'He went out with her for a bit and he was a right cunt to her.'

I very much doubt the story but I joke that it doesn't really narrow things down.

When we left I gave Murphy a kind of semi-emotional hug in the hall and I ended up talking about how I just want my kids to be happy.

'You're living in the wrong country,' grinned Murphy, and I laughed but it made it a long cab home.

★

Tonight we all end up standing, drinking beers over the wax township. I explain my original thinking was to come back to Glasgow and dominate a scheme. Employ agents who manipulated the locals and move them about the board. When it came down to it, the effort of doing anything with what I'd made, I just couldn't be fucked.

I look at them both over the top of my glasses.

'In this sense, I am like God.'

They both laugh, even though I am deadly fucking serious.

We talk about getting DMT. It's a kind of super-drug that we can never quite track down. It gives you a 20-minute high where you're in another reality talking to what have been described as 'the machine elves of Hyperspace'. Who doesn't want that?

'I mean, it's maybe not a party drug,' Stewart said, 'but I'd really like to talk to the little fuckers.'

'You should put it in your book,' monotones Murphy, deadly serious. 'Say you're looking for it, some cunt might give you some.'

'A drugs plea,' I agree. 'Maybe I could write a scene where we're all talking about how much we want DMT and then they turn the page and it's like my anguished face but made out of words and the words read "Get me DMT" over and over again.'

'The character of Boyle in the book bursts through into our reality like a literary astronaut,' laughs Stewart, in the intonation of a *Sunday Herald* review. 'The author's thirst for psychotropic substances literally transcends the page. A word golem leapt from my copy and began searching my house for drugs.'

I wheeze with laughter and when I stop, I say, 'But, seriously, where the fuck can we get DMT?'

★ ★ ★ ★

Ego is a structure that is erected by a neurotic individual who is a member of a neurotic culture against the facts of the matter. And culture, which we put on like an overcoat, is the collectivized consensus about what sort of neurotic behaviors are acceptable.

Terence McKenna

★ ★ ★ ★

08

Everybody now classifies themselves as having a 'public' and a 'personal' self. I'm sure that has always been the case on some level – you speak differently to your kids than you do to your co-workers or whatever. Now with Facebook and Twitter and even things like texting, we have a variety of different masks. We are never done selling ourselves, marketing a public personality but believing that our 'real' self is unaffected.

The one real problem with that is [drumroll] … that's how a psychopath thinks. I'll bet a psychopath does a lot of the same things you do. Sticks exclamation marks into a text because they don't want to admit the sheer lack of emotion they feel about the communication. Psychopaths must love Facebook. It's like a primer in shallow humanity. If you had to pick a psychopath out of a group of people, would it be more or less difficult if they all communicated in only 140 characters?

Each new generation seems increasingly comfortable about being marketed to, and about marketing themselves in turn. You don't even need to be in show-business anymore. What you're marketing might be your friend's band, a run you're doing for charity or even just an article you've read – but really it's you. It might be you as a great friend, as a person who cares about cancer victims or even just as being politically aware, but we all know what we're really selling.

This is encouraged because *guess what happens in that gap between the real you and the you that you pretend to be?* That internal wasteland – that's where they sell you stuff! You're not that sporty outgoing type you pretend to be but maybe with a new snowboard and an off-road vehicle you could be. You could be the intellectual you pretend to be if you bought a bunch of important books you piled beside your bed but never read. You're reading this one instead of *Gravity's Rainbow*, you fucking idiot. I'm not saying that being a psychopath is particularly bad for you – hey, if you want to be part of a society that bombs little brown people into mince, it's probably an advantage.

This is the reason actors are so foolishly over-celebrated. They're a metaphor for the general culture of unacknowledged psychopathy. The nearer the edge they are, the more we like them. You always hear about actors being 'vulnerable' as a compliment, and it's never particularly in reference to the characters they play. The idea that 'mask wearing' is driving them mad makes us identify with them more, because it's how we all feel.

I have a theory that all actors are pretty fucking crazy; it's just when they step out of line that they're allowed to talk to the press and reveal what a fucking nutcase they really are. You read about actors with 'painkiller addictions' and have this idea that they're taking too much paracetamol. They're actually crushing up and snorting powerful opiate pills and fighting the Withering King and his Memnoch Army as they traverse a swirling medieval landscape. Who'd have thought that pretending to be somebody else every day could send you crazy?

Take Charlie Sheen, who went on tour with his one-man show. Which is a neat trick when you have multiple personalities. Given how many voices he has in his head he could easily stage a production of *Les Misérables*. It says a lot about how he's treated his body that the last role he got offered was playing Martin Sheen's corpse. Charlie says he's confronted his drug demons, and the good news is that it was all a misunderstanding and now they're getting on brilliantly. He even provided a blood sample during an interview – after lighting the wrong end of a fag brought on a coughing fit. Because of his offensive comments and out-of-control behaviour, TV executives have cancelled his sitcom, and offered him his own reality TV show. With the blank, expressionless eyes of a snowman, he says, 'I'm on a drug and it's called Charlie Sheen.' Ironic, as he's taken so many drugs that the one thing no longer present in his bloodstream is his own DNA. He told an interviewer, 'I have one speed. I have one gear.' It sound to me like he actually has a lot of gear and only some of it's speed. He also said he's got 'Tiger Blood' in his veins. It's certainly a lot safer having a blood transfusion from a tiger than from Charlie.

At the moment Sheen's life consists of going on huge drugs benders with groups of porn stars. If he'd straightened himself out he could have a really mediocre career as a bit-part Hollywood actor. He's crazy like a fox! And also actually crazy. What a tragic waste, not being Charlie Sheen is. How majestic it will be for him to die, possibly quite soon, knowing that when they make a movie of his life, it will be a porno.

I think that I, like a lot of comedians and social critics, have taken a wrong turn somewhere in imagining that by slating our culture we're providing some kind of social critique. First up, I'm not sure that the two things are all that related. Ireland has always had a vibrant literary and musical culture, but it's a fairly horrible, priest-ridden, fucked-up society. More moral societies like Canada and Norway (I realise how brutally subjective that is, but don't care) have incredibly dull cultures. More than this, blasting *Britain's Got Talent*, or the Beckhams, or whatever, is something people can pretty much do themselves, and indeed the shiteness of those things is part of their appeal.

Also, let's remember that the public culture we are presented with isn't real. It isn't even real-ish. To give you an example, Celtic manager Neil Lennon was being sent threats, replica bombs and bullets with his name on, by the sort of people whose IQ goes up when they stand in dog shit. This was reported under headlines like 'Scotland's Shame', with various people characterised as being either terrified or outraged. I'd say the actual mood of people at the time was the standard human reaction to sectarianism in Scotland. Bored, disappointed, but not surprised. That doesn't work for the culture, though, because the culture is a soap opera.

Think of all the gurning and overacting soap opera actors have to do: telling their drinking partner that of course they put that bet on for him, then contorting their face into a parody of guilt. It's much easier to convey broad things like terror or outrage – as a result, the public's actual reactions are completely ignored. To be honest, it would be almost impossible to be truthful using the machinery of our culture. Tabloid headlines, talk-show monologues and Twitter posts aren't really capable of communicating something as complex as ennui, and the increasingly concise nature of all that stuff makes it almost impossible to convey an original thought.

So there we go. All those *X Factor* and Jordan jokes, all that shit is pointless. But look at it this way. In the old days, before automated abattoirs, there would have been a big guy who swung a hammer at the cows to kill them. A big, heavy sledgehammer that he'd bring up and down in an economical arc created by practice and indifference. I'm sure that other people in the abattoir would have kept that man at a distance socially, but sometimes they'd look up from their tasks on the bloody floor and admit that there was a certain beauty to those short brutal swings, those folding legs, those silent deaths. The following remarks should be taken in that spirit.

Julie Burchill said in the *Sun* that I had a face only a blind mother could love. She's wrong; they hate me as well. Unless I'm wearing their husband's aftershave. This from a woman who looks like The Penguin on human growth hormone. Blind mothers would love you too, Julie, if they could touch your face without getting their fingers eaten off. Reader, do you see the beauty in that? Good.

★

Show-business does have its upside. James Corden has managed to marry an attractive woman. I would say she lives in a perpetual solar eclipse but it's really more akin to strobe lighting. She spends so much time in shadow she has moss growing up the front of her face, and has developed her own rudimentary system of sonar where once an hour she will just scream into the darkness in the hope that someone will rescue her from her starless prison.

Superdrug have been selling record amounts of a new hairspray endorsed by Cheryl Cole. It's the hairspray she herself uses. Yes, you too could have hair like Cheryl's. Lonely hair. Hair with a void that can never be filled. Hair that will hold firm despite the fact that it's dying inside. I'd use a gel.

Cheryl published her autobiography, called *Through My Eyes*. Presumably the full title, *Through My Eyes You'll Just See the Back of the Inside of My Head*, wouldn't fit on the cover. I must confess I did find it difficult to put down. I was worried if it touched anything in my home that thing would somehow become fatally tainted by its mediocrity. The book's cover price is £18.99, but if you'd like to buy it just send me a cheque for £8.99, and I'll come round and smack you in the mouth.

Poor Cheryl, the Americans just didn't find her insincerity believable. Will the Black Eyed Peas still want to work with her if she heads for obscurity? Fear not, Cheryl. If they desert you too, I'll gladly provide the Black Eyes. And the Pee.

Cheryl was replaced on the judging panel by Nicole Scherzinger. That must be like coming home and finding your husband in bed with a plank of wood. Which must have brought back some painful memories for her.

She's reportedly been getting death threats. One threat carried the warning: 'Every1 has a bullet for you.' Which is plainly nonsense. I've got six. Louis was also very upset to receive death threats. Simon gets them, but merely runs them through his shredder and snorts them for strength.

Poor Chezza was so upset that for days family and friends were trying to coax her out from behind the sofa with a bowl of coins and a mirror. The last time someone bombed that badly in America they built a memorial at Ground Zero. She now can't walk down the street in the States without being unrecognised.

Cheryl told the American producers she *could* speak more clearly. They replied, 'Half past three'. She went straight to the airport and explained to the US staff where she wanted to go, which is why she's now in the town of 'Fek Kin Ootta Heer' in North Korea. I've always found it perfectly easy to understand Cheryl Cole. If my dog curls up into a ball and shits itself I know she's singing.

She only did four days' work. Doesn't sound much, but for some folk in Newcastle that'll do a whole family for a lifetime. In fact, her sacking has reduced total employment in the area by half. If it wasn't for Sid Waddell there'd be nobody earning a wage. Actually, I don't think Cheryl will struggle for work – it's just instead of advertising shampoo they'll probably be testing it on her. What will she do? Apparently she plans to continue her break from singing, which she started when she joined Girls Aloud back in 2002. With her extensive judging experience they'll be crying out for her at The Hague when the Ratko Mladić trial kicks off.

'... You made that massacre your own, pet.'

'... Never mind all them dead Muslims, pet ... can you sing us "Copacabana"?'

Cheryl was not only sacked from the US show; she's no longer a judge on the British one. But I'll only know for sure if my intensive delving into the world of Voodoo has worked if her legs fall off at Christmas.

There's a rumour she lost the UK show because her manager will.i.am didn't hit it off with ITV execs. Apparently, he borrowed a technique from his brother Sam, trying to sweeten the deal by offering them green eggs and ham ... and, despite their repeated refusals, just suggesting it again and again, changing either the location or the species of dining companion.

It would be difficult for Cheryl to go back to being a judge on *The X Factor* here again. I mean, how would she be able to criticise a contestant for their lack of talent and ability when she was sacked for not being able to sit on a chair? To be honest, I sometimes just stare at all the pictures of our Cheryl and wonder if maybe, maybe the deeper problem is that she's just too beautiful to live in such a heartless age. Then I slide the rifle back under my bed and think, 'Not yet, Frankie, bide your time, bide your time.'

Cheryl rebuffed Simon's attempts to contact her, completely ignoring all the flying monkeys tapping at her window. Simon was keen to apologise and bombarded her with so many texts it was almost impossible for the ones of Ashley's cock to get through.

Cheryl's doing her best to overcome allegations of racism in her past – she married a black guy, she caught a disease in Africa and has a body like fried chicken. I hope her malaria doesn't flare up before her heavyweight title bout in Vegas.

No sooner was Cheryl ditched by Simon Cowell than she apparently got back with Ashley. The whole Ashley–Cheryl thing is just like *Romeo and Juliet*. If Romeo had an etching made of his penis and sent it to Desdemona, Rosalind and Portia. I thought she looked loved-up lately but just assumed her cleaner had done a particularly thorough job on the reflective surfaces in her flat.

Ashley apparently missed Cheryl badly. He tried cheating on other women but it's just wasn't the same. Anyway, they didn't sleep together, they just sat and talked about the old days, Cheryl apparently dwelling on the rise of Prussia under Frederick the Great, while Ashley focused on Charlemagne.

Watch it, Cheryl. Ashley wants you to move back into a 12-bedroom house. He might still plan to pull women, safe in the knowledge anyone on a predominantly lettuce-based diet couldn't hope to open more than three or so doors. I reckon he's just turned on by the idea of that 25 per cent chance of getting caught … move back in and it could end up being like some giant, heartbreakingly pornographic version of *Deal or No Deal*.

But Ashley's taking his time. Friends say his tactic is 'softly, softly, catchee monkey'. Let's just hope it works with creatures of slightly less intelligence too. Ashley's planning to consolidate his wooing with the gift of a new Chihuahua. Cheryl loves the little dogs, as a dab of Bovril on her ankles means they can give her a well-timed nip if she can't muster sufficient tears in public.

Cheryl is like the Greece of the celebrity world. The game's up, but the press keep backing her because she now generates so much news copy that if we just admitted it you'd soon be paying your 30p for little more than a pair of tits and some racing advice. I doubt Cheryl will struggle for work; in a society as damned as this we will happily lay off teachers and nurses but there will always be a need for a perky-titted karaoke judge.

Cheryl got back with Ashley on her 28th birthday – pretty young for Alzheimer's to be setting in. They reunited at a barbecue. A barbecue is a fitting analogy to Cheryl's career. It initially burns brightly, then the embers fade. Often it makes you vomit and it's 100 per cent disposable. What's more, they won't let you on a plane to America with one.

You could vote in one of the *Sun*'s online polls on whether they should get back together. Alternatively, why not lower yourself into a mincer and have someone post the result to a landfill site? I wonder if Cheryl will one day be able to pass away peacefully without her life-support machine being wired up to a phone vote.

Ashley is a changed man. Nothing says commitment like a third wedding ring in four years. He's looking for a diamond worth around £160,000 – which is roughly three times the size of Cheryl's brain. Of course Cheryl wants to get back with Ashley – there's nothing that pleases a Geordie girl more than seeing their man shoot a student. Since splitting with Ashley, Cheryl has nearly died and lost two jobs. Looking back, sharing her rarely seen husband with a couple of hairdressers must seem like the height of humdrum contentment.

Ashley has agreed to Cheryl's list of demands. They include a lavish new home, a hi-tech recording studio, a house in LA and a no-expense spared wedding and honeymoon. So at least this time they're marrying each other for the right reasons. But in the end, it seemed they split because Ashley was shagging some air stewardess. Presumably, Cheryl found a pillowcase that looked like the Turin Shroud had been Tango'd.

Ashley is opening a restaurant with Jay-Z. The thickness guide for the steaks takes the form of photographs of Ashley's cock in different stages of arousal. 'My husband wants the "nail technician has sent a picture message" but I'm on a diet so I'll stick with a "Cheryl is walking towards my phone".' I confess I was addicted to sexy-picture messaging way back in the one-megapixel days. You never fully get over it – I still feel a stirring in my loins whenever we visit Legoland.

Cheryl's ex Derek Hough said he felt led on. He thought she was going to answer 'yes' to those four little words … 'Are you a man?' Derek made the comments in private phone calls to a female friend. We're not sure how the chat got leaked to the press, but if I were Derek I'd make sure his friend hasn't been murdered.

Cheryl says she may give up show-business. Yes, I think you might do that, Cheryl. I think you just might be able to fill the ravenous abyss at the centre of your being that means you need more love than a planet of newborn puppies and drags the attention of strangers towards it like a collapsing star. You might use the remnants of your tortured psyche to heal the shrieking anti-matter wound that passes for your soul. Or maybe you'll become a judge on *The Voice*, or something.

★

They say money can't buy you happiness. Jedward made £3 million last year. I think we can add talent, charisma and self-awareness to that list. I mean, they replaced the Coco Pops monkey on the front of the cereal box. I always said if those boys worked hard they would eventually be taken seriously.

JLS, another product of *The X Factor*, had their faces printed on packs of Durex. Presumably with the slogan 'Use a condom: don't let this happen again.' JLS say they're trying to persuade their male fans not to have casual sex with women. As your male fans are all gay, you've succeeded. Well done.

The band is passionate about tackling the important subject of unwanted pregnancy, unfortunately 24 years too late for their mothers. JLS are a great inspiration to wear a condom; their music has always led me to wish I had never been born. JLS feel they are well placed to teach other men about sex. After all, they did come second. Susan Boyle has also inspired a range of contraception. They're going to compulsorily sterilise everyone in West Lothian.

There was some hideous PR story where JLS singer Marvin tried to impress his girlfriend by making her some pasta, but he didn't know how to cook it. Quite frankly, I'm surprised that a member of JLS didn't try to impress a girl with pasta by glueing it to a picture along with some glitter. I can only imagine that going out with a member of JLS would be like dating one of those men that were in a coma since they were a baby. His girlfriend is a member of The Saturdays, so they've got a lot in common. They both go out with someone who they think is more talented than they are. And they're both wrong.

Nicola from Girls Aloud has been upset by people saying she has become too thin. We are worried that you have anorexia, Nicola, because we were using your body to distract us from your face and personality. 'Everyone talks about my weight,' she says. Wrong. Everyone talks about how they'd use you to try and pump one of the good-looking ones. The advantage is that after gigs she can be snuck out past fans in a poster tube. Never mind your figure, Nicola, I know that you've got a big heart – I saw it jiggling away through your paper-thin frame when you wandered in front of a spotlight. People say she could be the ugliest one in Girls Aloud. Which is unfair; she could be the ugliest one in Motörhead, too.

Britney Spears is pumping weights, doing yoga and kick-boxing. She will soon hold the title of fittest woman alive that no one wants to fuck. On her latest tour, Britney says she'll dismiss anyone working for her who is hung-over. That'll back-fire at her Scottish venues. Let's see how good a show she puts on after manning the ticket booth, hanging her own lighting rig and then selling her own merchandise. Then having to drive herself to her hotel, check herself in and the next morning cook her own breakfast before finally flying herself back to Florida.

Apparently Take That earned £15 million each from their latest tour. Everything's equal in the band this time – Gary, Robbie, Mark and Howard share the singing and songwriting duties. And Jason does the sarnies.

Robbie Williams laughed off criticism of his onstage swearing. At his last gig he shocked fans by announcing, 'My name is Robbie F***ing Williams.' What's the fuss about? That's always been his middle name in my house. Who wouldn't swear if they had to listen to Jason and Mark trying to sing every night? A friend was cross with him for teaching his toddler rude words. Robbie denies it, saying he just put on his new CD and the infant said, 'Oh, not that sh*t again' completely unprompted.

Take That are a mystery to me. First time round, their fans were 14-year-old girls and now they are all women in their mid- to late-30s. They quit when their fans became legal and re-formed when they stopped being fanciable. Police compared the fans at Take That gigs to football hooligans. The difference is football hooligans have much better songs to sing along to. Their gigs loked like a cross between *Loose Women* and *Dawn of the Dead*.

Teenage fans of Justin Bieber managed to sneak into his hotel room in Liverpool. Bieber was outraged as they could have been knife-wielding maniacs. I'm outraged too, as they could have been knife-wielding maniacs!

Madame Tussaud's (catchphrase: 'Underwhelming tourists since 1836') unveiled their waxwork of Bieber. I only really want Justin Bieber and molten wax to be brought together when he's being tortured by Al-Qaeda. The dummy weighs 60 kg and stands at just under 6 ft. And was in London for just a couple of days before resuming his tour. I'd love to buy Bieber's model when they're done with him. Then I could put him in a big suitcase dressed as a Nazi, take him down my gym and re-enact the end of *Raiders of the Lost Ark* in their sauna.

★

Lady Gaga showed up to the 2010 MTV awards wearing a dress made of steak. It wasn't the first time I've looked at a young female popstar and thought, 'Fill it'. There was a great afterparty, where the singer put the outfit in the washing machine on a hot wash and threw in a few carrots. Is it just the latest in a long line of attempts to stir up controversy? Apparently not; at least so says her publicist, the tormented ghost of Madeleine McCann.

Gaga visited Scotland and claimed to be celibate, a decision she made seconds after meeting her first Glaswegian. She says that girls should practise safe sex and get to know people before they sleep with them. It's true. That's why I make sure I always carry a condom, and fake ID. Gaga regularly wears net curtains, teapots and platform boots – it would be like trying to fuck the window display at Oxfam.

She says she's modelled herself on Princess Diana. It's just a shame it's not from how she looked before the crash. She seems to be going bald. Having dated a bald girl I have to say there are advantages. Draw a smiley face on the back of her head with a permanent marker and it really takes the sting out of her storming off after an argument.

Gaga is learning sign language so her deaf fans can understand her songs. Oh, come on Gaga, haven't these people suffered enough? Good luck with signing out her songs. When they attempt 'Rah-rah-ah-ah-ah! Rom-mah-rom-mum-mah! GaGa-oo-la-la!' it'll be funnier than the time the late-night signer had to explain Max Mosley's court case.

She caused mayhem recently after turning up somewhere in just a discreet jeans-and-jumper combo. Trouble is, we've seen her baps so much they're about as exciting as the back of my toilet door. And even that likes to tease me by being partially covered with a dressing gown once in a while. Poor old Lord Gaga, his monocle must be dropping from his eye on pretty much a daily basis. I suppose he might be blissfully unaware as he's probably a *Daily Telegraph* man.

Fashion genius Alexander McQueen famously dressed Lady Gaga. He hung himself in a wardrobe – how appropriate. I hope he popped some mothballs in his pockets out of respect for his cleaners. Gaga always looks like a cross between a Francis Bacon painting and a voodoo doll made in a secure mental home. McQueen's outfits were essentially a crocheted suicide note.

★

Duncan Bannatyne posted suicidal messages on Twitter. I know *Dragons' Den* is worried about its ratings – but I think the live tweeted death of one of its stars might mean it wins at reality television and we can go back to watching nice comedy plays in the evening. Bannatyne asked, 'Is death the end. Or is there more?' Like he was even negotiating with God. A man who runs gyms gets suicidal? You mean paying to constantly run on the spot while breathing in someone else's genital sweat won't bring me happiness?

Duncan is a very young-seeming 62. I don't mean he looks young, I mean he thinks it's appropriate to chat about topping himself on social-networking sites. I'm not worried about being out of line here; Bannatyne owns casinos and knows all about cashing in on people's marriage breakdowns. I think this was just a cry for help. And the British public have responded with a resounding, 'Anything on at the cinema? I fancy a coffee. Have you read the new Henning Mankell?'

Twitter isn't just a sublimated admission that the person you live with tunes your conversation out. There was that whole super-injunction malarkey. If your most secret and depraved acts can be described in 140 characters then you're not trying hard enough. My sex secrets could never be described in one tweet. You'd need a pair of 3D glasses and a Nintendo Wii controller with a tongue.

The names of celebrities with super-injunctions were being printed in foreign newspapers. It was a sad day for the British free press when I read the truth in the *Tehran Gazette*. This scandal has a lot to answer for. Mostly for burning the hideous image of Andrew Marr having sex indelibly in my brain. Even when I shut my eyes I can see the veins popping out on his baby bird's head as he grunts, 'You're dodging the question so I'll say it again, am I a naughty Mr Marr? Am I?!'

It seems all these celebrities are at it like rabbits, which raises a very important question for me. Why aren't I getting any of this? It's good it's come out because the injunction has been terrible for Imogen Thomas – like any ex-*Big Brother* housemate, all she craves is a quiet life, out of the limelight where she can relax in her pants in front of photographers.

Scandal is nothing new. In the 1930s you couldn't even hope to break into the movies unless you'd strangled a waitress in a motel room. It's clearly time for our celebrities' extra-marital sausage-hiding to be regulated and transparent. I propose a draw, like with the football. Number 6, Peter Andre, paired with Number 41, Sooty. All these revelations imply that celebrities are deeply troubled people, who only feel validated when winning the approval of strangers. At least I hope so. Their insatiable misery's all that keeps me going.

Then there are the celebrity drug scandals, like when George Michael crashed his car into a Snappy Snaps. George was quizzed by local police; I presume the main thrust of the questioning was, 'Why the fuck do you keep doing this?' George was very shaken and upset when he crashed – well, it's always horrible to be woken up suddenly, isn't it? George has only just come back from a two-year driving ban, which will be why he's out of practice. How long before the impact from one of his crashes results in him being seriously injured? When his passenger bites his cock off.

George was sentenced to eight weeks. Which is nothing, really; he's gone out to buy milk and nodded off in an NCP multi-storey for longer than that. Eight weeks! George could do that with his eyes closed, the same technique he uses when turning left at traffic lights. It's a tragic waste – all those drugs and not one decent song to show for it. I'd love to have seen him painting old folk's homes and clearing the leaves out of people's gutters. Though you could argue he's taken enough work off Andrew Ridgeley already as it is. Poor Andrew Ridgeley. He took up race-car driving to forget about Wham!, and George still ends up more famous for his car crashes.

One of the few moments when I was proud of being on the panel show *Mock the Week* was the time we were asked to slaughter poor old George for getting stoned and driving into something. I'd always had a real soft spot for him after he spoke out against the Iraq War. Of course, that's a ridiculous thing to do if you sang 'Club Tropicana', but, to be fair, you could see in his eyes that he knew it was ridiculous but felt compelled to do it. Anyway, the subject came up and I said I didn't want to do any jokes about him for that reason – that he'd done something vaguely heroic. Dara Ó Briain, who is a good soul, said that he agreed and we all just sat there in silence until the producer or whoever realised that we weren't going to loose any arrows at the big, slow-moving target he'd presented us with. Sadly, for a panel show that's like *Spartacus*.

So why, you're probably wondering, am I doing jokes about it here? OK, you know the story of the fox and the scorpion? Well, I am a scorpion. Wow, it really felt amazing to write that down. I advise you to live your life in such a way that one day you actually get to write that in a book, and mean it. *I am a scorpion!*

Photos of Tara Palmer-Tomkinson show how drugs have wrecked her nose. Everyone says it's because the cartilage is destroyed but I think it's because her head is so empty it's created a vacuum and her face has collapsed in on itself. This is the trouble with going to see a cowboy doctor – he took her money, he's knocked down a supporting wall and hasn't been back to finish the job. On the plus side, he did put a lovely serving hatch in the back of her head

Stephen Fry also admitted to '15 years of chronic cocaine taking' and would tackle difficult crosswords while high. A stark warning to Charlie Sheen of what could happen if he doesn't get help.

Charlie made his webcast debut with a show he called *Charlie's Korner*. Can't be long before the guest presenter is Charlie's Coroner. Charlie's live show didn't go well. He couldn't have crashed and burned any worse than if his act were as a fire-eater on the *Hindenburg*. Some said they expected the show to be funny 'cos they'd seen *Two and a Half Men*. What? If *Two and a Half Men* is evidence, I'd expect Charlie to be as funny as having my testicles stretched out behind a lorry then used as a show-jumping practice arena.

He fiercely denies Warner Brothers' claims his behaviour on set was unpredictable, saying you could set your watch by his on-the-hour moon-howls. The story's effects are being felt right across Hollywood – there is now not a single rehab clinic in the LA area still offering a money-back guarantee. Is Sheen any madder than the rest of Hollywood? I'd rather be addicted to cocaine and booze than Prozac and flattery. One thing's for sure, this is a lot funnier than *Two and a Half Men*.

Poor Amy Winehouse. The grief only really hit me a few days after her death, when Ladbrokes explained that for my accumulator to have paid out, Gazza would have had to have gone first. Amy was discovered by her bodyguard. It came as a huge shock to him that she was dead, as in the past he's seen her look far worse and still get on stage.

There was widespread grief, both from fans and shareholders in The Priory. To be honest, if I fall off the wagon I can't see me heading there. Judging by their recent results I think I'd stand a better chance getting back off the sauce by going on a distillery tour with Charles Kennedy and the ghost of Dylan Thomas. Among the tributes, some people were leaving bottles of vodka – the thing that killed her. But then again, I suppose it's no different really to Christians wearing crosses. The best tribute had to be a single carrot left in the middle of hundreds of bunches of flowers. It made it look like everything had been put there to memorialise a dead snowman.

There have been some moving tributes paid to Amy. My personal favourite has to be the one from a Glaswegian newspaper seller, minutes after the news broke. I was buying an evening paper and mentioned to him that she had been found dead in her flat. He stared blankly at me for a few seconds, then began shaking both his hands frantically in front of his chest, before shouting at the top of his voice, 'And that's jazz!' He then struck an applause cue with a big smile on his face.

Perhaps a more fitting tribute would be to re-examine both our nation's increasing reliance on the crutch of alcohol and the potentially destructive nature of fame. Or alternatively, just crack open a few more cans in front of *The X Factor*.

Her family said she hadn't touched drugs in three years, as touch was one of the many senses she'd lost the use of. Amy had even been off the booze for three weeks, which wasn't even enough time to sort out all her cans and bottles for recycling. Amy was given a medical examination 24 hours before she died. I say medical examination; she was looking so rough, the doctor started doing a post-mortem. He only stopped when he noticed that she had a return ticket for the tube. The toxicology report could take weeks to be delivered. Even if they left the printer on overnight.

Pete Doherty was genuinely shocked to hear news of Amy's demise. Up till then, he'd assumed they were both dead already and this was just some kind of limbo. *X Factor* creator Simon Cowell sent his sympathies too – I think it's particularly touching to have tributes from outside the music industry.

Amy died at the age of 27. As have other musical geniuses, such as Janis Joplin, Jimi Hendrix and Jim Morrison. What can I say, except Victoria Beckham is 37? When I was 27 I'd just had my first child and was appearing regularly on panel shows. Add my name to the list. I was dead on the inside.

'At Amy Winehouse's Funeral' sounds like the title of one of those upbeat Pogues songs about drinking, where everyone would dig up George Best's body and make it buy a round. Amy dying so suddenly would make you think that she was a sick person who needed help – rather than one who was dragged around the concert venues of Europe like a neglected perform-ing circus animal.

Ah well, I was honestly gutted when I heard the news. She was a real talent. I often wonder if drugs are as much a prob-lem in show-business as the addiction to fame and booze. I'm not sure that the place we call 'celebrity' isn't actually hostile to human life. There are people who seem to be battered by it physically, and others who get swamped spiritually. Fame is now such a universally accepted goal, people can't even run when it's eating them. And even outside of the people who want to profit from them, friends and family will throw them back to the monster just as surely. Who wouldn't want you to get your act together so you can make more movies, write more songs? Who doesn't want to be famous, right?

Some of my friends were a bit baffled at being so upset by Amy Winehouse dying, but isn't this what art is all about? Someone being able to touch people they don't know? Well, only if it's someone I like. If it's Princess Diana or something, you're just an idiot.

Still, it would be a stone heart that could watch her perform with such open vulnerability and feel nothing. But you've got to laugh, haven't you? We all know what you'd have to do if you didn't laugh. I don't know who I feel sorrier for, Amy or the lice who became junkies while infesting her hair.

Rolling Stone Ronnie Wood says he stopped boozing because he was turning into Victor Meldrew. Which reminds me of the episode of *One Foot in the Grave* when Victor falls out of a tree after injecting heroin into his scrotum. Although my favourite one was when Victor has an argument with his neighbour, gets incoherently drunk and ends up dragging his 22-year-old Russian girlfriend through the streets by her hair. It beats Del Boy falling through the bar any day of the week. You haven't turned into Victor Meldrew, Ronnie

– you've turned into a roadkill rook. Ronnie says since he's stopped drinking he's like a newborn baby – well, a newborn baby's ball sack.

Elton John's house is now home to the pitter-patter of tiny feet, as an army of Filipino nannies desperately try to raise a baby in silence so as not to enrage their masters. Chris Evans has admitted he feared that becoming a father at 21 would stop him fulfilling his dreams. Luckily it didn't – though it must help if your dreams are just talking over records like the bloke who does the waltzers at a fair.

Victoria Beckham gave birth to a baby girl via Caesarean. It's a shame, as a natural birth was probably the best hope she had of ever successfully hitting a high C. Doctors administered muscle relaxants. So that Victoria could smile when handed the baby.

It was weird seeing Victoria pregnant – with that bulge it looked like someone had trodden on a hose. It was a simple two-hour operation. 90 minutes on the delivery, and another 30 to remove her Dolce & Gabbana womb lining. At one point Victoria asked for gas and air. Then after lunch she gave birth. Like a lot of rich women, Victoria opted for a Caesarean, because she's 'too posh to push'. Even when she goes for a dump her Hispanic maid has to give her the Heimlich Manoeuvre. Her vag might be holding up but her stomach must be starting to look like it's been used as a breadboard. Top designer Christian Louboutin even designed a pair of booties for Harper, as Posh believes it's never too soon to corrupt her offspring's value system.

They named their new baby 'Harper Seven', partly because they thought 7 was a lucky number. Not sure anyone whose legs were blown out of Aldgate Station on 7/7 would agree. The proud parents probably felt there was some mystical element to her being born in the 7th hour of the 7th month. Forgetting that it was an elective Caesarean. David was said to have found the name in one of those baby-naming books. At the very bottom of a page near the front, tucked right in the corner. How nice of them to have rejected a *Hello!* deal for photos of baby Harper. Are they respecting her privacy? I suspect they may just have run out of room for any more money.

Victoria Beckham considered calling her new baby girl Santa, after one of her favourite places, nearby Santa Monica. And if you want to get a girl's name out of the words 'Santa Monica', Santa's the obvious choice. Brooklyn Beckham has appeared with three stripes on his wrist that people assume are a temporary tattoo. They're actually scars from self-harming while watching Calum Best on *All Star Family Fortunes*.

Michael Jackson's former British bodyguard claims he acted as a sperm donor for the singer after he told him he wanted an 'athletic' child. Whether or not that's true, Jackson was present at the birth, which involved a mammoth 14-hour labour. Apparently the baby saw him waiting and refused to come out.

Before his death, Michael recruited leading throat specialists to see if they could implant vocal chords into his pet chimp Bubbles. It sounds horrific, but it's probably not the worst thing he tried to put down that monkey's throat. The monkey did master uttering weakly three words through endless repetition: 'Please, Michael ... don't.' Bubbles was so close to Michael he was like the son he never fancied. He was just a performing monkey really, and Bubbles was his pet.

A new Michael Jackson album came out made up of any spare recordings found of his voice. Hence the tracks 'What Do You Mean the Doctor's Sick, Is there a Locum That Can Write Prescriptions?' and 'Now You Realise This Is a Special Secret between You and Me ... Why Does Your Chest Have a Wire on It?' Even the Jackson family aren't sure if it really is Michael.

Admittedly, they doubted whether it was really him every time he turned up for Christmas dinner for the last 15 years.

The album is called *Michael* – rather than the more honest *Songs Too Shit to Go on Any of His Other Albums*. In many ways it's great to know that Michael lives on through his music – rather than just through kids' nightmares. After hearing Michael perform on the recordings, his dad Joe decided, for old time's sake, to beat the tapes with his belt.

★

Oh, the paradox that is celebrity second-hand dartboard Jordan. Or is it Katie Price? How can someone with two such distinct personalities also appear to have less than one? Jordan observers say her recent activity suggests she may be becoming 'self-aware'. Apparently something boffins have feared ever since she was built for the *Daily Star* by Cyberdyne Systems to fill slow news days ... a story reminiscent of when *Daily Express* special forces had to hunt down their own creation, 'Home Counties Black Male Stereotype Re-enforcer Droid MK IV', more commonly known as Biggie Smalls, when it bypassed its own remote-command circuitry.

Jordan was named 'The most hated woman in Britain'. Don't worry about that, Jordan. You're 'The most hated *person* in Britain'. Give it time, baby. You'll eventually be 'The most hated object in Europe'.

There have been various tedious stories about Jordan's relationship with her new Argentinean boyfriend. I won't bother with the name, it's pointless you getting used to it. I hope this time Jordan finally gets the fairy-tale wedding she deserves and ends up locked in a dungeon for a thousand years before being eaten by a wolf.

Jordan clearly has a void that can never be filled. I only wish that was a psychological analogy. Apparently, the key to her relationship lasting is communication. They've both promised on no account to learn the other's language. If they reproduce, with their combined genetics that baby will be the idiot equivalent of Brazil's 1970 World Cup side.

Satellite intelligence seems to suggest that Katie is stockpiling semen in huge concrete silos at her mansion, it's feared in preparation for her transformation into a giant 'Queen', with plans to relentlessly pump out a huge mega-titted army to bring the world to an end as every man on the planet wanks themselves unconscious.

I do feel for her kids. Now they're at that age when they'll be asked at school, 'What does your mum do for a living?' and just having to answer with a blank shrug. Jordan has gone to tremendous lengths to preserve her children's anonymity, frequently drawing the fire of prying paparazzi by splaying her legs like a tipsy faun and filling her cleavage with vomit outside Chinawhite.

In the latest twist, Jordan's tits have announced that they're leaving to pursue a solo career. But the big shock was Jordan's previous marriage to cage-fighting tranny Alex Reid ending after eleven months. It certainly wasn't a long marriage. I've taken dumps that lasted longer. And photographed better. And that you'd rather sit next to on a first-class train journey.

Jordan says Alex ended up just wanting her for her fame. Presumably, she longed for the happier times when he just wanted her for her big rubber knockers. He surely doesn't deserve half her fortune – mind you, neither does she! Katie was apparently really upset about the whole thing. Or maybe really happy. It's impossible to tell. Her face doesn't move and she speaks in a robotic monotone. It's like trying to understand how your Hoover is feeling.

It must've been awful for Alex to hear Jordan say the marriage was over – hearing that from her cold, dull, monotone voice must be like discovering Optimus Prime doesn't love you anymore. Perhaps that explains why Alex has been putting on the lippy and mascara again. Not that feminine, it has to be said, but if David Lynch ever makes a movie about clowns he'll be straight in there. He's not so much female impersonator as female impersonator impersonator. I feel sorry for Alex. I know he's a hard man but he must have feelings. Not in the face obviously – there's no nerve endings left there – it's been tenderised like a cheap steak.

★

No matter how low you think you are in show-business, there's always another layer beneath you. An escapologist in Atlanta, Georgia, was lucky to survive after failing to get out of the chains and getting dragged behind a car. I think you'll find, mate, that you're actually just a pologist. The incident must've had Michael Hutchence wanking in his grave. The spectators in Georgia had never seen a man dragged behind a car before. Well, not a white one. The accident took place on a racetrack. That must've been a test for the pit teams – do you use slick or wet-weather tyres to get grip when driving over the layer of face skin on the back straight?

Hazel Maddock, an actress from Merseyside, left her dead mother's rotting corpse in the bedroom so she could collect her benefits. Which turned out to be a waste of time as she had to spend most of it on air freshener. All for £200 of benefits. She could have made a lot more money from a maggot farm. Thank God it was a pension. If her mum had been under 60 I suspect she'd have been putting on her pelt once a fortnight to sign on.

After failing in show-business, Hazel could think of no other way to earn money than to keep the corpse of her mother. I will personally pay to show this news report in the ad break of every episode of *The X Factor*. Living with a corpse can't be that bad – it's probably very similar to being married, except you'll actually get to have sex. Hazel worked as a TV extra on *Hollyoaks*, meaning she will be considered to have already served most of her sentence.

★

There's also the whole freaky, sleazy crossover we now have between show-business and politics. A website has been created where the public can vote for who they consider to be the sexiest MP. Finally something on the internet that I can't wank to. Looking at that list is not the first time I've imagined David Cameron having sex. But it's the first time he's not been getting raped.

Former Fugees frontman Wyclef Jean was shot in the hand in Haiti, where he's standing for president. When asked how many times he was shot, Wyclef was able to say, 'One time.' This is why, no matter what rappers tell you, you should always look around for snipers before putting your hands in the air like you just don't care.

Margaret Thatcher's handbag sold for £25,000. Thatcher had several bags, though by far her favourites were one made from the pelt of the last working miner, and one made from a 19-year-old Argentinean conscript shot while trying to defend his foxhole with a corkscrew and a chip fork.

And think about Comic Relief – a night where celebrities ask you to solve social deprivation that their coke habits have largely caused. To be honest, I only realised last year that Comic Relief doesn't mean being wanked off by a clown. Just a lucky coincidence it happened on the same day, really; it meant I could pass it off by shaking a tin at the same time.

The real irony is that Lenny Henry's life is worse than somebody's who's living in a Kenyan slum. They should do a show where one of those guys comes over and spends his whole week pitching game-show ideas to UK Living, scanning his wankbank and only finding memories of Dawn French swaying above him, coming like an electrocuted walrus.

Gordon Brown was interviewed by Piers Morgan. Piers didn't make a home visit like he did for Katie Price; Gordon had to come into the studio. His wife was sat in the audience and he had David Cameron as a 'Phone a Friend', in case he forgot the answer to the 'How did you feel when your child died?' question. It seems our leading politicians have learnt something from *The X Factor* – the British public like nothing better than to vote for the recently bereaved.

We are bringing up our children with a very odd concept of how it feels to be bereaved. We will soon have raised a generation for whom the stages of bereavement will be denial, anger, government position, recording contract, acceptance.

If my child died it would be so private, so personal, I would never try to get sympathy by talking about it in an interview. I'd probably tell a few gags about it on a panel show, but never try to get sympathy.

Once, on holiday in Romania, I sat and watched Romanian TV with my friend and his family. There was a show that involved a host doing a big topical monologue, so I got them to translate. He'd do a bit about the defence minister and the defence minister would actually be in the audience. The host would walk up into the crowd and have a bit of banter with him. Then there'd be a bit about some other government official and he'd be there too, and again they'd swap a bit of chat. It seemed incredibly corrupt. 'You could never have a show like this in Britain!' I scoffed.

'You do have a show like this …,' my friend said seriously. 'I saw it when I was over there … *Have I Got News for You.*' Another friend, a TV producer, told me that his company approached Lembit Öpik, the former Lib Dem MP who doubles as a bad hand at Scrabble and a banana with Down's syndrome. They wanted Lembit to appear in a series where he becomes a cage fighter, perhaps with one eye on having his face punched into a normal shape. What a tragic thing that you ask a production company what they think the public would like to see someone do and they reply, 'Being savagely beaten'.

I suggested that they tell Lembit the show had been commissioned but actually start filming something slightly different. There is a guy called Oleg Taktarov who won the Ultimate Fighting Championship for a couple of years. A story at the time (my source is a *Combat* magazine I read at a house party) went that he walked across Siberia and down through Alaska to enter the championships. Actually walked all the way there across the top of the world. A dead-eyed living weapon externalising the blankness he feels within through the medium of other people's pain. What we should do is get Lembit to train with a different trainer every week. We laugh at how he can't master basic skipping, smile as his trainer shakes his head in exasperation at his lack of cardiovascular fitness. Meanwhile, Oleg Taktarov starts walking from his home in Siberia to London for the end-of-series bout, where he will destroy Lembit. Minor training victories for Lembit would be intercut with shots of this grim mountain walking impassively. At the end of each episode Lembit's trainer that week will be flown out to fight Taktarov, wherever he is, and be left as a bloody smear at the side of a motorway. Through countryside, through rain, through waist-high snow, Oleg carries a perfect meat replica of Lembit tied to his back. He hangs it from trees and the doors of motorway-service toilets and practises killing blows and nerve attacks. Every episode ends with Oleg Taktarov on top of the dummy in his sleeping bag, slowly and powerfully fucking it.

'THAT SQUARES YOU WITH LITTLE RAY. FOR ME, YOU'RE GONNA
NEED TO FIND SOME PUSSY! SOME BIG PUSSY!'

I stretch in the morning and pick up the *Guardian* from outside the front door. £10 a week to bribe the paper-boy to come up here.

Paul Merton has been raped. He was introducing a silent film in a theatre and was raped behind the screen as the film started. The audience saw the shadows and were howling with laughter, thinking it was a stunt. It seems weird he's still famous. *Have I Got News* is pretty shite now, though. Perhaps the rapist has started to judge us artistically, as well as commercially. It might be the Valium, but there's something about that I find uplifting and I put the Wu-Tang Clan on the stereo, the *Iron Flag* album. Merton is in a coma or something.

Today the paper has a sci-fi writer in the insultingly titled 'Other Lives' section.

Ralph William Stead

Ralph Stead, who died from a stroke on Tuesday aged 74, was for much of the 1970s a household name as a novel-ist and screenwriter. He is best remembered for his fantasy novel *Dogs of Rome*, an imaginative triumph that saw the pet dogs of Roman senators weaving internecine plots against the backdrop of the struggle between Julius Caesar and Pompey. Satirical in nature, its amoral Schnauzer Cassius was a damning portrait of Henry Kissinger. Stead struggled as a writer for pulp SF magazines during the 1950s but the success of *Dogs of Rome* propelled him onto magazine covers. Overnight he became a very wealthy man but the book had a critically mixed reception. Jacques Derrida phoned him out of the blue to tell him it was rubbish. Hollywood called, and Stead and his young wife Barbara moved to Los Angeles in the summer of 1963.

Kaprowitz, his first project, was a major success, and he won an Oscar for best original screenplay. The film is the story of an actor who plays a famous TV detective. Developing Alzheimer's disease and believing himself to be homicide cop Mark Kaprowitz, he begins an investigation into the murder of a local waitress. The people he interviews respond to the character as if he were real, and the film received much praise at the time for highlighting how increased exposure to television was shaping the national consciousness. However, it's rarely shown now because of its dated depiction of Alzheimer's. The final scene reveals the whole investigation has been Kaprowitz talking to the condiments in the dining hall of a mental home, and that he himself had murdered the waitress, believing her to be Satan.

After leaving Los Angeles, Stead signed a deal to write more 'animal histories'. Despite being poorly received by the critics, *Dogs of the Aztecs*, *Dogs of the Mongols* and *The Mayans Kept Pet Monkeys* all sold well, but Stead's heart was not in his work. The books were increasingly poorly researched and perfunctory, becoming obviously autobiographical tales about Stead and his wife. *Dogs of the Soux Indians* focused on two dogs living with nomadic Native Americans, but their living quarters closely resembled Stead's New York apartment. The dogs were married, went to the library and argued about an affair the female dog had had with Norman Mailer. There were only infrequent mentions of Native American matters, largely factually incorrect, and 'Sioux' was spelt incorrectly. One of the reasons the books continued to sell was that, when placed together, the spine of the covers as a set formed a picture by Stead's friend Andy Warhol. It became clear after *Reich Snakes!* that the picture was of Stead slumped over a writing desk having shot himself in the eye, and sales tailed off.

★

For lunch I have a meeting with a producer from the BBC. He's producing his show in Scotland as some kind of funding wangle; nobody Scottish will be involved. I can see this includes me. His expression holds no promise, a playground in the rain. We meet in an empty West End pub, as he is afraid of being seen with me. He tells me I have recently been voted 'Most Offensive Comedian' by comics questioned for some internet publicity survey.

I'm not one of those comics who googles their own name. That stuff always reminds me of Lynda La Plante's *Killer Net*. Just after *Prime Suspect*, La Plante knocked off an exploitative sex-murder thriller, utilising an internet no rational mind would recognise. At one point a wee guy runs in and shouts to our hero, 'You'd better get home mate! You're being flamed in the newsgroups!' Whenever I hear bad publicity I always think *flamed in the newgroups!*

The producer cat is a 50-something meat sculpture poised somewhere between career peak and heart attack. He orders an expensive mineral water and, as he does that jolly pre-business chat, pours it slowly over cubes of tap water.

He's doing a kind of all-star sci-fi sketch show. Lots of big names doing a couple of sketches each over a series. Simon Pegg is doing one and so is Steve Coogan. There's no way I can get on this thing and the producer is meeting me as a favour to my agent.

I met him before when he was looking for prank ideas for *Balls of Steel*. I suggested seeing how close we could get a cardboard cut-out of Lee Harvey Oswald holding a rifle to Tony Blair. I only saw the actual show once and it had a guy pulling up in a car and throwing cheeseburgers at some people sat outside a café.I don't think they were real people, those shows worry about getting sued nowadays, it seemed to be actors having cheeseburgers thrown at them.

He tells me the show is called *Set Phasers to Laugh*, and I have a moment of panic that I'm being set up for some hidden-camera show. I picture the abject horror of the waiter turning out to be Rio Ferdinand or, worst-case scenario, Rufus Hound.

I swing into this idea I have for a running sketch where a Lex Luthor-type supervillain is sharing a cell with a low-level black drug pusher, like a character from *The Wire*. He starts trying to 'school' the super-villain on some chump-change crime ideas but then Lex Luthor hits him with some high-concept criminal shit.

We see the guy come out of jail and start reorganis-ing his gang with righteous supervillainous thinking. There's a montage of them getting hold of an Infinity

Gem so they can control a Sea Titan. We watch the Sea Titan collect moneys owed and then, in a huge booming voice, say, 'THAT SQUARES YOU WITH LITTLE RAY. FOR ME, YOU'RE GONNA NEED TO FIND SOME PUSSY! SOME BIG PUSSY!'

The gang do a drive-by on a mystical-quest team of a magician, young knight, giant, dwarf and wise woman. They open up with their gats and one of them is shouting, 'GET THE FUCKIN' MAGICIAN – HE'S HEALING THEM, THAT MOTHERFUCKER'S HEALIN' THEM!'

We see the gang boss having a meeting with Odin, All-father of the Norse Gods.

'YOU HELP ME OUT ODIN AN I CAN GET GET YOU SOME GOOD PCP!'

'WE ALREADY HAVE PCP!' screams the Allfather. 'HOW DO YOU THINK WE DO ALL THIS SHIT? LOKI IS JUST A PERSONIFICATION OF OUR PARANOIA.'

He gestures to 'Loki' a horned helmet and a cloak balanced over a big chair.

★

The next scene is the guy outlining a plan to his homies. They are relieved at its seeming conventionality.

'So we just got to use guns, no laser rifles, no atomic knuckles, no infinite cube?'

'That's right.'

'And we just driving the Mustang, we don't have to ally ourselves with no paradimensional lion and ride that mutherfucker in there?'

'That's right. How are we going to make the getaway?'

He produces a complex starmap. 'THROUGH THIS RIP IN TIME, MOTHERFUCKERS!'

So two black drug dealers have to escape from a bank robbery and hide out in the Wild West for a year but they're told it's very important that THEY DO NOT FUCK WITH TIME! They're stuck in the Wild West with a lot of money and a lot of crack, but they just have to lay low and NOT FUCK WITH TIME! We see them sitting on the end of a bed in a Wild West bordello, clutching handfuls of cash and crack and looking at each other uneasily.

The final scene is the two guys reporting back to their boss.

'I THOUGHT I TOLD YOU NOT TO FUCK WITH TIME, MOTHERFUCKERS!'

'We didn't boss, I promise …'

'WELL, DO YOU WANT TO TELL ME WHY WASHINGTON DC IS NOW CALLED CRACK DC, MOTHERFUCKER? HOW COME I HAVE THE CONSTITUTIONAL RIGHT TO STEAL? I TOLD YOU NOT TO FUCK WITH TIME!!!'

★

As I'm screaming 'DON'T FUCK WITH TIME!' into this guy's face, I suddenly feel happier than I have in years. My career is actually over, I can be alive again. I will be raped. Can that be so bad? It's just something going in and out of your arse. Is the problem that someone is getting one over on you by fucking you? He'll find no victory in my arse. I feel like crying, like holding this guy's hands and kissing them.

That night I finally watch the first episode of *The Game*. It starts with shot of a buff guy in his 40s making himself a cocktail by the side of a pool. He sits in a deckchair watching the sun rise while a smoky American voiceover says, 'When it came right down to it. As it always does. Roger wasn't so great at The Game …'

We see his hand click at a little remote unit in his hand and a mist rises on the swimming pool. We see a close-up of a smile.

'He made some mistakes. As we all do. Maybe he cared too much. That's what he likes to tell himself.'

The grin tightens as he sips at his cocktail.

'You can be living right there in the moment, then it can all just slide away from you'

The show proper begins with Derek getting in a fight at a taxi rank. The cops find a couple of grams of cocaine on him and when they get him down the cop shop he's being given a doing. Suddenly a senior-looking guy comes in and says, 'That's enough, just let him go.' When he picks up his stuff at the front desk there's a piece of paper with a phone number written on it. He calls the number from the car park and someone on the other end says, 'No problem Derek, just trying to keep you in The Game.' He doesn't understand but the voice just keeps reassuring him. 'Just like the way you play The Game, that's all.' He goes back to the taxi rank and there's no queue, and in the cab home he notices the cops have put the coke back in his wallet.

★ ★ ★ ★

The border between the Real and the Unreal is not fixed, but just marks the last place where rival gangs of shamans fought each other to a standstill.

Robert Anton Wilson

★ ★ ★ ★

09

I have this idea that all our current technology has been around for thousands of years. The 1960s and 1970s were just a period when it was all put in cold storage for a bit so mankind could try to get a grip on our phone flirting, social networking addiction and porn use. Old cylinder recordings of Hank Williams will probably show up some day, '… and we'll go sexy-textin', baby, sexy-textin'', or long-hidden hieroglyphs will emerge of aliens handing their mobile phones over to us, because they were doing their heads in.

The feeling of certainty we get with science comes because we have internalised religion. I have this idea that we are a decadent society in denial. We went to the moon and we're not going back. Ignorance, in an age where information is so accessible, is an expression of that decadence. TV previews in newspapers that admit they haven't seen the show, people dismissing films they haven't watched, getting angry about jokes they haven't heard. We all do it and, in a way, not showing us bin Laden's body is the perfect way to make us believe he is dead. We feel far greater certainty about things we haven't seen than we do about risking opinions on things we have.

★

Stephen Hawking said in an interview that there is no heaven. I can see why he wouldn't believe in God – after all, it looks like God doesn't believe in him.

Harold Camping, that California-based preacher who predicted Armageddon, was so embarrassed when the world didn't end that he must have just wanted the ground to open and swallow everyone else up. An 89-year-old preacher doesn't need a Bible to predict everything will end soon. Just a mirror. It was supposed to be the Rapture, where all the good people go up to heaven and the bad ones get left behind. I confess I was a little taken in and apologise for strapping myself so tightly to Michael Palin as a precaution.

It's been reported that a solar flare in 2013 could bring the earth to a standstill. Thousands of years ago the Mayans predicted a catastrophe would hit earth in December 2012. They're weeks out! The idiots. No one can be certain exactly when the solar flare will happen – I'm so worried, I'm going to keep a constant eye on the sun to see if it's started. The sun is sending out a flare? I think it's quite a bad sign for us when the universe starts signalling for help. Do you think after the flare another planet will show up with a rescue boat and huddle all the mountains and forests on board in silver blankets? There is a tense, silent ride into the galaxy until one of the oceans starts sobbing and breaks down … 'You don't know how terrible it was out there, we … we … had to eat Atlantis!'

The *Sun* even reported that sat navs and home freezers would no longer work. That's some apocalyptic vision of the future they've created – a lawless land where men roam without direction trying to prepare their own Yorkshire pudding batter.

The Large Hadron Collider started and the world didn't end – which means I'm going to have to stop using that chat-up line, and start buying condoms. The collider will close for a year at the end of 2011 so that some design flaws can be fixed. Thankfully, those design flaws mean that 2011 starts next Friday and will last a week.

In 2010 the world emitted 30.6 gigatonnes of carbon dioxide. If you want to know how big 30.6 gigatonnes is, look at your children and imagine them dying from skin cancer and lack of water, and then stop asking stupid questions and just do your fucking recycling. At least after the Japanese tsunami the world will see that hydropower is a much better option than nuclear power – that wave could have provided electricity for decades.

Scientists have been told to conceive a strategy where people can survive without computers. They have started handing out pens and paper. If the internet shuts down, will that actually mean the end of the world? Won't it just mean the end of the last 20 years? Does looking things up in *The Thompsons* qualify as the end of the world now?

Last year, PlayStation 3 was hit by the millennium bug ten years late. The editor of a gaming website said it was the same as the Toyota crisis – I imagine it's annoying, mate, but in fairness, you and your family aren't going to go crashing through a house because you can't finish *Medal of Honor*. It would be weird if it was the year 2000 again – you'd have just over a year to persuade Caitlin Moran,* the inventor of *Total Wipeout*

---

* The hotel I stay in when I'm in London will only bring you The Times. *Caitlin Moran's showbiz column always has exactly two jokes, the rest of it just being sentences. Some of the sentences are printed in a larger font, because she can't even think of enough non-jokes to pad it out. I read her book by being strapped into a chair with my eyelids held open, like in* A Clockwork Orange. *Apparently, her parents schooled her at home and I can't help thinking that her personality is exactly the sort of thing that bullying is for. Sadly, her whole 'What larks!' sense of humour has survived to adulthood, so if you see her you would actually be doing her a favour if you gave her a Chinese burn. Or, better yet, a hearty kick in the pie.*

and Vernon Kay to all take jobs on the top floor of the Twin Towers.

Some users of the new 3DS games console have reported feeling sick – as they realise they have wasted their entire lives. It's got a new game with Wayne Rooney in it – *Pre-Evolution Soccer*. You can get the Nintendo 3DS experience for your kids without the expense – simply give them a swig of Toilet Duck and let them stare at your mobile.

Apple had to pull an iPhone app that allowed you to pretend to glass someone, which is handy if you've already smashed your glass on an iPhone user's face or find yourself in a brawl with the Mario Brothers.

Researchers have taught a computer to recognise sarcasm. Next, they're going to try to teach Danny Dyer. The algorithm was taught to recognise patterns of words that are not meant to be taken literally. The words were taken from the Lib Dem election manifesto.

Cameron wants the Chinese to lift their ban on Facebook, Twitter and YouTube, and find out what makes their economy so dynamic. David, they're one and the same thing. Ban them in the UK too, and we might actually get some work done for a change. Mark Zuckerberg stands to make $25 billion from the sale of Facebook. That's unless the CIA can come up with a better offer than the Chinese government.

A model is warning Facebook users to be careful after she was duped into sending nude photographs to a man claiming to be Peter Andre. Her message is simple – you shouldn't send explicit photographs to people unless you're absolutely sure that they're a celebrity that you haven't met before.

New research claims that using the internet too much overloads your brain. It's called 'Divided Attention Disorder' – your attention is divided between what you're looking at on your computer, and whether your wife will walk in and see what you're looking at on your computer.

Porn could be blocked from every computer under government plans. It reminds me of when I was a young lad, and my mum put the Littlewoods catalogue out of reach on the top of the wardrobe.

Apparently if you spend hours with your laptop resting on your knees you can actually get burnt. The trick is to lift it occasionally. Porn usually does the trick. According to a new study, Britons now spend more of their internet time visiting news websites than looking at pornography, even though I am doing everything I can to unbalance these figures. Pretty much the only time I visit a news site is to find out if my internet pornography addiction has made the papers yet. Personally, I don't see it as an either/other situation. I can watch Fiona Bruce and crack one out. Then again, I can go onto a news site and read about a train crash and crack one out.

★

It's official. Attractive people are the cleverest. That explains why Wayne Rooney has Alex Ferguson spending each match shouting 'breathe in, breathe out, breathe in, breathe out' at him from the touchline. Wayne's IQ has been measured but they won't know the result for a day or two. They're hoping they can piece together the test paper from the bits they retrieve from his litter tray. They picked Natalie Portman as an example, because she's a looker and can speak Japanese. Anyone can fake that – you just have to try eating a couple of really hot chips.

There's a new bra to make boobs seem bigger. I think it's just wrong. If you do pull wearing it, ladies, there'll be nothing but disappointment. They should invent a bra that yanks your boobs right down and in different directions. Then when you take it off they'll ping back up and it'll be relief all round.

There's also a new pill out that helps ease the misery PMS can bring. You don't need tablets; it's easy to make PMS fun. I just dress up as Inspector Clouseau and shout, 'Not now, Kato', while she's chasing me round the house with a bread knife. A pill to cure PMS? I'd like to say I approve but it's messing with nature. It's called 'The Curse' for a reason, girls. It was your ancestor who ate that apple, so face up to your responsibilities and deal with it.

Test-tube-baby pioneer Professor Robert Edwards has been given the Nobel Prize for his ground-breaking work in IVF. Is it just me or if you were in his position wouldn't you just use your own each time? It'd be like *The Boys from Brazil*, but *I'd be Hitler!*

Asda have announced a plan to sell reduced-price fertility treatments from their in-store pharmacies. Aldi have their own plan, where for 20 quid a cashier will take you into the stockroom and pump you over crates of unbranded grapefruit segments.

Tesco are going to sell Viagra without prescription. Good idea. It'll give us somewhere to hang a couple of extra bags on the walk home … alright, one. Over the counter? Well, it is if they sell you the Viagra. Tesco are predicting sales in Viagra will rocket while sales of cucumbers will dramatically drop. Lidl are going to sell their own impotence cure: a pack of rubber bands and two lollypop sticks.

A third of over-75-year-old men are still sexually active. The only problem is a lot of them get up there, then can't remember what they went in for. I'm surprised. I assumed the only time old ladies had anyone rummaging through their drawers was when they let in two blokes with a fake ID, and one kept them distracted downstairs with some crap about a burst pipe.

Apparently, they've still got the patter too. Popular chat-up lines include: 'Do I come here often?' and 'Here's a ouija board. Go tell your mum you're staying out for the night.'

77-year-old Dennis Ealam has become a dad for the third time in the last three years. He and 37-year-old wife Cora were congratulated by well-wishers and family – and their 23-year-old live-in gardener, Raoul. This woman is some kind of OAPaedophile. To increase the chance of a man that age getting you pregnant it's claimed that you just have tiny benches installed in your fallopian tubes so their sperm can take the occasional breather.

The world's oldest calendar girl is stripping off at the age of 94. Her tits start in October and go all the way to December. It's tastefully done – nothing shown below the waist. Phew, no nipples then. The withered nonagenarian is 'Miss January'. Which, if you want to avoid throwing up into your mouth, sounds like good advice.

Sir Cliff Richard had the best-selling calendar of 2011. This is kind of strange, as the people who buy Sir Cliff's calendar are the people in society least likely to need one. I'm guessing the most popular entry will be 'hip operation' followed by 'purchase soup' and finally, around November, 'turn heating down'.

There's now a test that can tell you how fast you are ageing. It costs £700. If you can't afford that, here are two simple questions that will tell you if you are ageing too fast. Do you listen to Radio 2 and think Steve Wright is funny? Are there a dozen milk bottles on your doorstep that you can't get to as you've fallen and smashed your hip? Congratulations, you're ageing very fast. And saved yourself 700 quid – which I suggest you put towards a deposit on a coffin.

Scientists claim that baldness can be cured with a pig's bladder. At last, the mystery of what the fuck Donald Trump is wearing on his head has been solved. They also think they might have found the key to eternal youth by manipulating genes that stop internal organs from aging. Although, if you really want to stay young for ever, you should immerse yourself in a bathtub full of virile young men's seed. When it hardens, you'll remain trapped for eternity like a bug in amber.

Scientists have also discovered a cocktail of drugs that could help the elderly live longer. I'd love some for my nana. At least so she makes it through the current slump in property prices. Psychologists have said jigsaw puzzles help keep old people's brains sharp. I must pass the good news onto my nan, as she pieces together yet another 1,000-piece kitten while regaling me, through a blizzard of Hob Nob crumbs, with memories of our wedding day.

A report claims over 75-year-olds who drink a little every day can cut their senility risk. I suppose even if it doesn't, at least you've got an excuse for having your trousers on back to front. Tragically, my nan is a little senile. So, to help avoid the stigma attached to it, whenever I visit her care home I always leave a couple of empty Scotch bottles on her lap.

Earlier in the year, the BBC showed a documentary by Alzheimer's sufferer Terry Pratchett, which sparked 900 complaints. Though most of them were Alzheimer's sufferers phoning up to complain that they hadn't shown the documentary yet. People were worried that the programme would spark a rise in suicides – I think if we got through a week of *Britain's Got Talent* without killing ourselves, we'll be alright with this. I couldn't watch the bit where old Peter actually died, as I was coming so hard my glasses fell off. How do you schedule the showing of an assisted suicide? 'We'll pick Monday as it's the only night where this will cheer people up.'

Opponents of assisted suicide say that only God has the right to take a life, and if He'd rather show his boundless love by slowly destroying someone in front of their family and friends, that's His call. Currently, there's nowhere for seriously ill people to go in the UK to end their lives. Not since that report on Staffordshire Hospital came out.

A Belgian man diagnosed as being in a coma for 23 years was actually conscious the whole time. I've visited Belgium. Two hours in Ghent and I was diagnosed as being in a coma. Imagine being trapped in that useless, lifeless body desperately trying to communicate with the world but failing. It must be what it's like to be Chris Moyles. Apparently, by year 17 he put an amazing amount of mental effort into squeezing out some chest hairs so that they formed a word on his body. Unfortunately that word was 'Aggggggghhhhhhhhhhh'.

Jimi Heselden, the owner of Segway, died after test driving one of his scooters over a cliff. Who was he testing it for? Dignitas? It came just two days after the head of a mobility-scooter company tragically died while trying to jump the Grand Canyon. This horrific crash has already affected sales of Segways. Richard Hammond's bought a dozen.

★

A new drug called NRG-1 has been developed and, according to a professor, will 'kill enough British people to fill an Olympic stadium'. Now that's the opening ceremony I want to see. And, thanks to the assassination of bin Laden, probably will.

The doctor who claimed that the MMR vaccination had a link to autism has been struck off the medical register. He says that he's being persecuted and that sacking him will cause a dramatic rise in breast cancer.

Scientists have invented a patch to help people who faint at the sight of needles. Presumably, you stick it over their eyes. It was tested on mice. I didn't know they were particularly needle-phobic. I should imagine a more common fear with mice would be scientists repeatedly injecting them with cancer.

Research on rats has shown the best hangover cure is aspirin and coffee. If you're wondering how to get a lab rat drunk, it's easy. Just leave out some cans and tell it the boffins next door are injecting his family with cancer.

Five animal-testing activists were jailed earlier this year for intimidating people supplying Huntingdon Life Sciences. It's a victory for common sense – at last its staff can now get back to lip-sticking rabbits.

An Animal Liberation activist let a pet rabbit out of the hutch in a garden. The two owners, aged 10 and 13, were devastated that their pet rabbit Fluffy had gone. Not least because they'll now never know what effect Head & Shoulders will have on his eyes. I'm sure Fluffy will have absolutely loved the few moments of freedom he had until he was either eaten by a fox or died of starvation because he was tame.

Hungry sheep on the Yorkshire moors have taught themselves to roll three metres across hoof-proof metal cattle grids to raid villagers' gardens. Dawn French has a similar trick where she rolls over the night-watchman at the Kit Kat factory. 'Sheep are quite intelligent creatures and have more brainpower than people are willing to give them credit for,' said a sheep.

After years of decline, bees are making a comeback as more of us take up keeping them as a hobby. I keep them myself. Not for the honey. Their pelts make ideal puffa jackets for my gang of rapping ants.

Giant jellyfish have entered British waters. Apparently, if you get stung the best thing is to urinate on the stings. I recently found that if someone else gets stung the best thing to do is ask first. And a giant 55-foot 'sea monster' washed up on a beach in China. The authorities said it was so badly decayed they weren't able to identify the whale-sized, whale-shaped creature that came out of the sea, where whales live.

Scientists are to create a barcode for every species of animal on earth. Well, they say every; I'm guessing they won't have to bother with the zebras.

Japanese scientists believe they will soon be able to bring the woolly mammoth back to life using samples of their DNA. It seems odd when there are plenty of animals the Japanese could save from extinction just by not eating them.

★

Four astronauts have agreed to be locked away in steel containers for 18 months to simulate a NASA mission to Mars. In order to make things as realistic as possible, the scientists behind the mission will eventually pump out all the air in the capsules so they can die inside a freezing vacuum.

NASA banned astronauts on a recent shuttle mission from any intimate activity. NASA's come pretty close in the past, though. The *Challenger* space shuttle fucked the entire crew. They're right to ban relationships in interplanetary travel. How would you dump someone? You're hardly going to get away with, 'I just need more space.' Maybe better to go with, 'Whenever we get down to it I know the others are just behind that foil curtain sucking cottage pie out of a toothpaste tube.'

It's the end of the space-shuttle era. I always think it's sad they only started spacewalks in the 1980s. Long after they'd stopped sending dogs up. We've a lot to thank the shuttle programme for. Let's not forget, without its role in satellite launch, right now bemused villagers in remote parts of Nepal wouldn't be sitting in front of the village TV scratching their heads at a 1979 episode of *Knots Landing* and I wouldn't have been directed into a field last night screaming, 'This isn't a fucking petrol station … stop telling me this is a fucking petrol station!'

A photograph of a topless model that was smuggled aboard an Apollo mission is to be sold at auction. The astronaut who discovered it was shocked to find the picture after his capsule landed on the moon, but not as shocked as he was five minutes later when he discovered a cup of tea his mum had left for him on the side of the control panel.

A NASA probe has become the first man-made object to orbit an asteroid. The research could help develop techniques to divert space rocks away from a collision with earth. As long as they can give us a bit of warning, just so I can build a giant horseshoe out of papier mâché, write 'Asteroid Magnet' on it and point it at the sky while screaming, 'I, 'tis I killed the world!'

The first wedding officiated by a robot took place in Japan in 2010. It was all running smoothly until the robot asked the groom if he would now exterminate the bride. I think it's a great idea as they're highly efficient, follow orders and never question their instructions, but I don't know why Japanese people also see the need for robots.

A scientist who implanted a computer chip in his arm says that within the next ten years we'll have robots with human brains to help around the house. I'm not sure a machine that's capable of feeling jealousy and rage, and is able to snap your spinal cord like a cocktail stick and then wear your skin because it's taken a fancy to your wife, is really going to be worth all that hassle just to save on doing a bit of hoovering.

I'm not actually that convinced that our modern scientific outlook is a rational one. Isn't rationalism about using your own reason, engaging your own inductive and deductive mind? Most of the popular embrace of scientific culture seems to be about accepting other people's reasoning. Don't get me wrong: I'm not anti-science, I just think a lot of people imagine our culture to be defined by rationality and scepticism, when actually that strand of our thought is overwhelmed by our decadence, dogmatism and ego.

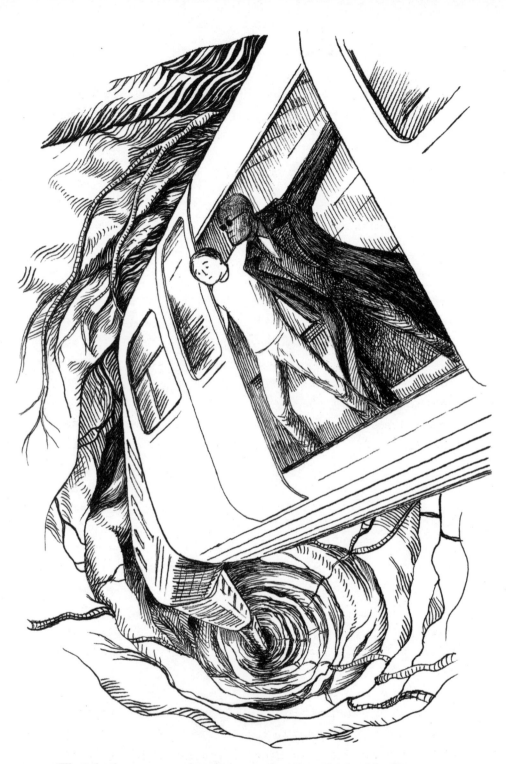

'The tube door opens and we hang our faces into the deathly slipstream,
hearing the strange whisper of our onward transit through the meaty,
sepulchral corridor'

★★★★

I spend a day in the stateroom moving the wee voodoo
men about the wax scheme and working up this short
story from ages ago. Maybe a smaller magazine might put
me on the cover, not the whole cover but on it somewhere. I look at the door again and I have got to do
something.

Mark Millar, the comic-book writer, is someone I know
from years ago, from a threesome at this really weird
New Year's Eve party in Dennistoun. Nobody really spoke
during it. In fact, the only thing he said that night
was when the woman first stood up and started undress-
ing. He turned round, his face emotionless, looked me
in the eye and said 'Victory' in a monotone so numb I
actually really laughed.

Changing CDs while he was fucking her seemed really
odd - after that I tried to straighten up enough to
leave. Sometimes I think he's not the guy from the
party. I got to know him properly about a year ago and
when I mention it he always affects not to know what
I'm talking about.

I email him and ask if he can put me in his magazine
CLiNT, and he says that actually there is a hole in the
next issue, so I sit looking at the sheets of A4, lying

on my back in the stateroom, wondering if the story is any good. I remember that I couldn't get started on it at first, then I thought of writing it as if I were Paul Marsh, and it just appeared. I wonder briefly if Marshy is a fictional embodiment of my personality, like Tyler Durden in *Fight Club*. Then I wonder if everybody is. Then I wonder how many comics are having that thought at this precise moment, and settle on 80 per cent.

My agent phones me from hospital, where she is in the early stages of labour. She's quite chatty about the Caesarean she's going to have. I laugh when she finishes talking and try to think of something to add. 'Fuck,' I say. I tell her that I placed a story but I don't know if it's any good.

'It must be good if Mark's printing it,' she assures me.

'But he hasn't read it,' I remind her, and she just gives that two-beat silence she does when I say something stupid.

Peeking Under the Hood

Things came to a head around the time I was having dreams about Laurence Fishburne. I remember him staring at me from the other end of an empty tube carriage. It was a place that looked like the London Underground but felt more like purgatory.

After losing my job at the *Bromley Courier* I realised I'd gotten fairly disillusioned with journalism. Well, I like writing but I don't have the temperament for that kind of work, the requisite aura of bullshit. My flatmate Martin had met some guys with crystal meth, a lot of it. We knew plenty of people who would be interested in buying. And we were pretty desperate for cash. At the back of my mind I thought it might also give me some ideas for the crime novel I was trying to write.

And that was when the dreams started, with Fishburne. Maybe it was the over-active imagination of a film obsessive but after the second time I did start to think there was something really strange happening. I've read about shamanism, people having encounters with their guardian spirit. Or maybe it was just something weird in that last batch of meth.

He never said anything, just seemed to be weighing me up with that strange, distant look. There was all this other stuff going on at the time, what with breaking up with Karen. And we'd come to the attention of some people. Well, the guy who came to the flat that night. I'd read about the Peckham Boys and gangs in the area, how ruthless they could be. I never thought I'd meet one of them, never mind having a gun waved in my face.

I suppose I'd been trying to rebuild the myth of myself, fuelled by regret about the past. Driving through New Cross with the windows down, the steady martial synth line of John Carpenter's *Assault on Precinct* 13 theme playing through the speakers, my nerves felt fine-tuned to the pulse of the city. I guess my head was quite far up my arse by this point.

We had a couple of big paydays in the beginning, and we partied. But after a while it seemed like a dark grey cloud had settled round the flat. Martin's 'craziness' was starting to grate. A bunch of student girls were in the flat one night and he starts waving around this replica Glock, doing his mad Latin American gangster voice, or whatever the hell it was.

I was becoming more like a ghost, obsessive about time keeping and household chores. Sometimes I felt like I really didn't belong in Martin's social scene, in which I probably cut a fairly spectral figure. 'Who was this pasty-faced indie-kid wearing Ecko Unltd T-shirts and listening to NWA?' I could sense people wondering.

I'd been going through an existential crisis of sorts. I remember thinking it would be good to try lucid dreaming, where you become aware of what's happening while you're in a dream. I could ask Fishburne what was up. Some paternal street wisdom is what I expected from him, I suppose, like Tre's dad in *Boyz n the Hood*. Or he might tell me to wake up, that I was in *The Matrix*.

Anyway, my memories of the event are hazy - can't remember much of what happened that day. But later I became aware that I was in a dream, and he was there too, just sitting on the steps outside Tooting Bec station. He regards me impassively. 'How can I find a way out?' I hear myself ask, as if it's another part of my brain that's composing the question.

He seems to be measuring me up with his cold gaze.

'You afraid of dying, brother?' he asks.

I answer honestly that I am, very much. He looks down at his feet ruefully, shaking his head a little. Then he gets up and beckons me into the station and down the escalator. We board an empty train carriage. The doors close and it starts to move.

I look at a tube map on the wall. The arrangement of coloured lines looks familiar, like it's the London tube system. But when I look closer it appears to be some kind of kabbalistic diagram, a map of my own psyche. Some of the stations are named after ex-girlfriends, or people I'd gotten batterings from as a school kid. There's a deeply familiar symmetry or sense to it all. The black line heading out the top of the diagram isn't the Northern Line, it's called *Thanatos*. And the Central Line - the red horizontal one - is now *Eros*. The erstwhile Piccadilly line is now *Justice*, which worries me. Fishburne beckons me to a seat.

'I'm gonna show you something, man,' he says, glancing out the window.

There's no one else in the whole tube system, it seems. Trains, empty. Stations, completely dead.

He pauses to take a couple of bottles out of a polythene bag. It looks like the cheap cider I used to drink as a teenager. He hands me one. I'm confused but I pop the top off it anyway. Before taking a sip I look closer at the label and it says 'Astral White'.

'This ain't exactly regular cider,' he says unnecessarily, before upending the bottle and taking a gulp. 'Got some hallucinogenic shit in it.'

He nods at my bottle and I take a hit. As I sit back I feel the tube accelerating, and I put a hand on the seat to steady myself. The stations start to flash past at smaller and smaller intervals, till there's only a fraction of a second between them. They're positively streaking past. Then the tube system seems to fall away, leaving inky blackness on all sides.

A few moments later it's like we're back in a different tube system, a 3D one this time, with no walls between the tunnels, which themselves come from all directions. The line we're travelling on is just one filament in a vast, cosmic head of hair, one of trillions of coloured flues streaming in to converge on a large dark object, like an asteroid, somewhere up ahead.

I look out the window as one of the other trains draws closer. The rail it's riding on is a thin cylinder of light, electric blue in colour. And the train itself looks more like a blue tic tac, with square windows. Its passenger appears to be a white fluffy lion, sitting upright like a person. It makes eye contact with me but seems vaguely bored.

'Is this the astral plane?' I ask.

Fishburne looks at me and nods curtly, as though rationing his information carefully.

'It's a little more complicated than that,' he says. He crosses the aisle to look out the window at the strange planetoid up ahead. 'It'll make sense when we get there.'

We whizz round the edge of the big asteroid and the slate-like surface appears mottled with what looks like stubble. It's a head! But we're too close to discern the face, to recognise it.

We enter the mouth of the thing. Inside, it's like some horrendous, fleshy Death Star. The tube train is speeding through an endless, heavily shadowed alimentary canal, several stories high and wide. The tube door opens and we hang our faces into the deathly slipstream, hearing the strange whisper of our onward transit through the meaty, sepulchral corridor.

'God, where are we? What is this thing?'

He looks at me, slightly incredulous. 'Well if you don't know,' he chuckles and shakes his head, 'I don't know how the hell the rest of us are supposed to cope with it'. My memory of his exact wording is a little vague.

A few moments later he grabs me. He looks spooked, like Tyrone in *Apocalypse Now* just after he has strafed gunfire across a boatload of farm animals and Vietnamese people.

'Look, I should have said something. It's a black hole in here. We can't get back out.'

'Well, who's driving? Can't we steer it out?'

Panicked, I rush through the carriage and reach the empty driver's compartment. I grab the controls and steer us sharply into the fleshy wall of the tunnel. We tear into the fibrous surface and burst out the other side into another passageway. Then another, and another. Soon we're hurtling towards a glowing wall lined with veins.

We smash into it, passing through 100 yards or so of pulpy white matter before ripping out the other side and back into the empty blackness of space. Behind us, the ruptured pupil of an enormous eye comes into perspective, then the rest of the eye, all framed by a titanic head, *my* head. I laugh insanely - a mix of terror and exultation matched by the expression on the huge head, just before it caves in on itself, as though consumed by a black hole inside.

The drip stand vibrated a little as I released the grip on my arm. My section of the room was enclosed by a section of blue curtain. I had been under heavy sedation for the past week, according to the female Indian doctor who appeared shortly afterwards. The double vision freaked me out at first, but she explained I'd have to get used to it. Damage to the optic nerve of my left eye, sustained by a blow to the face, meant that I would have lost much of the sight in it. But I was still lucky to be alive.

Karen came to the hospital that evening and handed me a copy of a newspaper. My eyes fell on the front page headline:

GANGLAND FANTASY WORLD ENDS IN TRAGEDY

It's some bullshit about how a taste for the high life had led two younger men from respectable backgrounds to operate on the fringes of a world of drugs and violence etc., etc. The high life? The article seemed to imply that Martin was a far bigger player in things than I had known. He had built himself a proper little empire, if this story was to be believed.

It's hard to believe it now, really.

★ ★ ★ ★

I don't know if it happened, but according to the account from Saint Augustine, a pirate was brought to Alexander, who asked him, 'How dare you molest the seas with your piracy?' The pirate answered, 'How dare you molest the world? I have a small ship, so they call me a pirate. You have a great navy, so they call you an emperor. You're molesting the whole world ...' That's the way it works. The emperor is allowed to molest the world, but the pirate is considered a major criminal.

Noam Chomsky, *What We Say Goes*

★ ★ ★ ★

10

They said they shot Osama B in da face. Are we supposed to feel safer now? I don't know if I do. It's like saying, 'You know that runaway train that has been hurtling down the track towards that bus load of primary-school children stuck on the level crossing? Well, good news. The train driver's dead.'

The US government has released pictures of bin Laden sitting on the floor, wrapped in a blanket, while watching himself on a portable television. On the one hand, they are trying to show that he was a pathetic, vain little man who lived in a hovel, while at the same time they're also saying that he was controlling the world's biggest terrorist network from his secret base. Osama had no internet access. It explains why he was so angry. He'd never seen a panda sneeze. Or a cat playing the piano.

That's the room from which he organised his network? He's not even organised enough to buy a TV table. Comedy is a strange business. It can only really be Barack Obama and myself who, when hearing the news that a 52-year-old man had been shot in the head, both thought 'Fucking Jackpot!' Osama bin Laden got his face shot off before being dumped into the sea. It's got to be my favourite-ever episode of *Celebrity Wipeout*. My biggest worry about the burial at sea is that if there's any truth in homeopathy, that whole ocean is now pure evil.

The US killed the Saudi Arabian bin Laden in Pakistan for atrocities that were plotted in Germany. Which strangely doesn't mean it's time to say sorry for invading Afghanistan. Abbottabad, where Osama was killed, is a popular summer resort. Bin Laden must enjoy the heat, which is good news considering where he is now. Argentina.

Afghan leader Hamid Karzai says terrorists should learn an important lesson. Presumably the lesson that it's possible to evade the world's most powerful army for almost a decade. Imagine the sort of information that bin Laden could have given about his network of contacts if he'd been taken alive. No wonder the US government wanted him dead.

Bin Laden was getting on a bit. Sooner or later he was either going to be attacked at home by US forces or by a teenager with a fake Gas Board ID.

The world is now a safer place, President Obama told us, from behind bullet-proof glass, surrounded by security. He also said there will be no photos released of Osama. Which means I'll have to buy the unofficial calendar this year. Come on CIA, it took you ten years to get all the plastic surgery done to that decoy, you might as well show us the pictures.

His neighbours first suspected who might be living in the compound when their football went into his garden and he said, 'If that ball comes over here again I'll put a plane through it.' The Navy SEAL attack wasn't all bad for bin Laden. He was about to redecorate his living room anyway and had chosen a brain-splattered wallpaper pattern. It seems amazing that the Navy SEALs managed to get inside the compound and shoot Osama so efficiently. I can only imagine they were told that the mission was to rescue a bearded British hostage and he must be brought out alive. His compound didn't have the internet or a phone. Apparently, the Americans located it by following all the pigeons he was using to make his Facebook updates. No internet? It's no wonder he needed more than one wife, then. If that was one of his main criteria he could easily have hidden out on the Virgin Glasgow to Euston train service.

Originally, they said he used his wife as a human shield. That's nothing. I heard he used a skyscraper as a runway. That'll explain that entry I saw on dating site Match.com – 'Bearded extremist seeks giant, wide, fat woman. GSOH.' I can't judge. I confess I once used my partner as a shield while being shot at. A stupid thing to do, as it was hard enough persuading her to go to that swingers' party in the first place.

There was a $25 million reward for getting bin Laden but, as the US Marines shot him on a Bank Holiday Sunday, surely they were on at least time and a half? Bin Laden refused to surrender and, because he was unarmed, they had no other choice than to shoot him in order to prevent him escaping on a getaway donkey.

Normally, the Americans like to parade their victims like Saddam's sons, who they stitched together for a photo call. This operation seems to have been designed to create maximum doubt. They say he was unarmed but resisted them. How? Is it Navy SEAL policy to ask nicely once and if he says 'no', then there's no other course of action but to shoot him twice in the face? The first soldier that found him cut his beard off and started wearing it, then next soldier came in and thought he was bin Laden and shot him, then he put on his beard, and so on until about five soldiers were dead.

Pakistan's government denied that they had any knowledge of bin Laden's whereabouts, even though in 2005 he appeared in the Pakistani version of *A Place in the Sun*. They're going to demolish his £1 million house. I hope they fit a couple of wings and a tail fin to the bulldozer, just for old time's sake.

The US is treating the fact that Osama was broken, old and grey as a victory. No, that just means it took them bloody ages to find him. Osama's final insult to the West – having a home life so boring that the news media scrabble around trying to find the evil implications of a man wearing a hat buying chickens. His house had trailing leads and extension sockets everywhere. This man just *toyed* with danger. Five videos have been described as the US's biggest-ever intelligence haul. That's because in previous operations the soldiers have burnt all the books they've found, while squealing like frightened chimps. If you find a haul of videos in a military genius's compound, all that proves is that Sky+ is harder to operate than a remote detonator.

Apparently Osama dressed as a woman to have important tactical meetings. Either that, or a woman actually did all this and, as usual, will never be credited for it.

Muslim extremists have supposedly set their sights on Prince Harry. Is beheading Prince Harry the biggest threat terrorists can come up with? At least kill someone who won't ejaculate when it happens. Harry's hardly scared of dying. He's a ginger that's desperate to go back to the desert. Seems Harry has grown up to be like his mother – fucking with Muslims might be his main cause of death. If Muslims' number one target is Prince Harry, it goes to show that David Cameron is as ineffectual internationally as we'd always suspected. I suppose Harry is doing his best to keep Afghanistan safe. While he has six SAS gunman following him around to parties, they're not in Afghanistan shooting shepherds.

★

A church in the southern US caused chaos in Afghanistan by setting fire to a copy of the Koran to commemorate 9/11. Of course it's their right to do it. As any student of pre-war Germany will tell you, book burning's just a healthy part of building a democracy. The pastor said he'd stop the book burning if it caused too much offence. And made sure he had a full bladder just in case. It just seems so unnecessary to burn a copy of the Koran. Especially when every bookshop in the world still has copies of Michael McIntyre's *Life and Laughing*.

If this is all about honouring the victims of 9/11, is it not a bit tasteless to set fire to a book? They might as well throw it from the 35th floor of a skyscraper. They are trying to send a message to Islamic fundamentalists, that message being 'Come and kill us.' Hillary Clinton said the plan did not represent American values. She's right. It would be far more representative of American values if Justin Bieber smashed a Blu-ray copy of the Koran to pieces using a turkey drumstick.

The church had planned to set fire to a large heap of Korans the previous year. I think they fundamentally misunderstood the nature of capitalism. If they'd just bought 200 copies, the publishers would have been thinking, 'Hey, there's a real demand for those Korans down in Florida. Let's print up another 5,000.' And, of course, they'd have been burned too, and more would have been printed. The cycle would have continued until, in the state of Florida, the only book you could've purchase would've been the Koran and the only items you could've legally purchased from a shop would've been a hijab and a cigarette lighter.

UK Islamic extremist Emdadur Choudhury was fined £50 for burning poppies at the last Remembrance Day parade. I say, if he wants to live here, he should protest about the occupation of Afghanistan the British way. Just shrug his shoulders and reach for the remote when it comes on the news.

Burning poppies is a pretty piss-poor way of showing disrespect to our soldiers. It's not a patch on failing to give them proper body armour. Lots of people desecrate the two-minute silence. At least Choudhury had an opinion about war – surely it's more offensive when people just continue browsing through the Disney Store? How dare he publicly protest against the occupation of Afghanistan? Especially after all our efforts to bring it free speech. Apparently, he had planned a more lavish protest to bring the infidel British puppet government to its knees. But he couldn't buy the fireworks as his benefit cheque didn't arrive in time.

I loved a couple of recent stories that described terrorists being uncovered after US spies picked up 'internet chatter' indicating an imminent attack. Internet chatter? That doesn't mean anything. We're probably running scared after a simple Twitter game of #terroristattackcheeses. The man who suggested 'Al Qa-Brieda' is in protective custody, while 'Gouda Meinhof' is still under investigation. Police have cordoned off Leicester and Caerphilly, just in case.

The government says that terrorist groups are hell bent on sabotaging our computer networks. Which means that Virgin Media must have been working as an Al-Qaeda splinter cell for some time. The National Security Strategy has announced the top 15 threats to the UK. A list of 15 major disruptive events to British government, and revolution is not one of them? Brothers! We can take them by surprise! The *Sun* said, 'Many services rely on computers – police and banks, to name just two.' Leading me to believe the *Sun* has done a new poll and found most of its readership to be time travellers from our destroyed, cave-dwelling future. It's bloggers I feel sorry for. Without the internet they'll end up walking round town just handing out typed sheets listing the shit they've been up to.

A man living behind Wembley Stadium was discovered to be funding Al-Qaeda. Living on the route to the shrine of the drunken, violent idiot? Do you think he started hating the West before or after his daughter's Wendy house became a urinal?

A plot was smashed to launch a Mumbai-style attack on Cardiff, inspired by Western decadence. What? In Cardiff? They haven't even got a fucking Starbucks! Police are now investigating whether a Mumbai-style attack was launched against Glasgow but no one noticed. You can't terrorise a Welshman by threatening to blow up New Look. The only things they're scared of is impotence, and having to move out of their mum's house.

Possibly the craziest scaremongering of recent times was the story that female suicide bombers are being fitted with exploding fake breasts by Al-Qaeda. Just five ounces of explosives in a breast would be enough to blow a hole in the side of a jet. This is going to make security checks at airports more interesting. 'Excuse me madam, but are your tits ticking?'

These women want to use the exploding breasts for terror but they could be put to a very different, much more positive use. As anti-rape devices. Think about it. You're being chased through the park, and both your rape alarm and Mace fails to put the attacker off. You then blow off your own tits like the fuel cells on a space shuttle. Nobody's getting raped that night.

A 21-year-old Islamic woman was found guilty of stabbing MP Stephen Timms because he voted for the Iraq War. That certainly trumps my effort – I just sent him a turd in a Pringles tube. I suppose on the plus side, unlike other MPs, his dry-cleaning receipt was a legitimate work expense. Mr Timms, who followed Blair's instruction to vote for the war, was lucky. Doctors think he could've been killed if he'd actually had guts or a spine. There are rumours she'd tried a similar attack shortly before. Crouching by the front door wearing a full burqa, unfortunately she forgot it was bin day.

The SAS are apparently to patrol shopping centres this Christmas in case of an Al-Qaeda attack. They need to make sure they are not stationed near any department stores, otherwise they'll waste most of the day dealing with men pleading to be executed.

Hopefully, the SAS don't have the same training for dealing with crowds as the Met police or else we can expect someone to be pushed over so they die every day till Christmas. They will target anyone holding packages and looking suspicious – looks like a lot of women will be getting that secret surprise gift straight from the coroner's office this year. It can only end badly. 'Why did I take him out, Sarge? He had a beard and a whole sackful of suspicious packages.' Remember – if someone in a shopping centre asks you to stop, do not run! Unless they're trying to sell you Sky Broadband.

I'm presuming this is part of SAS training in withstanding torture. Three weeks of strip lighting and being asked if they want a family portrait, and they'll be begging to be water-boarded. Can you imagine the grief, to find out your son's been killed in a terrorist incident, compounded by the fact he was found with gift-wrapped bath salts from Wilkinson. To know he was thinking of you just before he died, but not all that fondly. I'm glad the SAS are there. After two hours shuffling through all the mouth-breathing, track-suited scum with Slade, Cliff Richard and Band Aid as my soundtrack, I'll just have to whip out an alarm clock taped to a pack of sausages and bang ... peace at last.

East Midlands Airport shut briefly after someone there saw another suspicious object. But it turned out to be a book. I went through Heathrow recently and I was at that bit with the walk-through metal detectors. They made me throw my keys in a bowl ... everyone else threw theirs in, I ended up shagging a pilot.

Then there was the hysteria over explosives found in printer cartridges. It's terrifying you can get this stuff so easily on the black market. I googled it and got directed to Amazon.

Apparently, 'Customers who liked PETN also liked Semtex and Diaminotrinitrobenzene.'

We had to rely on an Al-Qaeda supergrass for this. Our spies should be infiltrating these organisations but budget cuts mean we now have to share elasticated beards with the Americans. I say the only way forward is to ban printer cartridges and reintroduce scribes. *I said, scribes, Brother Matthew. Come on, keep up! You're not going to Vespers till this is done!*

It didn't go off so maybe there was a mix-up. Maybe there was a real ink cartridge on board while a temp at a haulage firm in Swindon is currently trying to ram a hydrogen bomb into the photocopier.

Hiding a bomb in a printer cartridge could have been very nasty. Have you ever tried to get ink out of a corpse? There is a lot of speculation as to how the bombers came up with this plan. I blame that recent Al-Qaeda convert, the wee paperclip from Microsoft Word. Now he can often be seen popping up wearing a turban, a beard and a hook, shouting, 'I see you are trying to defeat the West. Maybe I can help.'

As a result, all packages from Somalia were banned from entering the UK. Right now, my bed is unmade because my new housekeeper is languishing in a warehouse and, from her text messages, it looks like she's only got about five more hours of air left.

★

You know – I'm starting to think there are some people out there who don't really like Britain and the US. Of course, the whole terror thing is just a way of keeping us frightened and suggestible. More alarming is the view that after dallying with the idea of investing in green stocks and the planet's future, international capital has fled towards investing in security.

Rather than saving the world, the rich seek to turn the part of it they'll be left with into a fortress. The security sector in the US has, post 9/11, gone from chump change to a multi-billion-dollar concern. With a passive Palestinian population to try their tear-gas launchers and body scanners out on, Israeli firms are cleaning up. Meanwhile, Britain has a quarter of the world's CCTV cameras, each one relaying a feed to a sleeping minimum-wage security guard, leaving us safe in the knowledge that when we're kicked to death by an escaped mental patient it'll end up on *You've Been Framed*.

'He starts pretending that he's controlling her from the backseat and she jerks about like a robot'

★ ★ ★ ★

I'm out in the shared garden bit in front of my son's house. He's trying to join in with the bigger boys, who're about 8 or 9. One of them comes up to me to tell me I'm better than Michael McIntyre. 'Yes, I am,' I agree. 'Everybody is.' He says we can play for a few goals and the wee man runs alongside whoever has the ball, until he eventually gets dispirited. We take our own ball and kick it for a bit, then he grabs it and sticks it in the middle of the lawn. He makes me sit up on a wee bank with him and we both have to pretend we're guiding some action with PlayStation controllers. 'No more PlayStation for you,' I say, but he's already running towards the swings.

I'm telling his mum about it when I hand him back. She stays in the car, which makes it feel like a Cold War hostage exchange. He starts pretending that he's controlling her from the backseat and she jerks about like a robot and we all laugh. Later on, when I'm swimming, I think about that and whether laughing at something horrible just makes it bearable, and helps it continue. Maybe there is a laziness in laughing about stuff instead of doing something about it. I decide jokes should only be about things you canny change, only about disabilities and death and human fallibility and the eventual heat death of the universe. I'm in a Jacuzzi thinking this. Anyway, the wee prick is not getting on the PlayStation again. It's fucking snakes and ladders from now on.

★

Gary O'Donnell, Facebook assassin, has been texting me in the belief that I am Amanda H. I've been fending him off and also, let's be honest, leading him on. There's half an hour to kill before the European Cup Final.

You watching the game, Gary?

Can't wait! comes the reply. *What are you doing/ wearing?*

Just bored, lying on my bed, trying to think of something to do with myself.

I have a few ideas!

I'm sure you do! Well, I have none, so I'm going to run a bath!

Send me a pic! Sorry, bit forward, pics!

That almost makes sense, Gary. I can see him looking forward to leering at photos of my pal Lindsay in her undies while watching the pre-match build-up with some cans.

I think Man U might have won last time if Fletcher hadn't been suspended, I text - the most stupid opinion anyone could ever have about anything.

Agreed. Didn't know you knew about football!

There's a lot of things you don't know about me!

Think how often this standard flirtatious sentence has been used. One of his victims probably said it to Jack the Ripper.

I hope so! says Gary, enigmatically.

I'm imagining you're here on the bed with me, Gary.

I'm there in spirit! What are you wearing?

A blue dress, knickers, that's all.

Send me a pic!

Desperate. He's probably torn right now, because it's nearly kick-off.

My nipples are getting hard, Gary.

A couple of minutes go by. He'll be finding somewhere safe to beat off. My phone rings. It's him. I dingy it.

I text. *No calls Gary.*

Gary texts. *If I was there right now, I'd lift you up against the walls [sic] and slip my cock in and out of you as slowly as I could bear.*

It has the air of a standard, something he says to all the girls.

What about your severely disabled daughter, Gary. I feel guilty.

Don't. What are you doing now? Are you touching yourself?

I am.

Beautifully parried.

I'm touching myself through my knickers Gary …

Go on …!

I'm putting my hand in my knickers Gary …

Are you touching your pussy Amanda?

I'm touching my cock Gary, my cock is so hard for you …

What?

I leave it a couple of minutes.

What do you mean?

I'm pulling my cock Gary! I'm pulling my cock and imagining you're lifting me against the walls!

A good five minutes.

You have a cock?

A big hard cock Gary!

I thought you were a woman. Is this Amanda?

I am a woman Gary, a woman with a cock. We should meet up … I can come down to Manchester tomorrow.

The whistle goes and the game starts. I go through to the stateroom and relax on a beanbag. The wee man is right, it does seem strange not to be controlling it. I'll probably feel the same if I ever manage to watch any comedy again. Gary texts 20 minutes into the half, during a substitution.

You're joking, right? I thought you were a woman … have I got the wrong end of the stick here?

YOU'RE A FUCKING TRANSPHOBIC CUNT GARY! I'M SENDING ALL YOUR TEXTS AND SHIT TO YOUR WIFE!

Fuck you! I'm no poof, I can find you you cunt.

★

A lot of couples get their phones on a contract together so the partner's phone is often one digit higher or lower. One lower than Gary's is a soft-spoken Bristolian called Carl. Gary's wife's is one higher. I forward Gary's texts, as well as one from myself as a hysterical spurned mistress. Half-time is a blizzard of threats but after that I get into the game, the wee triangular movements and I switch the phone off.

Barcelona bring on this guy who's just got over liver cancer and I think about how it would be funny if he was kicked in the liver so hard that he died. Or if he started glowing radioactively because of all the chemo and scored a screamer from 80 yards with a light trail behind it. I light half a joint Paul has left there. The commentator is saying these days there's microchips in footballers' shorts, so the manager knows how far they've run. How long before that finds its way into school? A computer decides not to pick you for five-a-side and a letter is delivered to your house on the day of PE.

★★★★

I lay sprawled and twisted where I had fallen, sobs of fury at
my impotence, my uselessness, my helpless, stunted, ugly
body, wracking me. There and then, my face buried in the
crook of my arm, I silently cursed – with every curse that the
Trastevere gutters had taught me! – the nameless and
malefic being who had imprisoned me in a cage of flesh and
bone and mucus. I cursed him, his minions and agents, his
principalities and powers; I cursed the pope, the pope's
cardinals and catamites and painted whores; I cursed kings
and emperors and bishops; I cursed everything and everyone
I could think of. And I cursed the suppurating, filthy womb
which had propelled me, reluctant and screaming, into this
abysmal world.

David Madsen, *Memoirs of a Gnostic Dwarf*

★★★★

11

Have you ever stopped to think about how stupid sport is? Have you ever thought how idiotic it is that the Champions League trophy is a really, really big cup, because it's the most important cup? Remember how bored you were in school games when you didn't have the ball? Perhaps you fell into a reverie where you thought you'd like to be sitting at home, ignoring your family, watching cunts doing this remotely, cunts you didn't even know? Not that I'm entirely anti-sport. I always make a few quid on the Grand National – I've got shares in a dog-food factory.

The 2012 London Olympics will give the country the extra boost it needs to finally get us out of the recession and into a depression. The route for the Olympic torch was announced. The torch will first be handed over by China, once they've finished burning Ai Weiwei's feet with it. The nationwide relay will end at the Olympic stadium in London, when a surprise guest will light a giant flame by pulling the rip cord on his suicide belt.

There's going to be an Olympic cable car spanning the Thames. That's just what's needed. Now, we'll be able to see Team GB getting thrashed from an entirely different angle. It's 50 metres above ground – apparently, that's the distance most people can't tell bronze from gold. The big worry is that it'll be redundant after the games are over. Nonsense. It'll be a perfect viewpoint for security guards to make sure no one's breaking into the boarded-up stadiums below.

It's easy to knock our schools for not producing Olympic athletes, but I'm sure we'll bag at least a couple of golds in the shooting. You can't have an Olympics in the East End of London without a lot of gear getting nicked. I fully expect to be sitting on the Jubilee line with some guy in a leather jacket next to me with a horse. As host nation, we get to add an event, don't we? What about diabetes? We could take gold in that, though they'd have to lower that podium a bit.

The Olympic opening ceremony is going to be drastically cut – all competing nations will now be asked to bring a dish to share with everybody. The athletes can look forward to stand-ing on the winner's podium and receive a medal made from sea shells and milk-bottle tops made by one of Seb Coe's daugh-ters. Looks like we've saved a few quid on the mascots Wenlock and Mandeville. Their background story tells how they were fashioned from droplets of steel left over from the construction of the Olympic stadium. Kids love nothing more than to cuddle up at bedtime with chunks of reclaimed steel. The runner-up design was a smiley face drawn on a breeze block.

When tickets for the London Olympics went on sale the organisers made sure that prices were kept down, so that people wanting to watch the games are only ripped off by transport and accommodation costs. The results of the ticket draw were released and lots of people were disappointed. Which should help soften them up for the games themselves. I'm lucky enough to be attending the 100 metres finals. Well, it's pretty much definite. I've still to shave 28 seconds or so off my time. Of course, there is an easy way of getting right up close to the action – just disguise yourself as a small white square of paper with a number on it.

Less than a day into the job the Olympic clock stopped working. It couldn't get any more British, unless at midnight every Friday it puked into Trafalgar Square. It would've been more reliable to have used Nelson's Column as a sundial. There must be something more relevant than a clock. Perhaps an effigy of a London council-tax payer on their knees, crushed beneath the weight of a rucksack stuffed with coins, crawling towards a half-empty shoebox of bronze medals.

The Afghan Olympic committee has announced they're sending female boxers to the games. Sharia law actually produces very good lady boxers. They're more determined to win, as the penalty for losing is 40 minutes in front of one of those tennis-serving machines that's been loaded up with dirty pebbles.

Perhaps the saddest thing in athletics recently was the pitiless attitude towards India's hosting of the Commonwealth Games. Steve Moneghetti, Australia's chef de mission, asked for a written apology from the organising committee, saying his team had been 'treated like cattle' at the opening ceremony. Not the best choice of words, considering that in India they worship cows as gods. He'd have been better saying that his athletes had been 'treated like Indians'.

★

A study has shown that first dates go down by a quarter during the football World Cup. That makes sense – any man up for a date then is a repressed homosexual or Scottish. Either way, it'll probably end badly.

Hey, my English friends. Think of what you achieved. 2010 was England's *worst-ever* performance in a World Cup! That's got to be a step up from not even qualifying for the European Championships. I think the England team could still have had a heroes' welcome – if they'd diverted the plane to Glasgow airport.

I often get the England flag confused with other ones with a simple cross design, like Denmark or Sweden. So if I ever need to remind myself, all I have to do is look in any rubbish bin shortly after the start of any major football tournament. People worry that the George Cross flag is in danger of being hijacked by extremists and I can't help but agree. Heaven forbid if the Knights Templar, raising it high above Jerusalem all those centuries ago, dirt streets strewn with the blood and body parts of the vanquished Arab, could see how terribly it has now been discredited on car aerials.

The Scottish football squad celebrated the English defeat with a big party – in their lunch hour at the car wash. Various photos appeared of the England team looking 'ashamed' or 'stunned'. These were obviously just pictures of the team's usually blank and bewildered expressions, with emotions ascribed to them. Gazza said he was sure England would be back, even offering to be on hand to advise them in 2014. Presumably, only if they've got a wine glass and a circular table with letters round the edge of it. One thing to do is buy up all that hugely discounted George Cross tat and keep it in storage. Then just sell it next time England win a major tournament. Your descendants would make a fortune in Interplanetary Space Credits.

If you really have to replace Fabio, there's only one logical choice: his interpreter, the only man who knows all of John Terry's safety words. Fabio said that he only needs 100 English words to talk to his players. How far can a 100-word vocabulary get you? Just ask Danny Dyer. But don't expect a coherent or understandable response. When you look at the record Capello's team has had for running off with women, sometimes you wonder if he's setting up a football team or launching a flotilla of Vikings.

A room containing John Terry, Wayne Rooney and Steven Gerrard was taped. There's nothing on there about England's training methods but a fascinating discussion about Carl Jung's theory that the human psyche is religious by nature. Insiders say the sound quality is very poor – apparently, it makes everything Wayne Rooney says sound like garbled nonsense. The tape could reveal vital tactics, like which member of the team distracts the husband while John Terry gets 'in the channel'. One revelation from the tape is that Fabio Capello is looking to experiment – he's going to try breeding a horse and a window cleaner's ladder in the hope of creating another Peter Crouch.

In a different leaked video, Lord Triesman suggested there were rumours that Russia and Spain might bribe refs. These were the words of an old man trying to shag a woman 30 years his junior. I should think he's grateful it's just a tape of him slagging off football officials and not of him sobbing that Mr Binky promises to stay up this time. Old rich guys – worried that your mistress might be untrustworthy? You can carry round a simple implement to help you decide. A mirror. If you, like Lord Triesman, look like a moulting giraffe with hay fever, that young girl probably isn't really enjoying bouncing around on you.

Triesman commented that Melissa Jacobs had beautiful eyes – I didn't notice the eyes because all I could see were the teeth like a vandalised graveyard. At least I don't have to worry about a mistress telling the world my secrets, not unless someone's teaching her English in that basement.

FIFA lunatic Sepp Blatter has agreed to look into the allegations of bribery, for 50 grand and an OBE. All the fuss over bribes means that England will have lost out on future opportunities to bribe for the World Cup. Blatter has appointed opera singer Placido Domingo to join their council. I'm sure that Domingo would be most people's first choice for rooting out corruption in a global footballing organisation, now that Pavarotti is dead.

Actually, Blatter put paid to accusations of corruption with his re-election, bagging 260 of the 240 available votes. Sepp thanked delegates and then explained he wouldn't see protesting officials ... not now, not ever! As he was having his eyes plucked out and replaced with shimmering rubies. Even Wayne Rooney expressed alarm when the story was explained to him, by changing the word 'money' for 'whore vouchers'. What could be less dodgy than having an election contest with only one candidate? It's a system that works across Africa and the Middle East, and no one ever kicks up a fuss about it there.

FIFA's Ethics Committee just doesn't sound right – it's like finding out Al-Qaeda have a health and safety department. I feel sorry for England. You gave football to the world. If only they hadn't gone and spoiled everything by being loads better at it. At least you can be proud of the England bid. What better person to demonstrate the virtues of a fair voting system and the scourge of easy money than Prince William?

FIFA officials would never take a bribe. They paid me to say that. I'd like to see the World Cup being held in a Third World country that could use the tournament to improve their facilities, develop better players and create much-needed jobs. Which is why I was backing England's bid.

David Beckham said that he believed passionately in bringing the World Cup to England, as then he can spend a month 5,000 miles away from where his wife lives. Beckham said, 'We have everything in place to hold the World Cup.' Yep, psychotic riot police and a solid industry of multi-lingual prostitutes.

There was the ludicrous story of Beckham being involved with a hooker. Victoria would know if David had been unfaithful, as when he was writing his diary he'd have to come to her to ask how to spell 'prostitute'. Beckham was described as 'furious' but 'calm' – that's exactly the stage directions I would give to someone if they were trying to do a Frank Spencer impression.

Apparently, footballer infidelity is now so commonplace that in parts of the North-West 'yo yo knickered party orifice' is one of the options suggested to female school leavers by careers teachers. It's Beckham's kids I feel sorry for. I'm most worried that this business could rob their children of their innocence and, what's more, disrupt the launch of 9-year-old Romeo's sportswear accessories line. Brooklyn has reached the age where he understands what's going on. He's just completed the 'prostitute wrangling' module of his youth football team.

Can David Beckham still be a role model to young boys? Of course. If there's one life skill I'm sure they'll all need it's strenuously denying you've been with another woman. I also feel for Victoria. She's uncomfortable enough watching him play for LA Galaxy, because the club's named after a chocolate bar. Sadly, despite her pleas, he just won't sign for the San Diego Rice Cakes.

The culture of using prostitutes is so ingrained in football that when Wayne Rooney scores he instinctively leaves money on a chest of drawers next to the goal. The revelations came, as you'd expect with Wayne, thick and fast. I suppose the attraction for a woman is there's a chance that half way through he might just be replaced by Joe Cole. If the stories are correct, then we can certainly see that Rooney has a type. Whores. I always thought Wayne Rooney and Peter Crouch would have to pay someone to sleep with them, but I just assumed that it would be their partners. Wayne's carefully nurtured a family-man image – well, he has since the last time he fucked some hookers.

Wayne's getting smarter because, although he left evidence by way of sex texts, at least he didn't leave an autograph saying 'I fucked you,' like last time. Coleen's family say the days of her being humiliated are over. I'm guessing she's not told them about the job modelling jewellery for Argos. Her parents said they'll never let him in their house again. They've even removed his special flap from the back door. Coleen can't very well turn round and have a go at Wayne for his sexual habits – she's the one fucking a monkey.

At the time, Coleen was pregnant and she did get suspicious. Every time she asked Wayne if he wanted a girl he said, 'Yes, please', and pulled out his wallet. In his defence, maybe Wayne didn't realise a woman can have sex when she's pregnant. It's fine, which was great news for my girlfriend – she was worried she wouldn't be able to keep up her half of the mortgage payments.

A well-known footballer is being blackmailed with a film of an orgy in Las Vegas. An orgy's quite classy for most footballers. If you're wondering, it's basically a gangbang with grapes. Apparently, the three players spent the evening playing the slots, then left the hotel room and headed for the casino. There's an easier way of getting money out of top footballers. Just find one who's about to retire and tell him you need a partner in some shit nightclub somewhere. Premiership players often film hotel-room sex. Especially the foreplay. Basically, the girl with her hand on a Gideon Bible saying, 'I consent.'

So are we going to dedicate an entire front page to every Premiership footballer who's had an affair? 'Cos we could just save the hassle and photocopy a Panini album. Of course, I'm doing them a disservice. I'm sure the vast majority of Premiership players still believe that sex is just a beautiful thing that happens between two, three or more people. You'll never get a Scottish player caught giving bundles of cash to a prostitute. They'd be much more likely to try and palm them off with coupons.

How the hell did Ryan Giggs think he could keep an affair with Imogen Thomas a secret? She was on *Big Brother*! This is a woman whose idea of keeping a diary is sitting on a gold throne in front of a TV camera! You do wonder how Giggs was able to do it but, in fairness, at his age you tend to be up in the night a lot anyway. Personally, I didn't expect this of him – mainly because I couldn't imagine a man could manage to pull with the physique of an under-nourished monkey and the unemotional stare of a cat looking at a penis.

What is it that tempts these men to have sex with attractive, big-titted, sexually available young women? Imogen said, 'He didn't know who I was at first but on the way back to the hotel he said, "It's just clicked – you're Imogen from *Big Brother*."' She thought it was true love from the moment he found out her name a couple of minutes before they had sex. I feel sorry for Imogen – what married footballer would want her now?

Although she said she would never date another footballer. Interesting it's not the fact that he's married that she has found stressful. And she reckons the scandal turned her lesbian. Presumably, she's not acted on it yet because of the current low profile of women's football. Apparently, Imogen's so upset by this new twist she's barely keeping things together at work, even having to ask for help ice-cubing her nipples before *FHM*'s 'A Thong for Europe' special.

Giggs was attempting to imprison people for talking about him, and Ashley Cole shoots people for fun. Footballers are quickly becoming like powerful concentration-camp commandants waiting to pick us off from their balconies. Thousands of fans were chanting his name on the terraces. They say you can't silence a crowd. They've obviously never been to a Partick

Thistle game. If Ryan Giggs was so desperate to keep himself out of the papers and television news he should just have changed his name to Miliband.

It does seem unfair that Imogen Thomas couldn't say what MPs and journalists were saying – but those are the pitfalls of a Welsh education. The papers kept describing her as a 'Welsh beauty queen', which has to be pretty much the definition of a backhanded compliment. Still, it's nice to see two Welsh people on the front cover for something other than a mineshaft disaster.

One of the penalties of fame is that you don't get to have sex with whoever you like. Oh no … that's marriage. People on Twitter liked chatting about Ryan Giggs because his short name didn't use up their precious characters. Jan Vennegoor of Hesselink can pump who he likes.

Are the front pages of the tabloids to be controlled by what's been talked about on Twitter? Expect in-depth reports into the quality of the pub some bloke you don't know is in, and how nice seeded bread is when toasted. TV presenter Lizzie Cundy proudly took up her mantle as freedom fighter by stating we should be able to 'say what we feel' and 'being imprisoned for stating a name is crazy,' which is why I'm sure she won't mind my feeling that I need to say Lizzie Cundy sucks the tiny penises of random farm animals.

I'm unimpressed that people on Twitter could describe what he did to Imogen Thomas in only 140 characters. If I'd spent the night with her, it could only then be described in a 4,000-verse vision-quest poem handed down from father to son. Twitter users have been told that they will face legal action next time they break privacy laws. Trouble is, unless this was announced in a blog about *Dr Who*, none of them will have read it. The law courts don't want social-network users to think they can break the law. I think we went past that point when people on Facebook started grooming and killing teenagers. But nice to see a story about a footballer having sex finally bringing about some regulation.

Ryan Giggs also cheated on his wife with his brother's wife. This is Giggsy at the top of his game – he's always clinical from close range. It's going to make Christmas Day a bit awkward in the Giggs household. Awkward and sexy. What I want to know is how on earth did Ryan Giggs find time to have all these affairs when he works a 90-minute week?

Giggs had insisted there was nothing more important to him than his family, clearly forgetting to add the words … 'not finding out'. He's has been called the Welsh Tiger Woods – you might think that's a lazy comparison, but having a mundane, eight-year affair with your brother's wife in an unfurnished flat is the direct Welsh equivalent of banging a silicone-pumped porn star in the car park of a waffle house.

This must be a real kick in the teeth for Rhodri Giggs. He's spent his whole life with his brother being better than him at everything, and now that includes having sex with his wife. Rhodri said that Ryan won't be able to understand the humiliation. Of course he does – didn't you see him against Barcelona? I can understand how Rhodri must be feeling right now. I used to get annoyed when my brother stole my Action Man. And I really used to love sticking my dick in that. He ruined that for me.

I think Giggs can rebuild his family-man image, providing we don't get too fussed about exactly which family. Poor Rhodri. First the betrayal, then you have to spend a few days with that bloke out of *Two Pints of Lager and a Packet of Crisps*. Is Will Mellor the right person to help cheer you up? The last eight series of *Two Pints* would suggest not.

Stacey and Ryan went to Marbella to try and sort things out, while his balls are taking a well-earned break in the

Maldives. The Giggses are an odd-looking couple. She could fit both his eyes into her mouth. They say a lot of Man U fans are turning against him. I can't confirm that though, as my Urdu/Swedish/Hungarian/Cantonese/Filipino/Arabic/Swahili/Kurdish/Inuit isn't what it was.

Rhodri has warned his brother to stay away from his wife, but Ryan doesn't care. He's shown time and again that he's capable of bending it in from 30 yards. It emerged that Ryan paid for his sister-in-law to have an abortion. Ever the crowd pleaser, Ryan put a smile on the face of the staff at the clinic. When they pulled the foetus out, he did a couple of keepie uppies before volleying it into the dustbin.

I think these revelations are just a clever move on Ryan's part. He's had a great playing career, but he's getting old. I reckon he's just hoping to get put out to stud. He just wants to end his days siring Wales's 2034 World Cup squad. He could be in for a shock. The realities of stud farming mean he'll probably just end up being shuffled by a bumpkin with a glass jar and marigold gloves, after being tricked into mounting a pair of fake plastic buttocks.

Forget all their shagging about, the real story about the Giggs brothers is why are they ageing at four times the rate of normal humans? Rhodri Giggs looks like Ryan Giggs has been dead for a month. Giggs spent £30,000 on hair treatments. He can afford to treat himself now that Travelodge prices have gone down. He spent £30,000 on a machine to prevent hair loss. Which sounds like a lot of money for something totally useless that doesn't work, but pretty good value compared with a super-injunction.

Wayne Rooney also decided to have a hair transplant. Someone ought to tell him they can do faces now, too. It seems a shame to jeopardise all that hard work they put in training him to stop fighting his reflection. Surely, the one advantage of paying for sex is you really don't have to bother about your appearance. Coleen wanted Wayne to have a hair transplant before they tried for another child – because she doesn't want to risk having another bald baby. The other United players are already bantering with Wayne – Rio Ferdinand's bet him he can't last ten days with a ponytail without being shagged by Ryan Giggs. Was Wayne even going bald? He might have just been losing his winter coat. Part of the operation was done with lasers. The smell in the surgery must have been lovely. Fresh chips.

Still, good to see that Rooney's found a better way to cover up his bald patch than paying two women to sit on it. He tweeted, 'I was going bald at 25 why not.' You've got an IQ of 25 but at no point have you ever considered reading a fucking book.

Think of the advantages of a bald head for a Premiership player. They're always getting done for speeding. You could just polish it up to a shine with Nivea then, if you were flashed by a camera, just claim an angel stole your car. It must be great being bald. So low maintenance. You just get up, have a quick half-hour cry in front of the mirror, and you're ready to face the afternoon. Rooney has been warned not to have sex until his hair transplant takes root. It was massive relief for Coleen, but for some other women it meant missing out on a major source of income.

Apparently, Wayne Rooney initially refused to sign a new contract with Man U. Come on, Sir Alex, is it really that hard to forge an 'X'? He hardly scored at all last season – as Coleen had moved his hutch into the spare room. When Sir Alex Ferguson heard about Rooney's insubordination his face was bright red, so it was impossible to tell if he was upset or not. Wayne should remember no one's got the better of Fergie, who even bounced back after those crystal meth problems in the

Black Eyed Peas. Ferguson wasn't speaking to Rooney for a month. I should think he's run out of things to say – there's only so many ways you can rephrase 'run after the ball, kick the ball'.

What can a man like Wayne Rooney possibly do with a quarter of a million pounds a week? Shred it to make a nest? Sir Alex has finally got to the age where people decide to leave all their money to a pet. He was overheard saying, 'I want to leave Manchester United' – but that's simply how Wayne orders a taxi. A quarter of a million a week and he's only 25. Then again, we mustn't forget that's nearly 60 in human years. This is the thing – you can give Wayne and Coleen as much money as you like, but they're always only one more missing tooth away from appearing on *Jeremy Kyle*. Is it immoral for one man to earn £250,000 a week when in Haiti the children of dirt-poor peasants have their coffins carried on the backs of battered motorbikes? Maybe, but on the flip side, what about that goal against Arsenal last year? I mean, wow.

★

Rooney was punished for swearing into the camera after he scored a goal earlier in the year. This sort of thing doesn't just bring the Premiership into disrepute, it tarnishes the entire spit-roasting community. Swearing's actually the safest celebration option for Rooney, as when he pulls his shirt over his head, he believes the world ceases to exist. I may sound unfashionable but I happen to think using the 'F' word on TV is unacceptable. Unless, of course, your blowtorch has run out of gas half way through caramelising a crème brûlée. Now Wayne may have to attend anger-management classes. Which will involve wiring a plastic banana up to a 9-volt car battery. I don't think shouting 'What do you want?!' at the viewers of Sky

Sports should incur a ban – I think it makes him one of Britain's greatest moral philosophers. In Wayne's defence, it must be very easy to get 'delight' muddled up with 'furious violent rage'. It was strange to see a player yell obscenities into a camera that wasn't being held by a terrified apprentice right-back filming an orgy. The Man U board are furious at the ban. After seeking legal advice, they said it was 'really not on' and a 'jolly poor show'.

Man U were also upset about losing the Champions League final to Barcelona. Ryan Giggs briefly tried to sue the concept of victory. Big matches like that can be very scary, as domestic violence soars. But at least the wives get a two-hour break while the players are on the pitch. So what if Barcelona's Eric Abidal had part of his liver removed? George Best had somebody else's liver removed! Lionel Messi was left unmarked for much of the match. He's quite small, so fooled the Man U players, who thought he was really far away. Following their defeat the Man U team had a restrained evening of introspection, apparently unable to even muster the enthusiasm to high-five each other during a spit roast.

Alex Ferguson says he has no intention of leaving Man U for the next few years. Well, he probably never had the intention to look like a mouldy blancmange in a suit and spend his life shouting at sex-cases to run towards a ball – but these things happen. I imagine that every time Alex Ferguson tries to get his players to gather round in a circle for a team talk they automatically pull their shorts down and start masturbating over the ball.

Man U striker Nani has a life-size statue of himself in his house. No doubt just vanity on his part, but a lot of other Premiership players use them. They leave them by the window so they've got an alibi when a teenage hairdresser goes missing.

Mohamed Al-Fayed has told any Fulham fans who don't like his statue of Michael Jackson to 'go to hell'. Er, if they don't like the statue they certainly don't want to meet him in person. It seems strange to have a statue outside the ground of someone who wasn't a player – although Michael did try to get into the youth team several times. If Al-Fayed creates a statue of everyone who visits the ground only once there will soon be a model of the guy from the Passport Office who delivered the letter telling him to fuck off. It would be in better taste to erect a statue of the Green Cross Code man at the entrance to that Parisian underpass.

Ashley Cole shot a young student in the stomach. He got the gun out and fired off a few shots to help former Liverpool striker Torres feel at home. It must have been an accident – I can't believe anyone would pull out a gun at the Chelsea training ground and not aim for John Terry. Of course, the real tragedy is that he lived with Cheryl all that time. There was a weapon in the house, and nothing happened.

Last time he scored for England, John Terry dedicated it to a strong little fighter he had met on the plane. There was an uncomfortable silence among the press, relieved by Terry bringing out a photo of an ill child, rather than the terrified air hostess they were expecting. Footballers have a simple outlook on the world – 'I see sick child I am good man, I see pretty lady I am bad man.' Just once I'd like to introduce a Premiership footballer to a terminally ill prostitute and watch their synapses slowly melt with confusion.

England footballing wunderkind Jack Wilshere was questioned over threatening a cabbie. In his defence, he's 18, on £50,000 a week and should be dead by now, three hookers having been rescued from a five-star hotel, trapped beneath his drink-and-drug addled corpse, his face having been lifted off and replaced with a glimmering emerald mask. He just needs a mentor. Maybe Gazza should put on a sheet with two eyeholes and turn up as the ghost of football yet to come. Or, if we just wait a month or two, he probably won't even have to bother with the sheet.

Gazza was charged with drink-driving again last year. The police suspected he'd been drinking heavily when they noticed he was Gazza. They asked him how fast he was going – he didn't know, but in fairness, he hadn't even realised he was in a car. Gazza will now face another trial for drink-driving – that'll be very worrying for him. I wonder if there's anything he can do to calm his nerves? Gazza has to keep driving because otherwise people see all the cans and bottles in the back and start chucking their newspapers in, thinking it's a recycling bin.

I hate to think of what might happen if he bent over in the showers! He'd lose his balance, slump to the floor and curl into a sobbing ball. It's tragic; he's now not only addicted to alcohol and Class A drugs, he's addicted to rehab, too. It's only £600 a week. The Priory costs two grand, so that's pretty much budget rehab. I'm guessing it's just a room in a Travelodge with a picture of Alex Higgins sellotaped to the mini-bar door. He's pissed away £14 million and he's been living off a lump sum he received in 2008 when he took his empties back.

To make matters worse, he's been evicted from his cottage. That must just involve the landlord spinning him round a few times so he can't find his way back. Apparently, Gazza's now arrested so often he's got his own push-button option when you phone Tyneside police. 'For incidents involving Gazza, press one, for all other crimes ...' Actually, I hope he doesn't die. His cremation would be like *Piper Alpha* going up.

It looked briefly as if Gazza would be the new manager of non-league Garforth Town. The first time a football team would be sponsored by the Samaritans. To be fair, Gazza's great at making substitutions. If he can't afford vodka, he just uses Mr Sheen window cleaner. Gazza has stressed that his booze problems don't make him a bad person. I agree. It's knocking women about that does that. He's worried he'll die from liver failure. I suspect there's more chance it'll just wait till he passes out, then crawl up his throat and escape.

★

Ricky Hatton snorted seven lines of cocaine in a hotel room. He worked out it was cheaper than eating the peanuts from the mini-bar. I thought the only boxer who was in need of being so heavily medicated was Frank Bruno. Hatton disgraced the sport. Most of the people involved in boxing don't take drugs – they're too busy selling them. Apparently, the cocaine made Ricky 'very paranoid'. Obviously not paranoid enough to notice a video camera six inches away. Hatton beat himself up over this – well, he beat himself up a bit, then hugged himself and lolled on the ropes until the bell went. Hatton has an advantage over most cocaine users – there's nothing much left of his nose to destroy. Who'd have thought you'd find it easier to go ten rounds with Ricky Hatton in a boxing ring than down the pub? Ricky now faces the biggest fight of his life – it's against Charlie Sheen, for a gram.

Emma Bowe, who exposed Ricky, said she contacted the *News of the World* for Ricky's own good. Well, drugs helplines don't tend to pay as much as the papers, do they? What a ridiculous nickname, 'Hitman'. It's hardly like he kills people for money. He just gives them brain damage. Tragic to see a boxer destroyed by drink and drugs. Rather than the traditional route, where their brain rattles about their skull like a pea in a whistle till they're only fit to do slurred meet-and-greets at Cinderella's nightspot in Ilford.

★

Tiger Woods held a press conference to apologise for his behaviour. It was either incredibly sincere and heartfelt, or incredibly insincere and cynical, depending on whether you're American or British. Loredana Jolie says Tiger Woods was a nice bloke because he wore a condom. Funny how women think that means you're gallant when it usually means you've taken one look at them and thought, 'What a dirty old skank.' Tiger has been successfully cured of his sex addiction. All it took was the love of his family and a gloryhole cut into a wasps' nest. Of course, I could never do what he did. I fucking hate golf!

At some fucking tournament, Rory McIlroy played the worst game of golf since … well, let's face it, they're all shit. It was horrifying, but at least it was interesting – which I find is par for the course when hanging out with a Northern Irishman. Apparently, he was playing with the wrong clubs all the way round – every time he asked for a nine iron they just thought he was telling them where he came from. On the bright side, if a 22-year-old from Northern Ireland can say the day his little ball bounced off a tree is the worst day of his life, that peace process must be working spectacularly well. There are no losers in golf, Rory, because there are no winners in golf. There are just lots of men walking around on some grass.

He made amends by winning the US Open. Mind you, the way things are going in Belfast, Rory, I wouldn't go cutting about in that green jacket. Petrol-bombing rioters in Belfast seem as committed as ever. In fact, at £1.34 a litre, I'd say even more so.

★

There was a betting scandal in cricket. Suspicions first arose when Pakistan sent John Higgins on to bowl. Mazhar Majeed has been accused of rigging the game for a gambling syndicate. He protested his innocence, adding, 'Two grand says I get off.' I say never trust an outdoor sport where you don't have to take your jumper off. Apart from Scottish dogging, of course. You can't risk getting your nipples frozen to the windscreen. Mohammad Amir kept getting wide balls. To be fair, it's not easy bowling when you're filling in a betting slip. Fans threw tomatoes at the Pakistan cricket bus. They all missed, and a man in Karachi picked up 50 grand from Ladbrokes. The owner of Croydon FC was alleged to be involved? The people of Croydon are heartbroken. Nobody has poured that much money into Croydon since the locals clubbed together have the town planner assassinated.

The *Sun* did a special piece focusing on all the moments when Pakistan played badly for no reason. Can you imagine sports journalists trying to do a piece about all the times English sportsmen have totally failed for no reason? Oh yes, that's just called 'sports reporting'.

★

After a sexist debacle, Richard Keys resigned, blaming 'dark forces'. Or, as Andy Gray calls them, 'women'. There's an irony in the fact that football's gained a female employee and lost a pair of tits. I hear Andy did pop down to try and apologise during half-time. And he was definitely sincere, because he decided against taking his ironing along. As a Celtic fan, I'm appalled that an official's ability has been questioned because of their sex, rather than their religion. I'm surprised at Andy Gray. I'm sure he's no stranger to women watching 90 minutes of physical exertion. Then enduring a couple of minutes more when he's managed to get his trousers off. The media is a strange world. Andy Gray said women don't know the offside rule and he never works at Wembley again, whereas when Michael McIntyre says it he fills the bloody stadium. Andy is the type of man who believes that there is no place in football for women. Which is just plain wrong. Who are they supposed to roast? The goalkeepers?

I'm sure Andy will enjoy the irony of his sexism over the coming months when he spends his time watching daytime TV, cleaning and getting the dinner ready. Keys and Gray made the mistake of thinking that people were tuning in to see them. Men would tune in to watch the football if it were presented by a sea serpent. Footballers from around the country were desperate to condemn the comments, which included, 'I wouldn't,' when looking at a female official. You can see why Premiership footballers have come out against him. You know that no matter what she looks like, they would. Where will Andy and Richard work next? Do Al Jazeera even broadcast football? Andy Gray tried to work out how his career was destroyed, by drawing circles and arrows on a copy of Germaine Greer's *The Female Eunuch*.

I hear it wasn't easy for Sky to sack Gray:

'Andy, we're giving you the sack.'

'If it's my sack you're interested in, sweetheart …'

'No, Andy, listen, we're downsizing.'

'Downsizing? I'll be doing the opposite if you keep bending over darling …'

'Here's your P45.'

'P45!? P69 more like …'

Some claim that Gray's position at Sky became vulnerable because he launched legal action against the *News of the World*. The *Sun*, where I write a column, is of course owned by the same company, but I can promise you that I have never been censored by the corporation. In fact, I have some very interesting gossip you might like to hear. Apparently, when having sex, Rupert Murdoch likes to have a kalsdjffnlk … Sorry I just dozed off there, onto my keyboard. What was I talking about? And why is there a dart in my neck? Two darts in my ne … dsfhiNKLcjkfbazzzzzzzz.

★

Wimbledon. Two weeks of sitting on the sofa drifting in and out of fantasies where the Williams sisters, beads of sweat trickling down their cleavages, help me shift that new wardrobe upstairs.

There are always arguments, but how can you expect the players to behave respectfully when the umpire is basically sitting in a high chair. You wouldn't catch me getting pushed about by a giant baby. I didn't say it doesn't happen, I just said you wouldn't catch me.

Andy Murray won his first-round match in the rain, becoming the only Scotsman in London with a roof over his head. With projected career earnings of £250 million, he looked grimly preoccupied all the way to the bank. I wanted him to win, just to see if he'd even fucking smile. My money's on a tiny grimace of triumph, like a rapist's cum face.

Andy Murray's success has persuaded a lot of people in Scotland to get out on the tennis courts. They aren't playing, but at least they'll be getting some fresh air while they take their crack. He bowed to the Queen. If I were the Queen, I'd drop that particular tradition. At her age, there's always the chance that if they bow their heads they'll notice a bit of wee on her shoes. No one's blaming her; maybe one of her footmen didn't get the chance to run the royal Tena Lady through the mangle that morning. Though, as I've said, she only costs us individually 62p each. So when I meet her I know my first line. 'Your Majesty, if you've got a quid I've got 38p change.' I wanted to see Andy Murray win Wimbledon – it would've been inter-esting to see someone from Dumfries work out how to handle a cup live on TV.

★

A balloonist keeps trying to float across the English Channel attached to nothing more than a collection of party balloons. All he's going to do is die in a way that'll put his children off going to parties for the rest of their lives.

A 75-year-old man had to be airlifted after attempting a 40-foot tombstoning stunt in Dorset. It's a drain on the rescue services to do things like this – I don't mind him having another go, but why not make his next jump directly into a grave? You'd have thought with the length and width of a 75-year-old's scrotum, he would've sailed gently down like a parachuting bushbaby.

A 13-year-old boy has become the youngest person to climb Mount Everest. A child shouldn't be allowed to do something as dangerous as that. He should be at home, using social networking sites to talk to people pretending to be his own age.

A Frenchman called Philippe Croizon swam the Channel, despite having no arms or legs. Philippe first had the idea to attempt his epic swim when he noticed there were steps to get on the Eurostar. Philippe volunteered to do the swim – well, someone at his swimming club said, 'Hands up who doesn't want to do it.' For crossing the Channel, swimmers are usually given a badge but, as he's got no sleeves to sew it on, they gave him a hat instead. He may have no legs but on the plus side at least there's no chance of him getting a verruca. He wasn't even able to practise at his local swimming pool – mainly because, without arms or legs, it's impossible for him to get into the water without bombing. A government minister phoned Philippe and said, 'Nothing is impossible.' He should watch Philippe try to scratch his own arse. Philippe's a terrific example to others. Hopefully, more people will look at him and follow in his footsteps – well, drag marks. I'm sad he missed the opportunity to pull himself out of the water at the end and shout 'Shark!'

★

Ah, sport. In the classical world I could have perhaps enjoyed watching it, as it was training for battle. I would have sat engrossed as lithe men leapt at each other with weapons, happy for them to be celebrated by my society because they would soon be dead. I would have watched their tricks and flips in a different light, knowing that they would soon be slashed to pieces to defend a trade route, their muscular bodies impaled on a stake as a grim warning, their hand-to-eye co-ordination counting for naught now that their hands and eyes had been taken as trophies, while I tried to get into their widows' togas by writing poems in their memory.

'I think about whether I care and decide that, on balance, I don't'

★★★★

Paul Marsh drives my daughter and me out to Mugdock Park. There's always something slightly sinister about a warm day in Scotland - like somebody's left something on. It's a bank holiday, even though it's a fucking Tuesday, and a bunch of schoolies who recognise me surround me in the playpark. None of them say anything. They just look at us silently, like the end of *The Birds*.

On the way home, my daughter remembers a game where we guess if people we see in the distance are going to look happy or unhappy up close. I guess unhappy every time and I'm right every time. We all start laughing a bit hysterically at how scunnered everyone is.

An old woman at a bus stop actually looks like she is having a laugh on a mobile phone, so I say happy, but she is mental and arguing with herself.

I say, 'People are always unhappy on their own, they're happier in groups.'

'You can't walk around smiling,' says Paul, distractedly. 'You'd look crazy.'

The most Scottish thing I've ever heard. When we get to the West End, there are some twos and threes laughing.

★

I go visit this girl I see sometimes. We order pizza and watch some Hallmark Channel movie about Ted Bundy. She chain-smokes in bed and, because she clearly has something to say, I pre-empt her.

'I don't mind sincerity so long as I can laugh about it,' I smile.

She tells me she's thinking of marrying her boyfriend. I mention J. G. Ballard's idea that marriage is something men came up with to restrain themselves from fucking everyone and killing each other over it, and that they pay a terrible price.

'That's sexist bullshit.' She's rolling up and looking at me with one eye closed. 'Women don't have any say in this? They don't have their own sexuality? They're just things for men to fuck or make rules so they can't fuck?'

'Well, men did make the rules. Marriage is something that men came up with, everything is, men are in charge …'

'It just denies that women have any sexuality, any desire to be unfaithful …'

'Statistically, men are more unfaithful than women …'

'And you don't think there's any trouble with that data in a society where women are taught to feel ashamed of their sexuality, that men who sleep around are a bit crafty and women who do that are sluts? You think they tell people with clipboards about who they've been fucking?'

'Hey, I'm not J. G. Ballard, I'm just saying … Fuck it, he's dead now.'

Her roll-up goes out and she reaches for the lighter, which won't catch. 'Is that what you're doing here? Fucking me because of some genetic imperative?'

'No. I guess … I think everything is a communication.'

'What are you trying to communicate then?'

'I guess I'm trying to say I can help. You could take some money, just take it, go on holiday for a few months.'

'I can't take your money. Really, I can't.'

'You can. You should just go.'

'Are you sure you're not here to exploit my unhappiness? By fucking me?'

'No … I mean, no, I'm not sure.'

I put my arm round her and she hugs me.

'What am I communicating?' she asks.

'That you're very, very unhappy.'

I lie in the dark. The lighter occasionally brightens the room as she sits smoking. I feel like a caveman and we're taking turns at keeping watch. I fall asleep quickly, even though she has been talking about killing herself.

★

On the commuter train home in the morning, every cunt hassles me. I don't know how unapproachable, preoccupied or fucked off I'd have to look to be left alone.

Gary texts me.

Amanda Hugnkiss, I FUCKING GET IT! I KNOW WHO YOU ARE! A DEAD MAN!

I don't know how he figured it out but he is, I reflect, the least of my worries. I think about whether I care and decide that, on balance, I don't.

I'm in the stateroom playing *FIFA* when my agent phones. She'd stopped ringing me for quite a few months, but nowadays I have to answer. She says I'm going to be on *8 Out of 10 Cats* with Jonathan Ross. I'm momentarily tempted to pull it but I can't. Any time I meet Ross, or Jimmy Carr, they pull me aside and address me conspiratorially about a Scottish terrorist organisation they claim to belong to in thick Ayrshire accents. At first I found this a bit wearing but they are so insistent, their accents so accurate, their knowledge of Scottish history and sense of injustice so comprehensive, it's really quite overwhelming. Ross keeps saying he's going to shoot the Queen on the Royal Variety and I honestly don't know if he's fucking joking.

She tells me I'm getting asked to do *I'm a Celebrity*. 12 celebrities marooned deep in the Australian jungle a full 50 yards from Ant and Dec's hotel. You might as well just fill a big fish tank with urine and drop in eight labelled turds, removing the loser each week. Seeing the line-up in the paper of who's going there always feels like the bit at the BAFTAs where they show who died this year. I watched *I'm a Celebrity* last year and Gillian McKeith had a jungle breakdown that made Marlon Brando's character in *Apocalypse Now* look like Tarzan.

I say, 'That programme's … demented.'

She says, 'They don't really pay much any more because of the rapist.'

I'm filling a mug at the tap and my hands are shaking. I lift it up to my mouth and I suddenly think, FUCK THIS. Is this what I worked so hard for? To be frightened in my own flat, to drag this feeling of dread around with me? I know there's something I can do about this. I decide I'm going to turn this around. Showbusiness isn't going to get me like this. Slowly the dread goes and my hands steady and I feel just the general anxiety I have when I focus on work.

I'm out running round the Botanic Gardens. There's two student lassies smoking a joint on a bench and I try to speed up every time I go past that bit. It's really bright but so early that it's still cold. I go out for runs every morning now. The first few were terrible, walking and trotting like an old bastard, but now I'm going three times round the park and even doing push-ups when there's nobody about.

It took me a couple of weeks but now I'm on top of everything. Yes, the police have been in touch a couple of times and, yes, it's worrying, but I'm taking steps now. I started by hiring a yoga teacher. Every morning she comes round and every evening I work at it on my own. I also went to a sex shop with a gay guy I know from the Stand Comedy Club and got a butt plug. It's uncomfortable at first but it's really starting to have an effect. This rape is going to be nothing for me, I've taken it into my own hands. I have a kind of femidom thing for my arse as well.

I jog right down to Kelvingrove Park, have coffee then get a taxi back to the flat. I put on a Bonnie Prince Billie record and warm down. I'm stretching my hip out in the stateroom when my mobile goes. It's my pal Stewart. The papers say the comedian Richard Herring, who used to be in Lee and Herring, has been fucked to death.

★ ★ ★ ★

I believe ... that the real truth that dare not speak itself is that no one is in control, absolutely no one. This stuff is ruled by the equations of dynamics and chaos. There may be entities seeking control, but to seek control is to take enormous aggravation upon yourself. It's like trying to control a dream.

Terence McKenna

We are so much the victims of abstraction that with the Earth in flames we can barely rouse ourselves to wander across the room and look at the thermostat.

Terence McKenna

★ ★ ★ ★

12

We each of us live in our own little reality tunnel, seeing things through the prism of our own prejudice and expectations. Look at *Star Trek*. To us, the Federation is benign, travelling the galaxy in a quest for knowledge. Wait a minute, though. Some planets are just holiday worlds. Umm, did they choose that, or did the Federation tell them that suddenly their whole planet was going to be washing beach towels and handing out cocktails? Is that what the USS *Enterprise* is flying about the galaxy looking for – new sex worlds? Perhaps the formal name is 'holiday world', but of course they are actually sex worlds.

If we take the *Enterprise* as being representative of the Federation, it seems to have three approaches when it discovers new alien life. FUCK IT, STUN IT or KILL IT. And, wait a minute, that ship they fly about in seems to be pretty much a giant floating gun. That's not good, is it? Often, they are so keen to shoot something as powerfully as possible that they *divert energy from their life support systems* to the gun. Yet we see them as being altruistic, floating about in the USS *Peacegun*, looking for places to go on holiday.

I'd imagine the Federation looks quite different if you're living on an undiscovered world with a lot of beaches. And maybe *Star Trek* looks different if you live in South America and you have a history of explorers being the first stage of colonising invasions. Does that sound stupid to you? That's because I'm from a different reality tunnel. One where I swim up and down all day thinking about the ideology of *Star Trek*, when I'm supposed to be writing a fucking book.

One of the things we heard during the global financial crisis was that nobody could have foreseen this. Everyone was queuing up to tell us how unexpected this was. But that's just the view from their reality tunnel. Remember those anti-globalisation riots? Weren't they saying that the global financial system was unsustainable? As Slavoj Žižek points out in *First As Tragedy, Then As Farce*, in Seattle 14,000 extra cops were drafted in to deal with the sheer number of people saying that the international financial system was unstable. That's more troops than we sent to Iraq. So, while we are told that nobody could have foreseen the dangers, if we were trying to quantify how many people were actually predicting the collapse, it would be fair to say that there was an army of them.

Let's not forget that with environmental disaster, profiteering on commodity prices, the risks we take with the food chain, and mobile-phone masts springing up everywhere, it's a lot more likely that you'll be killed by a bank or a big corporation than by Al-Qaeda. What we call Al-Qaeda set itself up as an operation that individuals would come to with terror plans and bin Laden would decide whether or not to invest. It's interesting that if you want to create worldwide chaos and perpetrate widespread evil, the ideal model is that of a venture capital firm.

It seems to me that the world financial system is now geared towards privatisation. Countries borrow money and the price for keeping the rate of interest down is to privatise stuff. Who do we borrow the money from? Hedge funds, bankers, speculators. Why do they want us to privatise? Because it opens up areas of enormous profit for them. You can choose not to drink

Coca-Cola but you can't not educate your kids. You can't not go to the hospital when you're sick. You can't not drink water.

Look on the upside for a moment. The world is being destroyed by corporate interests but we're just at that point in the horror movie before we work out how to kill the monsters. Of course things look bleak now, but ask yourself this – how do you kill a corporation? One of us will work it out! And what then? What if we win? I mean it, have you thought about what the world could be like if people took control of their own reality? We can forget about war. We can evolve, we can explore the stars and we can focus on hating the people who really deserve it – our fucking parents.

Branded goods always get me. People paying to walk around like sandwich boards. I imagine that the FCUK logo started as some corporate guy making a *Trading Places*-style bet. 'Bet you I can get them to wear at hat with FUCK on it. I'm a STUPID FCUK. Right there on their STUPID FCUKing head. Ahhahahhhaa!' In a few years' time they'll be burning those logos onto them like they were cattle. 'Here you go. It says I'm a stupid CNUT.' Sizzle. Scream. Sizzle. Sizzle.

More websites than ever are selling fake designer clothes, luggage, DVDs and perfume. Let's not forget there are real victims here. It breaks my heart to think of Mr Dolce or Mr Gabbana having to return to their hovels in Milan to tell their families that, because of copyright infringement, there'll be no diamond sauce to go with the terrified homeless teenager they're eating for tea tonight.

Remember, people. Pirated goods come at a price. Usually a bloody good one. I know from experience that stuff bought off the internet often turns out not to be quite as described. Still, if I turn the light out and 'she' wedges it right back between her thighs I can hardly tell. So, the next time a little Vietnamese man comes up to you in a motorway service station and offers you cheap DVDs, say 'no' and keep saying 'no'. It's the only way to get the price right down.

A French court has ruled that Renault can call their latest car 'Zoe', despite objections from the parents of Zoe Renault, who claim their daughter will be teased at school. It happened at my school to Henry Hoover. And Max Stength-Anusol nearly killed himself. Bacardi have a similar legal dispute with me. Over my plans later this year to become known in the tabloids as the Bacardi Coke Rapist. Presumably the biggest problem isn't that you'll be named the same as a car. It's that you'll be named the same as a serial killer. That's what happened to my best friend Dennis Nilsen. Woke up one morning to find hundreds of people with the same name were angry because he'd eaten all those men. I give fair warning now that if you're called Frankie Boyle and don't want the stigma of being named the same as someone associated for ever with horrific crimes, you have until the next *X Factor* final to change your name.

A Spanish woman even registered ownership of the sun and wants to charge people to use it. Ridiculous. You can't own the sun any more than you can own the oil in the ground or charge people for the water that falls from the sky.

BP attempted to stem the Deepwater Horizon oil spill by pumping water into the mouth of the leak faster than the mess came out. Actualising Donald Rumsfeld's fantasy of water-boarding the earth.

They tried to stop the oil spill with a giant funnel, underwater robots and firing cannons of rubbish at the hole. Is it just me or did BP's troubleshooting decisions seem to be decided by a primary-school competition? I was waiting for a machine made of thousands of tiny ponies that turn the oil into choco-late drops. The one good thing about the leak is that people will be forced to eat more oily fish, as there's no longer any other kind.

BP was worth half as much as it was before the accident. Which is ironic as they'd discovered more oil than they had in years. Just unfortunate it's not in barrels, but in the lungs of hundreds of thousands of pelicans. Barack Obama presented BP execs with the financial reparations they should pay the people of the Gulf Coast. They presented him with JFK's brain wrapped in next week's newspaper and a BP points card.

A Chinese tanker ran aground and spilled oil into the Great Barrier Reef. Environmental groups called it a tragedy for the world's ecology that could have incredibly far-reaching consequences for life on earth, while the Chinese authorities called it 'Stage Two'. If the tanker breaks up and oil continues to flood out, the Great Barrier Reef may no longer be the world's largest living organism. Instead that title would go to the Chinese. Fair play to China – it has lifted 350 million people out of poverty this year. By shooting them for theft.

Developing nations say that rich Western countries aren't doing enough to help them deal with the effects of climate change, but that's not the case. We're going to help them deal with drought by submerging them under the ocean.

People in Germany were dying from E. coli-infected salad. Across Scotland everybody was going, 'Told you that stuff was dodgy.' I confess I caught an infection from an unhygienic cucumber. Just one of the perils of my particular method of shoplifting. The trick is just to wear a cowboy hat, then walking out that way looks a little less odd … it's up my arse. I've wedged the cucumber up my arse. My arse.

★

Chancellor Angela Merkel says multiculturalism hasn't worked in Germany. She added her government would search for a solution, some kind of final … then the mic went dead.

In France you can now be fined for having your face covered up. This is going to be extremely unpopular with bondage fetishists and gimps, which, let's face it, is most French people. Fortunately, they are also masochists, so a fine will only add an extra thrill to the experience. Any French women seen wearing a burqa will be fined 250 euros. So, if you're a black nun in Paris have your purse ready, this could get expensive. They're actually arresting women who wear them. The mugshot photos will be interesting. You can say what you like about burqas, but without one I'd never have got into that Muslim women's knitting circle. Damn, that was good hummus!

This story affects us all, not least me. All of a sudden it's 'burka' with a '-ka'. And I'd only just got used to spelling it '-qa'. Still, in the spirit of Raoul Moat, they'll have to prize that Scrabble trophy from my cold, dead hands. Banning the burka is taking away women's freedom of choice about whether they want to look like an evil shuttlecock. We would never persecute a minority in such a way. It's just not British. I should imagine we'll stick to pushing burning rags and dog shit through their letterboxes.

That said, Tory MP Philip Hollobone launched a bill at Westminster to make it illegal for people to cover their faces in public. Have a quick look at a photo of Philip's face so you can see why he thinks this. It's like a police Identikit computer has crashed and given him the features of every major paedophile of our generation.

★

Just when I thought Tony Blair couldn't get any more mental, he converted to Catholicism. That must be fucking weird, listening to confession with Tony Blair. 'I lost my temper with the kids, missed church on Sunday, killed a million Iraqis, was rude to the wife … Sorry, Father? Go back? Which one?'

He even wrote an autobiography. A lot of people couldn't put Blair's book down. They are the same people who can't pick it up. British soldiers and Iraqi children who've had their arms blown off. He revealed in the book that he was a bit of a drinker. When Tony was quizzed over what was the worst thing he'd ever done while pissed, he simply answered, 'Cherie'. It's no wonder Gordon Brown got so frustrated – every cabinet meeting was taken up by Tony singing 'Magic Moments', then claiming the next day he didn't even know the words. Blair describes the early years with Brown as a relationship as close as lovers. Can you imagine making love to Gordon Brown? He was so creased and wrinkled. The image I have in my head is that pumping him would be very similar to when you are camping and, in order to deflate the air bed, you have to lie on it to get the last of the air out.

Tony Blair donated the book's profits to the Royal British Legion. Which is a bit like Emperor Hirohito donating air miles to his kamikaze pilots.

Peter Mandelson also published his memoirs. You've got to admire him. It's not easy to type with hooves. To be honest, I always found him untrustworthy but, after reading it, well, how can you dislike the man who invented the internet and kidney dialysis?

Blair promoted his book in an interview with Andrew Marr, where he looked like a howler monkey enraged by the smell of his own farts. Footage also turned up of Carla Bruni on *Eurotrash* talking about sex books. Like that's the most embarrassing thing that's ever happened on *Eurotrash*. Her item was bookended by Jean Paul Gaultier enthusiastically demonstrating a pair of dildo boots and Antoine de Caunes interviewing a willy hypnotist.

We've all done sexy stuff in our past that's came back to haunt us. I know I have, I changed its nappy this morning.

Samantha Cameron would never ask a French TV presenter if he liked her titties, as she has been bred for power. You look at Samantha Cameron and realise her favourite children's books must have been *The Very Silent and Subservient Caterpillar* and *Spot Nods Sadly while Meeting Brave Children*. The book Carla was talking about taught French people to say to the English 'You make me very hot.' Of course, a woman saying that to the average English bloke would simply lead to a mumbled apology and an attempt to bleed your radiators.

Carla's husband, French president Nicolas Sarkozy, requested shorter security guards. That'll be a tough request to fulfil – for much of the year most potential candidates will be appearing in panto. Why doesn't he just stick with his normal security guards? Those guys are prepared to take a bullet in the knee for him. Sarkozy's rival, Dominique Strauss-Kahn, the ex-MD of the International Monetary Fund, was arrested in the States and charged with attempted rape. I say, let's not rush to judge. I mean, why should we think that being a banker might make him more inclined to behave in an unethical way outside the decent values of society?

Strauss-Kahn has denied any wrong-doing. The US has taken the line that he is innocent until proven French. The maid picked him out at an identity parade. 'Identity parade' always sounds like so much fun, like Mardi Gras or Gay Pride. You imagine she was forced to identify him despite the fact that he was dressed as Captain Jack Sparrow and hanging from the makeshift rigging on lorry driving past at 5 mph.

He was charged with an illegal sex act. That's impressive. In the midst of a serious sexual assault, imagine going off road and inventing sex acts that haven't even been put on the statute books. During a clumsy, frenzied sexual attack the last thing you want to be doing is dealing with the straps on harnesses, unruly livestock and uncooperative midgets. Some people say you should never joke about rape, that it can never be a subject for humour. I ask those people to picture this: Piers Morgan being raped by Bungle from *Rainbow*.

Italian Prime Minister Silvio Berlusconi is alleged to have slept with a 17-year-old prostitute. Prosecutors in Italy say that in exchange for sex, Berlusconi gave her cash and jewellery. He also gave her nightmares and a lifelong phobia of sun-dried sausage. He's denied the allegations – surely it's just a question of matching the teeth marks on the hooker's bum with his dentures? He's old enough to be her granddad! I worry that if he did pay for sex, he sellotaped the money inside a birthday card. In Silvio's defence, when you're 74 you don't want to be having sex with someone your own age – all those wrinkles rubbing together, it'd be like jogging in corduroy. When he cums it must be like having a handful of sand thrown in your eyes.

If Berlusconi did give a teenage prostitute £7,000 to just sit on her bed and talk about politics then he's a bigger pervert than I thought. It's also alleged that Berlusconi had sex with a weather girl while a handful of people watched. Could have been the one off *Daybreak*, then.

It's been claimed that Arnold Schwarzenegger has three secret love children. This was inevitable. How on earth can a sex-mad Austrian possibly keep all his love children secret? Oh, wait a minute … The photos don't show much of a resemblance. Then again, Arnie doesn't look much like Danny DeVito either, and they're twins.

The allegations came out after Arnold Schwarzenegger stood down as Governor of California in a ceremony that saw him lowered into a vat of molten steel before being cut into pieces by a giant metal press.

★

Robert Mugabe was re-elected as the Zanu-PF party leader in Zimbabwe. He won by a landslide when the opposition to his leadership was mysteriously killed by a landslide.

There is something odd about our ranking of life according to nationality. How we're supposed to really care when a bomb goes off in America, kind of care when it's Palestine and not even look up from the Xbox when it's all kicked off in the Ivory Coast, the last African country still named after the Dulux Mellow Moods range.

David Cameron's pledged £800 million for vaccinating Third World children. I must say I tire of these constant pleas for assistance from the Third World. Especially after we've already put in so much effort tidying away all their messy rubber, gold, oil and diamonds for them. There are some saddening statistics – apparently in Congo two in five children don't survive long enough to be conscripted as child soldiers. Or the tragedy of Zimbabwe, where many young people are now too ill to survive torture.

In North Korea, leader Kim Jong-il showed off his successor – son Kim Jong-un – at a military parade. Kim Jong-il is called 'Dear Leader' – that's makes it very tricky to write him a letter, isn't it? It's quite an achievement getting a double chin in a country where Sunday lunch consists of four grains of rice and a sausage made from toe-nail clippings. A brutal dictator, but a better dad than me. A whole country! I just palmed my boy off with a DVD of *Finding Nemo* I found stuck on the front of the *Daily Express*.

The previous favourite candidate was elder son Kim Jong-nam – he fell out of favour for forging a passport to go to Tokyo Disneyland. Kim Jong-il despises Disneyland, with all its 'You must be this tall to go on this ride' signs.

North Korea is incredibly secretive – apparently it was they who taught the Chinese how to whisper. That's what I heard anyway. Of course, in our own way, we're every bit as secretive.

I'm not sure exactly what WikiLeaks is, but it seems to be the political version of Popbitch. They came under a huge cyber attack. That's what you get if you publish ridiculous claims that governments are involved in cyber attacks. WikiLeaks couldn't have uncovered more embarrassing material if they'd received hacked messages from Jason Manford's Bebo account. Hillary Clinton ordered diplomats to collect phone numbers, email addresses and even DNA from UN diplomats. Well, just dress like a hooker and I promise within an hour you'll have all three. Of course, diplomats are two-faced. That's what diplomacy is. We all do it. 'Your baby looks lovely,' 'I loved your novel,' 'Yes, darling, I agree – she did look too thin.'

According to WikiLeaks, Prince Andrew is said to have insulted both the French and the Americans – a shocking breach of protocol for the royal family, as both nations are predominantly white. And I am stunned by the Saudi bribery allegations. To think the sale of electric batons, thumbscrews and explosives should in some way be tainted by financial impropriety.

★

The late Pope John Paul II was beatified. It's claimed he cured a woman of Parkinson's disease. She said it was such an amazing feeling that she's not been able to stop shaking ever since. If they're looking for a second miracle, I'd suggest keeping a lid on decades of kiddy fiddling would be in with a shout. When JP II becomes a saint it means people can pray to him directly for help and advice, such as, 'I've got a dead kid bleeding from the arse in my vestry. Who should I call?' Coincidentally, the Vatican is updating its policy regarding sexual abuse. It's finally made it into the top 100 commandments.

80,000 people went to see his successor, Pope Benedict XVI, in Hyde Park. I bet he hasn't seen a crowd as big as that since

Nuremberg. There was the assassination attempt that wasn't. They were bin men. Even if they had tried to do him in they'd have turned up on the wrong day. I confess I had a religious experience while he was here. I looked down at my tea and I swear I could see Jesus' face in it. Granted, I had to move the mash about a bit, and use peas for eyes and a sausage for a mouth.

Why are we making such a fuss of this man? If the Archbishop of Canterbury went to Rome they wouldn't even bother to defrost a tiramisu. Of course, Catholics derive enormous comfort from meeting the Pope. The McCanns say they found great relief from their audience with him. I suppose when your child's missing, contacting the head of a global paedophile ring is very useful.

David Cameron said he very much enjoyed meeting the world's favourite bead-jiggler. Apparently, he was desperate for tips on how to make people take shit in the hear-and-now in exchange for hazy promises about things being better in the distant future. The Pope's open-air mass was held in Glasgow and had a massive attendance – word got round that a guy was handing out free wine. He was only in Glasgow between 4 and 8 pm. Smart move. As the kids had only just got out of school no one would have been drinking, for more than about an hour.

The *Sun* likened the Pope's tour to that of a pop star – though they didn't specify whether it was Gary Glitter or Jonathan King. In papal doctrine, a pope cannot be wrong about faith or morals, but he can be wrong about other issues. What other issues are there? Ah, yes, science. My first reaction to the visit was that I don't want to listen to the mumblings of an old man – and then I realised his war stories are probably quite interesting.

Barack Obama also toured Britain and Ireland recently. When in Ireland he went to meet his eighth cousin. To give you an idea of how far removed that is, my seventh cousin is Jackie Chan. Michelle drank Guinness and did a good job of blending in with the Irish women – mainly by marrying an incredibly charming man who's actually killed quite a number of innocent people. Obama was in Ireland to see how his ancestors lived. So they slapped him in manacles, stuffed in him in a tiny cellar and sold him to the highest bidder.

I feel that as somebody who is 100 per cent genetically Irish I can say this. I fucking hate Ireland. The cunts never stop talking, and they bullshit. Do you know why? Because they ran out of true stuff ages ago. I can't imagine what the talks with the IMF were like.

'Ach sure, the economy will be all roight. We have a giant – do you want to make the giant angry? I know Derek and he's going to be fecking ragin! Think of the fucking songs we're going to get out of this! Mary, sing that one about how your grandfather ate himself!'

Shut up, you Irish cunt. Stop fucking *talking*. As Scottish people know, there is a time and a place for sharing your feelings, when one of you is drunk and the other is dying.

In Glasgow I formed a deep and abiding loathing of St Patrick's Day – loads of people out and about with ridiculous-looking Irish headgear. Or, as they call it, 'ginger hair'. According to legend, St Patrick chased all the snakes out of Ireland – well, we've all done some pretty crazy stuff when we're pissed. St Patrick's Day is a great chance for Irish people to be proud of their country and throw off all the misguided stereotypes by getting pissed and avoiding work.

After his trip to Ireland, Obama was then welcomed to Britain with a 41-gun salute – to display all the soldiers we have left. The president was intensely briefed on the flight over, with aides holding up pictures of the PM while he said, 'Cannington? No? Cameron ... OK ... Clegg? That's the same guy, ain't it? Tell you what, I'll just alternate between "Champ" and "Big Fella".'

Obama would have visited sooner but it's taken that long to train up a Prince Philip lookalike. The Obamas stayed with the Queen, as she's used to commoners now. Cameron still tends to get an asthma attack. It's interesting to note that the last such high-profile donning of a glove to shake a black man's hand was at the 1936 Berlin Olympics ... and as Hitler only put a glove on just to shake Jesse Owens's hand, and the Queen puts one on to shake everyone's, we can only conclude that the Queen is worse than Hitler. Obama told them he's black and Irish. Prince Philip said it's why the double-barrelled shotgun was invented.

Over at Downing Street, Obama and Cameron had a barbecue and played ping-pong – which to me seems a little insensitive, considering we're fighting several wars. Do you think if bin Laden had met Gaddafi, the first thing they would have done is crack open the Pringles and have a swingball tournament? Ken Clarke appeared to doze off during the president's speech. Although knowing him, he'll probably claim he was date raped.

During his visit to the UK, Obama rode 'The Beast'. Something Prince Philip hasn't done for almost 60 years. After three days of British weather, its food, moaning population and intolerable traffic jams, I'm surprised Obama didn't order the Navy SEALs to fly into London and shoot him in the face. Did you see him being interviewed by Andrew Marr? Marr was as excited as if he'd been told the pretty new researcher likes doing it with her eyes closed. Cameron and Obama were trying to work out how to leave Afghanistan. The UK's in a difficult position, calling for a more ordered exit; as for the US, anything better than dangling from a chopper that's plucked you from the embassy roof is considered a bonus.

Cameron and Obama agreed that the Taliban must either surrender their arms and introduce a parliamentary democracy … or, at very least, change their name so when they take charge again it's not quite so embarrassing.

★

After the earthquake and tsunami, the Japanese were told to 'head for the hills' – isn't that where the volcanoes are? Of the 450 missing Brits, about 50 were language teachers. The other 400 were TV crews making documentaries about how quirky the Japanese are. Hopefully, they will soon be found, keeping warm by giggling over a vibrator they found in a vending machine by the gutted wreckage of a primary school. Tragically, until then, we will have to survive on archive footage of Graham Norton and Jonathan Ross.

It was just devastating. British rescue dogs were brought in to help. Not sure how much use they were – Japanese disaster victims don't tend to smell of beer and chip fat. It just shows how fragile we humans are … especially the ones who live in earthquake zones next to nuclear-power plants. The power-plant manager tried to reassure people that levels of radiation weren't dangerous, with the words 'Hulk mad! Hulk smash!' 50 Cent (one half of 80s pop duo Dollar) and various comedians got in trouble for making fun of the events on Twitter. It's almost as if getting all your news in 140 characters from bored TV presenters, Justin Bieber fans and your stalkers doesn't manage to convey the full tragedy of a country being destroyed. Of course, it's not the first time 50's let us down. After the release of his debut album, *Get Rich or Die Tryin'*, he got rich.

Radiation from Japan was detected in Glasgow. I was worried at first, but thankfully my newborn Siamese triplets are fine and their laser vision is unimpaired. Hopefully, it won't create any superheroes, as the city already has enough people fighting each other in their pants. Glasgow has nothing to worry about – it takes many months to die from radiation poisoning, and there are very few Glaswegians with that length of life expectancy. What's the worst that could happen if the radiation levels rose in Scotland? 'Mr McCreedy, it's bad news, I'm afraid. You're lung cancer has cancer.'

I read that the new Japanese prime minister's wife is apparently proving to be quite eccentric. She claims to have been abducted by aliens and taken to the planet Venus. Still, our prime minister's wife finds David Cameron sexually attractive. Who's the freak? The Japanese prime minister's wife came out with a lovely phrase on TV, when she told viewers that every morning she 'eats the sun'. Much as her grandparents once did at Hiroshima.

Chinese Premier Wen Jiabao was in the UK for trade talks with the PM. A 35-strong delegation came over for the tour. That's the trouble with Chinese – you always get too much. The Chinese premier is looking to improve British rail networks – that's good thinking. Even the Romans didn't get the transport sorted out before they invaded. He's keen on improving the rail link between London and Birmingham. Or, as he calls them, the Inspection Centre and MegaPrison Compound One.

Mr Wen was accompanied by colleagues from the more liberal side of the Communist Party, and was seen laughing and joking with the minister of human rights and free speech, the hooded and inscrutable Doctor Pandemonium. Cameron said it was important only to raise human rights abuses at the right moment – when the translator had gone off on a fag break. I feel for Dave. It can't be easy to lecture China about human rights abuses when you're hoping they'll order a load more of our electric batons and nut clamps.

Apparently, child labour is now so rampant in the People's Republic that even Premier Wen is actually a 9-year-old boy standing on another boy's shoulders. Which would explain why, at the state dinner, he wouldn't take his coat off and seemed to be spooning every other mouthful into his belly button. Of course, the UK already plays a huge part in Chinese manufacturing, supplying an essential part of the millions of mobile phones they produce. The consumer.

★

I've never been surprised by low voter turnouts. In fact, I'm surprised anybody ever votes at all. Politicians seem so alien to us, their insincerity taken as a given, behaving inhumanely while they pretend to be human in some symbolic way. If, instead of a nation, we were 500 people living as a tribe, or a bunch of survivors in a lifeboat, would anyone elect Miliband or Cameron as leader, with their choppy hand gestures, lack of conviction and bizarrely automated range of emotions? In a normal social gathering, most of our leaders would seem to suffer from a hysterical personality disorder.

That video of Ed Miliband repeating the same thing four times is final proof that cameras do steal your soul – you can pinpoint the exact moment his conscience chokes on its last breath and dies. The only opposition we have to our bleak government is a man who would recite 'Jabberwocky' while wearing a mask of Nutella if his handlers told him it was the best response to the social-care issue.

Of course, if someone normal and sympathetic stood for office the white heat of the military entertainment complex would be brought to bear. Dave or Pam or whoever would be flattened within moments of announcing their candidacy by a giant tumour the size of a car falling out of the sky like a meteorite. On a brighter note, not having much political agency means less responsibility, too. All this pish from politicians about our deficit and how we'll have to work till 70 to pay it off.

No, cunts, it's your deficit; we could all fuck off to Spain en masse with our sense of humour and our work ethic and watch you fuckers, who are the least among us, briefly campaign for the votes of Britain's animals before succumbing to thirst and dysentery.

'There is a slurping noise coming from Dara's arsehole, like a mouth eagerly drinking soup.

★ ★ ★ ★

I'm in a little windowless dressing room with no toilet and the temptation is to piss in the sink. I'm about to do it when I think that I need to keep my dignity, however wired I'm feeling. I walk down the corridor to the bathroom but it's being cleaned by this young black guy, so I go back and piss in the sink.

Dara Ó Briain has got me onto his *The Apprentice* reaction show, which I'm almost certain is called *You're Fired*. I could only watch five minutes of it on iPlayer, but it rates quite well. I see Dara briefly in the corridor and thank him for his help. He laughs off my thanks but I want him to know how much I appreciate it. I grip his forearm and look him in the eye.

'Thanks a lot, big man. I was OK until I heard what happened to Richard Herring.'

'Oh yeah, car crash, horrible,' he nods.

I wonder if he thinks Herring was killed in a car crash, then I realise he means his arse looked like it had been in a car crash, which it did.

'I'm surprised at how little it got reported,' I tell him. 'He was doing quite well with that podcast thing …'

Dara shakes his head, and I know that this is both a sadness at Herring's death and a dismissal of my idea that anyone can be doing well with a podcast.

I realise it's a bit serious for a corridor conversation.

'I'm really grateful. This could well save me from having an arsehole like a cat flap that someone's forced a sofa through,' I beam, and he nods. Later I worry that he doesn't know anything about the rapist, that he seemed unsure of what I meant. Then I think that it's the kind of thing I usually say anyway, so fuck it.

I'm eating the little chocolates that they've left me in the dressing room. It's weird but when you do a TV appearance they give you a little gift. It's often something like facial-care products. Sometimes it's flowers. I'll take those with me even if I'm going back to Scotland the next day, give them to my girlfriend or my daughter, pretend I bought them. It's never choco-lates, I think numbly, my tongue feeling like it's swelling in my mouth. I'm standing, looking for the chocolate box but it's gone and my legs are trembling. The room tilts and roars and there's a tremendous smell, like a wet animal, and I'm trying to get to the door but I'm asleep.

I'm in a bigger dressing room, propped up on a sofa, my head resting on the wall. I should be rehearsing my jokes for the show. I want to panic but I don't, and I can't help feeling that I've had a lovely, relaxing sleep. There's a big guy draped over two of those little upholstered stools. He's in a suit but his trou-sers are off. I think it's Dara. I'm aware that some-body is sitting beside me on the sofa and I'm pleased to have company. I turn round and the swimming sensation makes me grin.

He's wearing a beautiful black suit. Armani, I think, and he's a big fluffy white lion. He seems pleased to see me and raises a beautiful gold-topped cane to his brow with a wink.

'Francis,' he chuckles in an impossibly deep voice. 'I have a feeling you've been avoiding me.'

I laugh a long, ridiculous laugh of relief and agree that I have. I stretch out my legs lazily and feel that rush you get when you're coming up on ecstacy, or acid. He knows what I'm thinking.

'Acid, yessss,' he growls. 'A bit of MDMA in there to take the edge off it.'

I see he has the box of chocolates on his lap and pops a couple of coffee creams into his mouth with a paw.

'Are you going to rape Dara?' I giggle. I'm honestly feeling that it would be interesting, maybe even exciting, if he did.

'Rape?' He seems surprised. 'Goodness me, no, this is something that he wants … Rape? No, I wouldn't call it that.'

'Who are you?' I ask, and it seems strange that I haven't asked already.

'It's pronounced Showbiddnnnessss…s,' he purrs.

'Do you appear differently to everybody? Does everybody see something different?'

He looks at his own paws in puzzlement. 'No, I'm a lion.' He seems thrown. 'Do I look like a lion to you?'

'Oh yes, absolutely.'

He stands up exactly as a man would, his thigh muscles bulging through his trousers, and his tail, which drapes from a neat hole in the seat, suddenly whips about excitedly.

'Fucking watch this,' he grins conspiratorially and produces from his fly a huge, red, animal penis. Semi-erect it's about the length of a policeman's truncheon. He unscrews the top of his cane and replaces it with a gold attachment from inside his jacket, which he screws on with a practised motion. Placing the stick in front of the sleeping body he slides his now-bulging cock into the attachment. It seems to function like a snooker rest.

'Why did you rape Paul Merton?' I blurt, and he seems a little put out. 'He's pretty famous, and normally you seem to …'

'I know, I know …' He shakes his mane apologetically and turns to look at me. 'I just hate all that fucking boring shit he does about silent films.'

I feel myself nodding. 'That's no reason to rape him …,' I start.

'And he does all those adverts for insurance and stuff.' He's growling now and stiffening along his cock rest as he gets angrier. 'And *Have I Got News* is shite now!'

'IT'S BEEN SHITE FOR YEARS!' I open my mouth to say something else but he roars.

'NIGGER'S GOT TO BUST A NUT, AIN'T HE?'

My vision blurs, like the acid is hitting me in a big wave. I feel like I'm looking at a single colour that's every colour in the room, then my vision comes back sharply and the lion is fucking Dara, pressing his arse cheeks back gently with his paws. The lion seems very much an animal now, bending over the body like prey as he thrusts rapidly along the rest into the jiggling mass beneath him. The room fills with a colossal purring noise and it slowly dawns on me that it's coming from Dara.

'Yesss … They purr … They purr when they want it …,' whispers the lion, slightly out of breath.

'I don't think he wants this,' I say, trying to stand. I have some idea that I can talk us both out of here, even do the show.

'He does, he does …,' the white lion groans. 'It's the mask, the face you wear, it takes over, it wants this.'

I try to pull at his shoulder but I'm fucked, and it's almost as if I'm patting him on the back, congratulating him.

'Those masks you wear to deal with your producers, your agents, your crowds, you are those masks …'

He is giving an extra-hard thrust every few words now, emphasising his points.

'Think about how much airtime you give your mask … It's the fucking AIRTIME! That person you think you are, when are you him? WHEN ARE YOU HIM?' he demands.

Underneath the purring, there is a slurping noise coming from Dara's arsehole, like a mouth eagerly drinking soup. My legs just aren't working and I fall back on the sofa nearest the door. I can see Dara's face now and his eyes are open. He's asleep but he has exactly the ironic smile he'd have presenting a show.

'This is what he wants!' shouts the lion. 'To be a living cipher, to be recognised by strangers, a high as blank as the purrrest heroin. Rrrrrrragghhh.'

As he thrusts faster, his words become incomprehensible, just a lion growling. 'Rrraggghhh' he says to me, nodding vigorously. 'Grrraggghhh!'

I think of going to Dara, 'This is definitely Red Button material.' It seems so stupid I actually try to

say it, but it's slurred and I can't really hear myself.
I reach across and try to squeeze Dara's cheek to wake
him but he keeps smiling ahead with the same glazed
eyes. I pull myself up by the door frame but slump back
down uselessly. I'm suddenly aware of how I can leave.

★

I'm walking through the centre of Glasgow, rattling my
suitcase along and nobody recognises me. There is something about Glasgow in the sunshine, and I hold onto
that feeling even as it starts to rain. I break into a
jog and it's a light little bounce, like running when
I was a kid, like there was never any age in my legs,
just work. I know that if I wanted to I could move
faster than this, that this is not even my body and I'm
not tied to it.

I stop to look at a newspaper board, which has something about Alan Hansen in big letters, with a picture
of him. A guy comes up to me and my chest flutters, but
it's just change he wants and I give him a few quid.
He's freaked a bit by me smiling and laughing, and he
doesn't even say thanks.

I've been saving this bit, but I stop in front of the
darkened windows of a music shop and I look at myself.
It's not me. It'll pass a passport check and nobody who
doesn't really know me will notice but it's not me. I
get back to the high-rise and phone an estate agents,
and put the flat up for sale. He asks a lot of questions
but I insist, 'Really mate, you're going to have to
come and look at this.'

I make a cup of tea and take my little joint-rolling
tray down into the stateroom one last time. The new
episode of *The Game* has Neil meeting up with this guy

in Soho who shows him how the game can work. A man hails a cab, then has to answer his phone, so they just walk right into it. At the bar someone has just ordered a drink they can't stay for. They sit down at the table and the drinks arrive without ordering. Neil is told of the value of living in the moment, of how life can unfold around you.

The man suddenly has a hunted look, glances round quickly, then grabs Neil by the wrists, sees the two rusty brown marks there and seems relieved. He tells Neil that soon he will tell him about the secret rulers of the world. A beautiful woman at the bar has been stood up and the man leaves with her.

Neil phones someone.

'No,' he tells them. 'I checked it out. He knows absolutely nothing about *The Game*.' Neil wets his thumb and starts rubbing the marks off his wrists.

'Secret,' he giggles to himself. 'Rulers,' he giggles louder. 'World!' and it finishes on his hysterically laughing mouth.

Just washing the mugs in the sink, I have a really brilliant idea and I try to forget about it.

Acknowledgements

Thanks to Anna Valentine, who came to Glasgow to have a look at the book while I was in the middle of a throat infection so extreme I was literally gargling with codeine. I was off my tits and my memories of the day when put together make little sense. I admire her tolerance of the whole *Jacob's Ladder* experience.

Much gratitude to Grant Morrison, whose inspiringly mental *Final Crisis* comic is where I took the book's title from. The 'Fuck it! Stun It! Kill it!' line in the *Star Trek* bit was something Grant said to me too, and now that I think about it, that would have made an even better title. I recently re-read *Final Crisis*, and tripped out on a bit that made the whole of my vision break down so I could almost see reality as a construct or projection – like I could almost see on a molecular level. It was amazing! Thank fuck for people like Grant, Terence McKenna, Bill Hicks and Robert Anton Wilson. To me, they're sort of the antibodies the planet creates against fear and dogma.

All the people I've quoted in the book are worth a look. Everyone evinces some kind of boredom or ennui these days – reading something more interesting would really fucking help! Seriously, if you want to be happier just switch your fucking TV off and read Gene Wolfe, or James Ellroy, or whatever you can get into. It's just got to have some complexity, some density of ideas. We're supposed to be challenged and, sadly, most of the time we don't even have the guts to challenge ourselves.

Many thanks to Meryl O'Rourke, who had a look at a couple of early passages. And just generally for being inspiringly funny. Thanks to Nick Morley for his illustrations. Bizarrely they really are as I'd imagined, including a chilling likeness of Paul Marsh, who he has never met or seen.

The idea for *The Game* TV show came from my friend, the screenwriter Rae Brunton. Rae is one tenacious son of a bitch when it comes to ideas. He had the idea for the whole first episode described here. I thought I'd flesh out the series and try to imagine what good TV might look like.

Most of all, to my real audience. Treehouse and Mike, you make me laugh every day. Thanks for showing me how to be happy. You doofers.

FRANKIE BOYLE